RELENTLESS PURSUIT

Inside The

Escape From Dannemora:

New York State's Largest Manhunt

Incident Commander

Major Charles E. Guess

New York State Police (Retired)

First published by Dog Ear Publishing
4011 Vincennes Rd
Indianapolis, IN 46268
www.dogearpublishing.net

ISBN: 978-1-4575-5595-4

This book is printed on acid-free paper.

Printed in the United States of America

For Elinor, Jennifer, and Rebecca, without whose love and support,

none of what I have become in life would be meaningful.

"It is not the critic who counts, not the one who points out how the strong man stumbled, or where the doer of deeds could have done better. The credit belongs to the man who is actually in the arena; whose face is marred by the dust and sweat and blood; who strives valiantly; who errs and comes up short again and again; who knows the great enthusiasms, the great devotion and spends himself in a worthy cause; who at the best, knows in the end the triumph of high achievement; and who, at worst if he fails, at least fails while daring greatly; so that his place shall never be with those cold and timid souls who know neither victory or defeat."

Theodore Roosevelt
Sorbonne, Paris
April 23, 1910

TABLE OF CONTENTS

THE AFTERMATH

AUTHOR'S NOTE

My objective in writing this book, was to establish an accurate, comprehensive written record of the events surrounding the escape from Clinton Correctional Facility, the ensuing manhunt, and the formative, salient moments of my career.

This book presents my views and does not represent the views of the New York State Police or anyone else. My role as the Incident Commander during the search provided me with a unique perspective on which to draw, and this is my point of view. Certainly, there are others.

The events depicted in *Relentless Pursuit* are based on my own memory. Conversations have been reconstructed from my recollections. Still, I attempted to be as accurate as my personal reflection and research would allow. Due to the frenetic pace of events at the time, and my singular focus on the mission at hand, rather than note taking, I have utilized multiple "open source" documents to verify events, time frames, people involved, and relevant quotes. I have made every effort to depict events and persons accurately and afford full credit to many outstanding people aiding me throughout my career. I have cited my sources in the endnotes and credited photographers and governmental entities providing images.

Importantly, I have <u>not</u> disclosed confidential information or tactics, techniques, and procedures, which would compromise or detract from future investigations. There are many who contributed directly and tangentially to the successful outcome of this mission, and I have attempted to recognize their efforts. Unfortunately, I may have inadvertently overlooked someone, and I thank <u>you</u>, for your support.

To the men and women of the New York State Police and Troop "B," I salute you.

Charles Guess
May 12, 2017

GETTING ESTABLISHED

CHAPTER 1

NOTIFICATIONS

Saturday, June 6, 2015

At 6:06 AM, I was awakened by a phone call. As I groped for the BlackBerry on my nightstand, I immediately thought, *This can't be good. No one calls a troop commander this early on a Saturday morning just to chat.*

Answering the call, I was greeted by one of my subordinate zone commanders. "Major, Brent Gillam here. We have two unaccounted-for inmates at Dannemora."

"Unaccounted for?" I said. "What the hell does that mean?"

The captain continued, "DOCCS (Department of Corrections and Community Supervision) just called and advised that two inmates are missing, as of the 5:30 AM cell check."

"Missing," I repeated. "You mean escaped?"

"DOCCS is saying 'unaccounted for'…," he corrected. They think the inmates may still be hiding out within the prison. A search is ongoing."

To me, this seemed like wishful thinking, at best. By this time, my senses were firing and the captain had my full attention. Expecting the worst, I asked Captain Gillam, "Who are they, and what are they in for?" He didn't yet know. Information was sketchy, and while the prison was engaged in a full lockdown and internal search (aka "frisk"), prison staff seemed to be hoping for the best and attempting to minimize the situation.

I did not share their optimism and knew the clock was ticking. "Well, what are we (State Police) doing at this time?" I probed.

Gillam advised me that he had people "headed that way" and would be en route himself momentarily.

Good first step, I thought. Gillam, a highly competent zone commander, and former Academy classmate, had immediately initiated a response upon receiving the preliminary notification from his subordinate sergeant. "Brent, I've got to notify Field Command. I want a full-scale response. Follow the plan. Notify the Border Patrol and our other LE (law enforcement) partners. Get whatever assets you need rolling. I'll notify HQ. I'm on my way. Keep me advised," I said.

With that, Captain Gillam responded, "WILCO," shorthand for "will comply," and we ended the call.

Son of a bitch. I thought to myself. *This is the big one.* One of those incidents you plan and train for, but pray never happens on your watch. Significantly, as the State Police major-in-charge of the 8,335-square-mile region of Northern New York known as the North Country, it was all going to rest squarely on my shoulders.

As in most states, the state-level Department of Corrections is solely responsible for inmate welfare, activity, and security while <u>inside</u> the facilities of the state prison system. But, God forbid, should a prisoner escape, the ensuing search then becomes the responsibility of law enforcement. Not that Corrections doesn't play a role, they do, a significant one. In New York, DOCCS remains fully engaged and invested as partners, not only in the physical search outside the walls, but also integrating with State Police Investigators conducting the overall investigation into the mechanics of an escape and assisting with required interviews of staff members and inmates. However, make no mistake about it, once an escape is confirmed, due to law enforcement's overarching responsibility for public safety, resources available, jurisdictional protocols, and the corresponding network of criminal investigative assets, Corrections rightly defers to law enforcement as the lead agency. In Northern New York State, an escape just 20 miles south of the Canadian border, in the heart of the Adirondack Mountains, would fall squarely on Troop "B" of the New York State Police, of which I was the Commanding Officer.

After hanging up the phone with Captain Gillam, and before saddling up for the ride north, my next order of business was to notify the Superintendent of the New York State Police (NYSP), Joseph A. D'Amico. Of course, the structure of the State Police (SP), being a paramilitary organization, would require me to make this advisement via the chain of command. While I would speak directly with the superintendent countless times in the hours, days, and weeks to come, my first phone call was to my immediate supervisor, and future superintendent, Lieutenant Colonel George P. Beach II, the Assistant Deputy Superintendent in charge of the Uniform Force.

Even without much to go on, and knowing this would immediately raise more questions than answers, I knew bad news doesn't get better with age. It was essential that Beach and the superintendent hear from me before getting blindsided by some well-meaning staffer from the Governor's office. News like this would sky rocket to the top, and DOCCS would eventually have to fall on their sword and make "the call," when their internal search efforts were exhausted. The bottom line, no boss wants to get caught out of the loop, and should an escape be confirmed, the State Police would be expected to take the lead immediately.

I rapidly searched my phone's contact list for the colonel's number and pressed the call button. Observing an incoming call from me on his caller ID, a professional colleague and old friend from years in the State Police, Colonel Beach answered with a pleasant, "Good morning, Chuck."

I said, "Colonel, sorry to bother you so early, but Clinton Correctional Facility in Dannemora is reporting two <u>unaccounted-for</u> inmates."

"Unaccounted for…," he said. "What exactly does that mean?"

"Good question," I responded, filling him in on what little intelligence we had. I added that Captain Gillam was en route, and that I had directed him to initiate a <u>full-scale</u> response, in accordance with our joint, pre-approved plan and provided a quick overview of what that entailed on our end. The conversation was brief. Beach, also a former troop commander (TC), knew I had my hands full and did not want to delay my response playing twenty questions. He told me he would notify his boss, the field commander, and ensure Superintendent D'Amico was advised forthwith. Knowing that this would generate an overwhelming plethora of questions, I assured Beach that I would keep him updated and hung up.

Upon terminating the conversation, I observed I had a missed call and contacted Captain Bob LaFountain, my right-hand man in Troop "B", and supervisor of our Bureau of Criminal Investigation (BCI). I said, "Sorry, Bob, I was on the phone with Colonel Beach. What have you got?" He didn't know much more than I did, having just received a call himself from a subordinate investigator, and shared my sinking feeling. I reiterated we were responding according to plan, and I would meet him at the Command Post (CP) in Dannemora. "Bob, we need to get the pedigree (physical description/criminal history) and facts on these two inmates ASAP. I just got off the phone with the colonel, and although he's good for now, we're flying blind here."

Bob said, "I'm already on it," and that was all I needed to hear.

Captain LaFountain, who had been the BCI Captain in Troop "B" for 10 years, knew the job inside and out, and was a consummate professional. I was confident in his abilities and figured my tactical and operational experience was well-complimented by his investigative acumen. Deep down I knew this mission would require everything we could collectively bring to the table.

By now, my wife, Elinor, beside me in the room where I took the call, was awake and dialed in. She had been by my side for the past 31 years of combined military and law enforcement work and knew intuitively that it was "go time." She understood that hitting me with a bunch of questions, no matter how well-meaning, would be non-productive. Besides, at this point, based on what she'd overheard, she was as well-briefed as anyone in the State Police. So, recognizing I was faced with one of the biggest challenges of my life, she simply told me she loved me and wished me good luck. With that, I felt secure in the knowledge that her unmitigated support and quiet confidence in me would sustain me in the days to come, as it had so many times before.

The last thing I heard her say, as I descended the steps to the garage was, "Wear your vest!"

Driving north, I ensured I had the necessary communications established to receive and relay updates and orders. Communications consisted of the NYSP radio system, Division cell phone, and an old-school car phone, which often provided extended range and reception. Information would flow through an amalgam of voice, text, e-mail, and NYSPIN (NYSP Information Network) messages. Even with those bases covered, I knew there would be dead zones. Throughout the ensuing mission, despite the numerous IT workarounds between law enforcement and commercial providers, such as Verizon, coverage and communications challenges would exist within the area of responsibility (AOR) that would complicate and plague operations during the search. But, for now at least, I had what I needed to maintain oversight of command and control remotely.

The fact that we were effective at all, during our initial response, was due to the application of a leadership model employing three specific factors. First, prior planning. The NYSP and DOCCS construct joint Escape and Pursuit plans, which are reviewed annually by key regional leaders to ensure effectiveness. Second, both agencies conduct regular drills, exercising appropriate facets of the response team, from boots on the ground, inclusion of special operations units (such as Aviation and tactical teams) and command and control for leaders and decision makers. Third, and *most importantly*, once these steps have been taken and the plan initiated, troopers, including their respective first-line supervisors are empowered to make fluid and appropriate leadership decisions in accordance with the "commander's intent" (vision) for the mission. This, in my view, is the true strength of how New York State Troopers respond to evolving incidents. The fact that this leadership model was applied during the manhunt, afforded outstanding young troopers and exceptional non-commissioned officers (NCOs), the flexibility to get the job done, *and* created opportunities for successful outcomes.

Updates known as Situation Reports (SITREPS) came in sporadically. By 7:15 AM, the status of the internal search for the missing inmates was officially confirmed as "escaped," after a steam pipe, and once-secured manhole cover, was found to have been cut. This occurred when a team of correction officers (C.O.s) and one of my State Police K9 teams completed the track of the escape route, starting within the walls of the facility and ending with the canine exiting the street-level sewer system at the intersection of Bouck and Barker Streets, approximately 400 feet south and <u>outside</u> the walls of the prison. What would later be described as an impossible, improbable, and first-of-a-kind escape, was now a confirmed fact. Two dangerous inmates were on the loose, and, as the troop commander, it was now *my* job to find them.

Just how dangerous are these two individuals? Information was now coming in via Gillam and LaFountain, and much more would be learned about them going forward. However, at this early point, facts and photographs were coalesced into an APB (All Points Bulletin) and released identifying the two escapees as Richard W. Matt and David P. Sweat. Corresponding pedigree information was immediately broadcast as:

RICHARD W. MATT

Age: 48 (49 when shot)
Race: Caucasian
Height: 6' 0"
Weight: 210 pounds
Physical descriptors: Hazel eyes, receding black hair
Scars, marks, tattoos: "Mexico Forever" tattoo on back and USMC insignia on right shoulder (never a Marine)
Incarcerated for: Murder 2 – for killing his former 76-year-old employer

DAVID P. SWEAT

Age: 34 (35 when captured)
Race: Caucasian
Height: 5' 11"
Weight: 160 pounds
Physical descriptors: Green eyes, receding brown hair
Scars, marks, tattoos: Tattoos on left bicep ("Rebel") and "I," "F," "B" tattooed on three fingers of his right hand
Incarcerated for: Murder 1 – killing a police officer

An accompanying **State Police Advisory** was issued: *"Both inmates are considered to be a danger to the public. If located, do not approach them. Contact 911 or the NYSP immediately."*

"These are dangerous people, and they're nothing to be trifled with," New York Governor Andrew M. Cuomo would say later that day, at a hastily arranged press conference on the steps of our Command Post, the Clinton Correctional Facility Training Building in Dannemora. As the public, would soon come to know, no truer words have been spoken.

In short order, we would come to learn the nature and most significant elements of their despicable Criminal Histories as follows:

Richard Matt - had been incarcerated for the kidnapping, robbery, and murder of North Tonawanda, NY, businessman William Rickerson, on December 3, 1997. After kidnapping his former employer, Matt, and an accomplice, drove him around in the trunk of a car for 27 hours, bound with duct tape, intermittently stopping to beat and torture the 76-year-old in attempt to extract money from him. Ultimately unsuccessful, Matt snapped Rickerson's neck with his bare hands and dismembered him with a hacksaw, dumping his body into the Niagara River. Matt then fled to Mexico, where he was later arrested, convicted, and imprisoned for the 1998 stabbing death of another American businessman. In 2007, the U.S. extradited him, to stand trial for Rickerson's death; upon conviction, he was incarcerated at Clinton Correctional Facility (CCF) in July 2008, where he was serving 25 years to life.

David Sweat - killed Broome County Sheriff's Deputy Kevin Tarsia, on July 4, 2002. Sweat and two accomplices had burglarized a gun store and were transferring weapons between vehicles in a nearby park, when they were interrupted by Deputy Tarsia. Tarsia, a 13-year veteran of the department, was shot more than 10 times, and was then run over by Sweat several times, before being shot in the face. Sweat and his accomplices fled after stealing the Deputy's .40-caliber Glock handgun. Sweat was tried and convicted of First Degree Murder and had been incarcerated at Clinton Correctional Facility (CCF) since October 2003, serving life without parole.

The pair was reported to be close prison associates and were last seen prior to lights out, at the 11:00 PM bed check. Given that fact, it became immediately apparent to those of us on the outside with the responsibility of finding them, that they were not only extremely dangerous men, with nothing to lose, but may have had as much as a six-hour head start. And, at that same press conference, I acknowledged the fact that, given the length of their head start, Matt and Sweat *"...could literally be anywhere..."*

As I weighed the enormity of the task in front of me, my mind briefly considered what led me to this point...

CHAPTER 2

EARLY YEARS

G rowing up in Henrietta, NY, a suburb of Rochester, as the first of two children of Edward and Dolores Guess, I was fortunate to be raised in a supportive, loving environment, with a strong sense of compassion and respect towards others.

Both parents modeled a solid foundation of family and exuded a sense of fairness, decency, and responsibility. I was imbued at an early age with a strong competitive spirit, sense of duty, and ideal of patriotism. From the onset, I was inspired to serve my country and community.

My mother, Dolores, formed the center of our nuclear family. An administrative assistant and "working mom," before it was common place, she was a devoted wife and mother, raising two sons, while tending to the myriad of job, home, school, sports, and other extracurricular activities that two boys would be engaged in during the 60's and 70's. Mom kept all three of us in line, Dad included, ensured I knew the meaning of unconditional love, and taught me how to relate to and respect women. The degree to which I am a good husband to my wife, and father to two wonderful daughters today, I owe chiefly to her.

My father, Edward, was the leader of our family. A man who grew up attending the school of "hard knocks." He joined the U.S. Air Force at age 17, serving in the Air Police (today's Security Forces), and upon returning to civilian life, he went to work in a factory, since he failed to meet the now-antiquated six-foot height requirement of area police departments. A hard worker, over several decades he would rise through the union ranks of his organization, the IAM & AW, to become an International Business Agent, responsible for representing his co-workers during the negotiation of complex, corporate labor management contracts.

Additionally, my father was an avid reader of World War II history. I recall several early discussions about some of America's greatest, and sometimes controversial, leaders and generals: FDR, Kennedy, Nixon,

Truman, Eisenhower, Patton, MacArthur, etc. The lessons often including even "great" men are fallible. True leaders must serve selflessly; their successes are only made possible by the inspired efforts of those they are entrusted to lead.

My younger brother, Brian, was my early partner in crime. Five years my junior, I have many fond memories of us playing sports in the backyard, building one of many "forts" from scrap wood or snow, hanging out at the lake during summer vacation, or watching late-night scary movies, during which he would often hide behind the chair in the living room, as a precaution.

In school, I gravitated toward history and social sciences. I viewed my study of history, and the lessons learned therein, as an opportunity to gain valuable perspective and insight on life, that most other disciplines lacked. I believed that, to live a worthy and productive life, it was essential to understand where you come from and attempt to determine your interconnected place in the world, both literally and figuratively, to chart your own course forward. The study of history afforded me that opportunity.

At an early age, my parents interested me in Cub Scouts, from which I later transitioned to Boy Scouts. Two tremendous pursuits, the latter of which I credit for developing my sense of adventure and appreciation for working as a member of a unit. I spent many years in scouting, attending every wilderness outing available, chasing one merit badge after another, while rising through the ranks to become my troop's senior patrol leader. Unfortunately, at the age of 17, just three merit badges shy of Eagle, I left scouting to focus more intently on athletics and girls. If I'd only listened to those advising against that shortsightedness, I would have avoided what would turn out for me to be life's single biggest self-inflicted regret.

I had always been competitive and like many kids, worked hard to balance school, sports, scouting, and life in general. But, it was on the athletic field, one of life's most fleeting of pursuits, where I most fully expressed my commitment and passion in the 70's. While I loved all sports, owing my exposure to my parent's passion for football, regular viewing of ABC's Wide World of Sports programming, and the Olympics, I focused intently on football and lacrosse. As a sophomore, on the varsity football team in 1976, I was fortunate to experience, for the first time in school history, our team's recognition as New York State Champions. It was an almost ethereal experience. Not simply because we won, but because at the beginning of the season we weren't supposed to win. Our success was predicated upon the leadership of our coach at the time, Werner Kleeman, now a legend in Rush-Henrietta Football, who took a diverse group of high school kids with some talent and transformed us into a team who believed anything was possible, *if* you worked hard enough for it. According to his model, simply desiring success and talking loudly about victory was not going to cut it, you had to *earn* it! Under Kleeman's tutelage and inspiration, we came together as a team and *worked* tirelessly to achieve it. That lesson stayed with me for my entire life.

During successive years and seasons at Rush-Henrietta, many of the same kids worked together to achieve other championships in lacrosse and football. While I would later be fortunate enough to be selected as an All-County Lacrosse Player and All-Greater Rochester Honorable Mention Football Player, my proudest achievement in high school sports was being voted Captain, of *both* my football and lacrosse teams, my senior year, for one simple reason: the caliber of fellow players and students who made those selections.

Throughout high school, I had caught the attention of a number of major college scouts and coaches in both football and lacrosse. One school in particular drew my attention, the USMA at West Point. After visiting during my junior year, I was impressed with the honor and tradition of the Academy. Since I had viewed the armed forces as a potential career after high school, I thought, *What better way to start?* Here, I reasoned, I could play major college football and lacrosse, and become a soldier! Considering my affinity for military history, I felt it a perfect match.

Well, I had a lot to learn and would learn it the hard way. Notably, what was missing from the equation was strong math skills, no pun intended. I had struggled in high school math classes and managed to get by with B's and C's, but this would hardly stand up to the rigor of the Military Academy's renowned engineering programs. And, West Point Admissions did not overlook that fact. Subsequently, I was offered an appointment, upon graduation from high school in 1979, to the United States Military Academy Preparatory School at Ft. Monmouth, NJ, where I would work on getting my math skills up. Prep School was the place that a couple of hundred less-than-stellar students, such as myself, could spend a year immersed in the USMA culture, while undergoing rigorous academic prep. Afterward, while not guaranteed, successful cadets could apply to West Point with a high likelihood of acceptance. On the plus side, the Prep School also had competitive sports teams, and I would be able to play both football and lacrosse.

After weeks of basic military indoctrination, athletics and academics finally commenced. Suddenly, our plates were full, but no different than what would be expected at West Point. To say that I was a good fit in the military environment would be an understatement. I loved it! To say that my least-favorite subject, math, was kicking my ass, would also be an understatement. Only here and now, for large blocks of time each day, math instructors, doing their level best to educate us, had us at the chalk board as we tried to work our way through computations. Invariably, it seemed, the harder I worked, the farther I fell behind. To make matters worse, I dreaded the daily, public humiliation I felt at the board. Unfortunately, in my case, whatever mental block I was experiencing with mathematics at the time, became a game changer.

After being set on where I was going to school far earlier than any of my fellow recruited high school classmates, I was ready to pull the plug. To this day, I remember the pay phone call to my parents and the disappointment in their voices. While I naively assured them that I would easily transition into one of the many schools that had recruited me the previous year, that would not be the case. Those coaches, understandably, had filled their rosters and moved on.

Turns out, it is far easier to remove yourself from West Point Prep, than get in. While I was contacted by both the football and lacrosse coaches at the Academy, one even driving down to New Jersey in a final effort to intervene, I was not to be swayed. Frankly, with West Point's emphasis on engineering in those days, I couldn't imagine life getting any easier. Besides, of one thing I was certain, I wanted to be a soldier, and if push came to shove, I could simply enlist.

Looking back, with the value of hindsight, my approach to this issue and opportunity may have been flawed from the start, but it was a salient part of my personal growth and professional development. A difficult experience for a young 18-year-old, but one that delivered important lessons I would never forget.

So, in mid-fall of 1979, I found myself unexpectedly in what is today known as a "gap year." My father had another, more derogatory, phrase for it at the time, but the consequences of immediately going to work, moving out of the house, and enrolling in night classes ultimately paved the way for my future. In fact, it was during this time, that I met the most influential person in my life, my future wife, Elinor.

Here I was, a former, standout high school athlete who had left town months earlier believing the immediate future was bright and cast in stone, only to return home prematurely, uncertain of the next step. However, it was this very departure from the "norm" that presented me with my life's greatest opportunity and blessing.

On Halloween night 1979, I had just returned home from a night school class in psychology at a local college, when a friend called to ask if I was interested in going to a bar across town. My initial response was, "No, I'm good", but fortunately, he didn't take "No" for an answer.

"I'm picking you up in twenty minutes," he replied. Shortly thereafter, true to his word, my friend Mark and his brother rolled into the driveway. I knew that with these two, it would simply be easier to get in the car than attempt to weasel out at the last minute. The stage was set…

Sometimes, life has a way of throwing you a lifeline when you need it most. Here I was on Halloween, when most of my peers were engaged in their freshman semesters; I had no costume, no concrete school plans, just nursing a beer. Truth be told, feeling a bit sorry for myself. Even so, after a perfunctory reconnaissance of the bar, I had noticed an attractive young lady, adorned with "bunny" ears and a cotton tail sitting several tables away. I don't know if it was her beautiful smile, deep brown eyes, or perfectly styled short hair, unique in that heavily "made up" disco era, but I couldn't take my eyes off her. Just as I considered my options and plotted how best to get her attention, my pal Mark gets up and approaches her table. *Damn.* I thought to myself. *Too slow…just not on my "A" game.*

Then, unexpectedly, I see Mark turn and point my way saying, as if in slow motion, "My friend wants to dance with you!"

I could have killed him. First, I had not said a word to him. Second, I was a long way from proposing we dance, primarily because I was still working on my first beer and I *suck* at dancing. Thirdly, and worst of all, I really *was* interested in this girl, and Mark, I thought, was about to blow it for me.

Fortunately for me, she locked eyes with me and mouthed the words, "OK…"

Normally, I would have reflexively declined out of embarrassment, as I hadn't yet worked up the courage to ask her to dance, but something inside me caused me to get to my feet and walk over to her. Come to find out, she initially only agreed to his proposition to save face for me, because she sensed he was engaged in some form of jackassery. Fortunately, it ultimately worked out for both of us.

That night and countless others flew by. There was an immediate chemistry. It may have started as a fluke, but the magic was real. We became inseparable, and now, the reality was, that I had another factor in my life's equation. I knew I would eventually figure it out, but I also knew, I needed her to be a part of whatever *"it"* was.

In fact, at the time, I wasn't even convinced full-time school was my next move. Increasingly, I had thought more and more of just enlisting. I had recently taken the ASVAB, a military aptitude test, and according to the recruiter, I had scored very high.

In fact, to make his point, he said, "Son, with that grade, you can sign up for anything! Hell, even Underwater Typewriter Repair, if you want."

Fortunately, that clearly fictional Military Occupational Specialty (MOS) didn't interest me, but I figured, I'd evaluate my options. So, armed with my new test score, I was an easy mark as I made my rounds at the Armed Forces Recruiting Office.

First, as I recall, I met with a Marine Corps gunnery sergeant, a particularly imposing figure, all but grabbing me by the collar and pulling me into his office. After a brief discussion, I informed him that I'd had an interest in law enforcement from an early age, and he slapped a six-year

Military Police contract down on the desk in front of me, telling me he could have me on the next bus out of town, if I signed on the dotted line. Compelling, but this seemed a bit hasty to me. With the stroke of a pen, it would be a done deal, and I hadn't even spoken to another recruiter about a job. When I informed the sergeant I had an appointment coming up with a Navy recruiter, he about lost his mind. I don't know if it was the end of the month and quota was coming due, or he was on caffeine over-load, but he was amped up and losing me fast. One thing I know for sure, I have always had the ultimate respect for the USMC, and if not for this guy's approach, could see myself wearing the coveted globe and anchor, but not if he was the gatekeeper.

So, I extricated myself from that situation in time to see the Navy recruiter. Now, this guy was the polar opposite; as gung-ho as the Marine was, this guy was low key. After a brief introduction, he handed me the Navy's version of a job book and left me to breeze through the glossy pho-tographs accompanying the brief job descriptions. It didn't take me long to stop on the page featuring a frogman carrying a machinegun and another jumping out of a helicopter. *Huh*, I thought to myself, *Navy SEAL?* I didn't know the Navy did such cool things. (Remember, this was the late 70's, Vietnam had recently ended and most of the talk was about the Green Berets back then.) With job book in hand, I went over to the recruiter who was BS-ing with another recruiter and paying me little mind. "How 'bout this?" I asked. "This looks like fun!"

He, looked me square in the eye, probably the first eye contact he had made with me all day, and said "Kid, you don't want anything to do with that!"

"Why not?" I asked.

He said, "They're not normal. They do a bunch of crazy shit, and it's harder than hell to get into."

I thought to myself, *Perfect!* but further inquiries proved fruitless.

"Besides," he said, "your ASVAB score is too high for that!" He then snatched the book from my hands and proceeded to show me stuff on sub-marines, radar, missiles, etc. Respectable, essential jobs, that I couldn't have cared less about. I was out of there.

Next stop, the Air Force recruiter. Talking to this guy seemed a lot like interviewing for a job at Costco. He was a personable guy and knew his stuff, but told me straight up, "These are the openings I have to fill. I can put you in any of them with that score. Are you interested in any of them?"

I had never considered going to the Defense Language Institute, learning Russian, flying along the Arctic Circle, and listening to the Soviets (it sounded frigid), so I passed. There was one, Air Force Pararescue, that looked intriguing, as the video featured some stud jumping out of an airplane, but after expressing interest in that, the Air Force "suit" reiterated, that he has certain openings *he* is looking to fill. If I was interested in one of them...let him know.

The Army recruiter wasn't in, but hanging on the door was a poster of an Airborne Ranger in a black beret; they didn't change to tan berets until 2001. I walked out of there thinking that square-jawed dude looked *bad ass!*

With no solid prospects and more than a little disappointment regarding how the various recruiters had represented their branches and interests, I continued to work my entry-level, minimum-wage job and talk, when possible, to college coaches. This led me to Brockport State College, a mid-sized liberal arts school in Western New York, in relatively close proximity to where I grew up. The coach of the Golden Eagles had attempted to recruit me in high school, but as previously mentioned, I had already committed elsewhere. I went out to meet with him and his assistants, tour the campus, and evaluate my degree prospects. Fortunately, although I had respectfully declined his overtures back in high school, he was still looking to add "talent" to his roster, even if he had to wait until next fall to realize the gain. This time around while considering college, I appropriately elevated academics as the pre-eminent concern. I found that as a liberal arts school, they had a wide variety of programs of interest to me – far beyond engineering. Realizing I could pair a major in history with a minor in military science, by joining ROTC, I felt it offered the best of both worlds. Not to mention, the fact that I was in a committed relationship with a wonderful girl, so remaining local allowed me to pursue what I viewed to be a long-term prospect, sealing the deal.

Moreover, Brockport offered me a fresh start, and I intended to make the most of it. I focused intently on academics from the beginning and immersed myself in Army ROTC. I thrived during the classes on tactics and strategy, weekly PT on campus, and especially, the monthly leadership drills and outings. Working with a series of on campus military instructors and advisers, I realized I could be as busy militarily as I wanted to be. Additionally, I could voluntarily compete for summer training slots, well before the mandatory cadet training camp required during the summer of the junior year, and start building my military credentials prior to graduation. The Army even offered a nationally competitive three-year ROTC scholarship, to which I immediately applied. Shortly thereafter, I was awarded a full, three-year Army ROTC scholarship, assuring me of an active duty role upon graduation.

Throughout college I excelled, making the most of the experience. My only setback occurred as a result of a football injury and resulting knee surgery my freshman year. I'd had a previous knee surgery in high school, while playing lacrosse, which was now part of my ROTC medical record. The possibility of a reoccurring knee injury concerned my ROTC instructors, and it was communicated to me, directly, that any subsequent injury would likely result in medical disqualification and my scholarship being revoked. I did not view it as a threat, but certainly took it seriously, acknowledging the need to minimize further exposure on the football field. Recognizing that the military represented my desired plan for the future, I decided not to return to football. Giving up football was disappointing, but I had made the decision to go *"all in"* with the Army, and never looked back.

My next challenge was to educate and position myself for a successful bid at my chosen branch or career field. I figured the best way to show the Army what I wanted to do, beyond excelling academically, was to compete for and attend every training opportunity available prior to graduation. So, each summer, and during the winter break of my senior year, I attended schools. First, in 1981, Basic Training at Ft. Leonard Wood, MO, followed by Northern Warfare School at Ft. Greeley, AK, in '82, then, Ranger and Airborne School at Ft. Benning, GA, in '83 and '84 respectively. By the time the Department of the Army conferred branch selections, I had locked up the Infantry slot I sought and was granted a Regular Army Commission as the Distinguished Military Graduate and George C. Marshall Leadership Award recipient at my college.

Everything had come together. Upon graduation, Elinor and I were married after dating for five years, and the only open question was, where would we be assigned. During the last four years of my exposure to the military, I had determined that my dream assignment would be to one of the Army's two, existing Ranger Battalions. The 1st Bn, 75th Rangers, located at Hunter Army Airfield in Georgia, or the 2nd Bn, 75th Rangers, at Ft. Lewis, WA. The 3rd Bn, at Ft. Benning, GA, did not yet exist. In addition to our desire to experience the Pacific Northwest, I knew from consultation with career counselors, that: 1) second lieutenants were not assigned to a Ranger Battalion straight after commissioning due to their corresponding lack of experience, 2) only first lieutenants, with highly successful platoon leader time would be considered, and 3) Infantry officers assigned to 13-month, unaccompanied tours in Korea represented the typical pathway. They would have the requisite experience and been recently promoted upon leaving that assignment, a sort of free agent, if you will.

As a newlywed, I did not particularly desire an unaccompanied tour. However, after consulting with an assignments officer in Washington, DC, I judged my course of action to be less certain, but doable. Accordingly, I opted for assignment to the 9th Infantry Division at Ft. Lewis, WA, which is also home to the 2/75th, with the notion that during my four-year commitment, I would have the opportunity to achieve the necessary platoon experience and, upon promotion to first lieutenant, request an intra-post transfer from the 9th Infantry Division to the Ranger Battalion. That was the plan.

Prior to arriving in Washington State, I made the obligatory stop at the "Home of the Infantry," Ft. Benning, GA, a place I had been many times before on training assignments, but this was for Infantry Officer Basic Course (IOBC), required of all newly minted Infantry lieutenants, regardless of previous experience. Like it was yesterday, on the date I reported in, I recall a wooden plaque above the door welcoming new officers that said simply: "LEAD, FOLLOW, OR GET THE HELL OUT

OF THE WAY!" I was riveted by that statement, potentially the single greatest one-liner I've witnessed as a student of leadership. I took it to heart and have applied it ever since.

Following four months in Georgia, we arrived at Ft. Lewis, WA, in proximity to Mt. Rainier, one of the highest mountains in the continental United States. My first assignment was as a rifle platoon leader in 2/2 Infantry, followed by anti-tank platoon leader in a sister company, within the same battalion. Both presented me with a tremendous learning experience and an opportunity to serve with some of our nation's spectacular young soldiers. Upon promotion to first lieutenant and 14 months in the 9th Infantry Division, a quick visit to the adjutant (aka personnel officer) of the Ranger Battalion across the airfield confirmed that they were indeed projecting platoon leader openings in the very near future. Based upon my status as a Ranger-qualified first lieutenant with two successful platoons under my command, all I needed going forward was an "approved" release from the 9th ID. Naively, I figured I was about to reach my goal.

Army Regulations laid out, in sum and substance, the straightforward procedures to request a transfer. At the time, I had satisfied my initial assignment requirements with the 9th, was not requesting a PCS (Permanent Change of Station) move which would cost the Army money, and I met the requirements of the next available open position. Therefore, I completed a DA Form 4187 requesting transfer and submitted it through channels. For the preceding 14 months, I had been a model officer, substantiated by "Top Block" Officer Efficiency Reports. In fact, as part of the 9th's transition to a Motorized Division, as 2/2 Infantry's Anti-Tank Platoon Leader, I had developed and conducted a Tow II Missile Field Training Exercise (FTX) for the entire battalion's successful certification required for anti-tank mission readiness. In short order, my request was approved by my company and battalion commanders, both Ranger-qualified officers themselves, and forwarded to Brigade HQ.

Days went by, and I had not yet received an endorsement or reply from the brigade commander, a full bird colonel. So, I asked my commanding officer if he'd heard anything. He hadn't, but had a staff meeting later that day and said he'd check with the battalion commander.

Hours later, I remember being summoned up to Battalion HQ to see the "old man." There, in the lieutenant colonel's office, sat my company commander. The battalion commander waved me in, and I centered myself in front of his desk and "reported" with a salute. He returned the salute and told me to have a seat next to the captain. The Boss did not mince words, he said, "Chuck, your request has been disapproved by the brigade commander. He won't entertain it." He could tell I was shocked by the look on my face, especially knowing the positive endorsements he and my captain had provided. He said, "You've done a nice job for us, so when I got the response, I called him."

"The brigade commander said, quote 'My brigade is _not_ a fucking training brigade for Ranger lieutenants!'"

"So," my battalion commander continued, "I'm sorry. We may have an opening in the Scout Platoon or S-3 shop coming up, if you're looking for a change."

I came to attention, thanked him for his effort and requested permission to be dismissed. My company commander exited with me and waited till we got out of the building before he said what I was thinking, "That's bull shit." I just looked his way in disbelief. He knew it was my longtime goal to serve in the Ranger Battalion, among, in my view, the best of the best. Then, like a flash, it entered my mind that the brigade commander was not a Ranger. I had heard of the animosity that existed between "tabbed" or Ranger-qualified, and "non-tabbed" Infantry officers, and by the tone of the colonel's response to my battalion commander, it was hard to see it any other way. It was a long walk back to the company area. From that moment on, I vowed, NEVER to hold back a fellow soldier in any professional quest or aspiration.

I was devastated. For the same reason Ranger Battalions do not take newly promoted lieutenants on as platoon leaders, they do not take on new captains without a prior successful company command. The problem is, there are a lot of captains looking to punch their ticket for a second command with the Rangers, and due to the natural order of selection, the Ranger Battalions can (and should) be highly selective taking their future company commanders from a pool of captains who have also _previously_ *served* with them as a Ranger lieutenant. Makes sense. So, while it's a big Army, with lots to do in the conventional Infantry, I reckoned, this was very likely the end of my dreams of serving with either Ranger Battalion.

A brief period of time passed, but the disappointment continued to resonate. Then, one day, I was reading the "Army Times," the popular military journal, and noted an advertisement to become a U.S. Army Aviator. The article went on to say that a Department of the Army selection board would soon convene to select active duty officers for flight school. All that was needed was: 1) a passing score on Flight Aptitude Selection Test (FAST), 2) a Class 1 flight physical, and 3) endorsement from local command. *Damn, there it was again.* I didn't even know how the first two would go, when I saw the third bullet, and realized that I would probably be blocked again. But, nothing ventured...

As an officer, I could schedule the first two screening requirements across post on my own, as neither required unit approval, just to see where I stood. In short order, I had an excellent FAST test score and Class 1 flight physical in hand. Now the hard part.

As luck, would have it, by the time I assembled my completed package, my brigade commander, yes *that* colonel, had gone on Christmas leave. I took this as a sign, and submitted it through channels. In no time, I had my company and battalion commander's endorsement (again) and hand carried it up to Brigade HQ. This time around, the brigade executive officer, a lieutenant colonel, had been designated as the "acting" brigade commander, and signed off with a smile and sincere, "Good luck, Lieutenant!" I had the necessary "approval" and wasted no time ensuring it got all the way to Washington, DC, in time for the board.

One month later, "Official" Orders from the Department of the Army arrived assigning me to flight school. A phone call from the brigade adjutant saying that the commander wanted to see me quickly followed. I knew the risk going in and that there could be a price to pay. I reported directly to the brigade commander. As I recall, he kept me at attention for the terse and intense exchange. He was livid, but could not argue with the fact that I had followed all the rules, even if brigade endorsement occurred in his absence. But, he made it perfectly clear, "Lieutenant, you better hope you do well in flight school, and they don't send you back here to me...Now, get out of my office!"

So, I was off to the Initial Entry Rotary Wing Aviator Course at Ft. Rucker, AL, for another life-changing experience. Over the years, I've had ample time to review my conduct relative to that transfer. Frankly, the only regret I have is that I loved the Infantry! The camaraderie, discipline, and *"Can do!"* attitude of the American Soldier is second to none. I do not regret submitting my flight school request to the brigade executive officer. The brigade commander, who had never even met me prior to the very end, dealt my request to transfer to the Ranger Battalion, a career objective, a crushing blow, without a second thought. And when my battalion commander inquired on my behalf, lit into him with an F-bomb laced tirade, as if I had no business even asking. Good riddance.

Flight school was the real deal. I've got to hand it to the Army. Nobody does helicopters better than the United States Army. It was an intense experience, made all the more difficult by the omnipresence of mathematical calculations, but I was not to be denied. At Brockport State, I had no choice but to take math courses as part of my early core curriculum graduation requirement, but given a phenomenal professor with a gift for explaining math to "right-side" brained guys like me, and without the pressure of going to the blackboard every day, I managed two A's, checking the box toward graduation. Besides, this was different, the calculations were applied in the form of aerodynamics, aircraft systems, instrument flight, and weather effect. Not easy, but relatable and workable.

In fact, my earlier experience with "failure," at the Prep School, kept me on guard. I took nothing for granted and spent so much time studying that my wife, who had accompanied me to Alabama, felt like a geographic bachelorette. When I wasn't on the flight line, I kept myself locked in the spare bedroom of our apartment studying. The only interruptions I recall, were the occasional meal together or when she convinced me to finally take a break to join her at the pool at our complex or the beach in Panama City, FL. Even then, I was never without my 3" x 5" index study cards. We still laugh to this day about her quizzing me late at night on my EMERGENCY PROCEDURES and her nodding off while

I recited a multi-step procedure to counteract the condition. She told me, long after the fact, that she would have felt *responsible* if I'd crashed!

In those days (circa 1986) we started training in the TH-55 Osage, a small, two-seat helo, with barely enough room for the student pilot and instructor. Painted orange, so the rest of Army Aviation in the state of Alabama knew to avoid you, it was an exciting platform to learn the fundamentals of helicopter flight. For the uninitiated, flying helicopters takes slightly more hand, eye, and mental coordination than flying fixed-wing aircraft. In certain models, one needs only to *think* about making a control input and the slightest, virtually imperceptible, movement will transmit into the controls resulting in a change of flight attitude. Truthfully, it takes some time to get the hang of it, and it is not for everyone. I still remember the afternoon I got it. My grizzled Vietnam-era instructor pilot (IP) was attempting to teach me how to hover (over a fixed point on the ground) with only a few hours in the aircraft, giving me simultaneous responsibility for all three control inputs. As he transferred control of the helicopter to me, he said, "Try to keep it in the state of Alabama, kid!" Initially tensing up, I drifted slightly fore and aft, side to side, and up and down. The more I fought to keep the aircraft in one spot, the farther off the mark I drifted. The IP reiterated, "Just relax. Relax…" With nothing to lose, I "forced" myself to relax, which is a completely mental and physical exercise. With only a soft touch on the cyclic, a firm, but steady, grip on the collective lever, and subtle pressure on the pedals, I found the "hover button," as they call it, and stuck the hover.

That exercise proved the value of mental affect and conditioning. Whether it pertains to flying, completing an Ironman, taking a precision sniper shot, or televised public speaking, mindset is the key.

By far, the most rewarding moment of my flight school experience is when we supported the Ranger School during a FTX out of Camp Rudder, FL. While this activity served our training purposes as Huey student pilots in the areas of mission planning, tactics, and formation flight, the best part was we would be transporting actual Ranger students, during an airmobile assault of their final training evolution, during "Swamp Phase." It was at this point, after approximately nine weeks of training, sleep deprivation, and minimal food intake (forced caloric restriction), the Ranger students were physically at their lowest point, but were expected to perform flawlessly at the highest, company-level missions. Having recently completed Ranger training three years earlier, I knew firsthand how they were feeling and what the prospect of an airmobile mission held for them. First, it meant the opportunity to fly from point A to point B instead of walk. That was an obvious bonus for soldiers reaching physical exhaustion. Second, and most important, was the unofficial tradition of flight school students handing out food to starving Ranger students, once they boarded the helicopters.

This time-honored tradition depended largely on the Ranger Instructors. For those students boarding a helicopter without an instructor, it was five to eight minutes of heaven. In that instance, the crew chief would hand out the pre-made baggies of food (M&Ms, peanuts, oatmeal creme pies, beef jerky, etc.), with the understanding that it ALL had to be consumed prior to landing. In any event, NO student was allowed to take contraband food with him on the ground; a violation of course regulations. For those students boarding with a Ranger Instructor (RI), it all depended on the RI. He either looked the other way, or gave a thumbs down, dooming the students. Any soldier going through that experience will tell you, they looked forward to the airmobile for days, specifically because of the prospect they may get some extra food into their depleted systems. Those who missed out were devastated.

While that aspect was out of our control as student pilots, being the only Ranger in my flight school class, I ensured each helicopter was well-stocked with an Aviator's kit bag full of snacks. As we landed at the pick-up zone (PZ), the students boarded the helicopter, and without an RI to accompany them, we were free to hand out the snacks to the ravenous soldiers. As they tore into the bags, one student noticed the Ranger tab Velcroed on back of my flight helmet, got the attention of his fellow soldiers in the back of the aircraft, and give me a big thumbs up. Priceless!

My academic perseverance in Flight School was rewarded in two ways: First, posting the top GPA, I was the Distinguished Graduate, and I had the honor of having my silver wings pinned onto my uniform by CW4 Michael J. Novosel, a Vietnam-era Medal of Honor Recipient; second, I was awarded my choice of aircraft transition or duty location. As a Huey pilot, I requested a Black Hawk transition, but was advised the only place they were being assigned, at that time, was on an unaccompanied tour in South Korea. Or, I could have my choice of worldwide geographic assignments. After consultation with my wife, I chose Hawaii, and never looked back. *Somebody's got to take those hardship assignments!* Prior to arrival, with some experience as a first lieutenant who had already served in a previous duty assignment, I reached out for the 25th Infantry Division (Light) Aviation Brigade S-1 (personnel officer) at Schofield Barracks, HI, and requested assignment to the Air Cavalry Squadron. It had been my experience that the intensity and tradition of the Air Cav would be a good fit for me, plus, it came with another desirable aircraft transition to the OH-58 Kiowa Scout Helicopter.

Elinor and I arrived in Hawaii at the end of 1986, just before Christmas. We found the Island much to our liking as it offered a plethora of activities and opportunities to explore.

The Air Cavalry made me feel right at home with its mix of ground troopers and aviators. Traditionally, a Cavalry Squadron presented a structure of one mechanized or armor (tank) troop and two helicopter troops. As the 25th ID had recently converted to a LIGHT Infantry Division, our ground troop consisted of Cavalry Scouts with HUMVEEs. Collectively, our squadron, the 3/4 CAV, later redesignated 5/9 CAV, was a highly mobile and lethal combined-arms task force, supporting the Division's Infantry soldiers with two troops of aerial OH-58 Kiowa Scouts and accompanying Cobra Attack Helicopters and one ground Reconnaissance Scout troop.

Nearly four years in Hawaii flew by, with two deployments to Team Spirit in Korea, serving as a Scout Helicopter Platoon leader, and one deployment to Japan, where I served as captain – Flight Operations officer. Toward the end of my assignment, it was time to serve as a primary staff officer, and I was selected as the battalion adjutant of the 25th Attack Battalion.

These were busy days. Elinor and I thoroughly enjoyed our time in Hawaii, the highlight of which was the birth of our first beautiful daughter, Jennifer.

By this time, I had been a captain for approximately two years, and my six years in the Army was quickly coming to an end. I knew that the time was at hand to choose between attending a Branch Advance Course, followed by another PCS transfer, Functional Area, and joint-assignment, thus solidifying my career as a soldier, or consider options in the civilian world. With a young family, including a two-year-old born in Honolulu, the prospect of moving back to New York State, where both our families were located, tugged heavily at me.

Since I was 16 years old, I had had an interest in law enforcement, particularly in becoming a State Trooper. Indeed, my entire plan to go to college was based upon the fact that applicants had to be 21 years old to enter the NYSP Academy, and that meant there would be years to productively fill between high school graduation and applying to the New York State Police. During late 1989, while still in Hawaii, I contacted a recruiter with the State Police assigned to my home region of Rochester, NY. He seemed quite pleased to have an Army officer with a Secret Clearance (which meant I had a clean background as a candidate) on the line. He advised me that they had an exam scheduled for early 1990, and back in the days before the Internet, he put an application packet together for me, to be picked up at my local barracks, when I was home on leave. Easy enough.

Weeks later, I stopped by the barracks, introduced myself to a trooper at the front desk, who looked rather unimpressed. He was not the recruiter I had spoken to previously, and I asked him for my application packet. He took a very brief look around his immediate grabbable area, that is to say he didn't get off his ass, and said, "Nope. Nothing here."

Now, I knew that the recruiter on the phone had ensured the package was waiting for me at the desk at SP Henrietta, but I didn't want to piss this guy off either. I said, "Would you mind taking a second look trooper; I was told it's here."

Without a word, he stood up, a good start, and delved into the assemblage of envelopes behind him on the counter. Expressionless and without apology, he spun around and slapped it down in front of me, with a, "Here ya go."

Other than my conversations with the recruiter, and two tickets I got when I was seventeen from a road trooper, this was the first contact I'd had with the SP. I could tell by this interaction, that it would be pointless to ask him how he likes the job, so I collected my envelope and headed out. In all honesty, sometimes you learn more from certain people about how *not* to lead, or how *not* to interact with the public. Disappointing to say the least. Fortunately, I did not let that dissuade me.

I returned to New York in early 1990 for the exam and was promptly told that 30,000 people had signed up to take it. I knew I had what it takes, but for this effort to be relevant for me, I'd have to hit the proverbial "homerun," as classes are typically 100-150 recruits per year. I went in focused and gave it my best. The old-school troopers administering the exam did not give a rip. No pleasantries either: sit down, pick up your pencil when we tell you, and put it down when we tell you. If you need to use the "head" (bathroom) a trooper will accompany you. "Any questions? No? Good. Begin." Hours later, upon conclusion, it was very much, "Don't call us, we'll call you. See ya."

I returned to Hawaii, the Army, and life. Months went by and my decision point for the military was coming up rapidly. The Army waits for no one. Today, in the age of the Internet, there's a New York State Police website, and not only recruiters give a damn about recruiting, but *everyone* in our agency cares about recruiting and putting the State Police in the best light, as we compete for the best of the best candidates. But, back then…not so much. Then, one day in May 1990, I got a letter in the mail advising me I got a "99" on the written exam and was invited back to New York for a physical fitness test and medical evaluation. I had the score I needed and knew I'd crush the physical stuff, as I was top physical shape, competing locally in triathlons in Hawaii. The only step left, or so I thought, was to schedule a trip back to New York for what the SP refer to as Processing Weekend.

The weekend flew by, and I aced the physical components. After having sat through several hours of written psychological testing, we met back in the main lecture hall (auditorium), where the subject came up regarding scheduling the Psychological Interview; three weeks hence.

Three weeks from now?! I thought. That means flying back to Hawaii and returning a third time for further processing. *Heck,* I reasoned *I'm tentatively scheduled to get out of the Army in six weeks! I wonder if I can defer it...?* So, although I didn't want to be *that guy,* that holds everyone up, I had to raise my hand. The proctor reading the instructions looked like he'd never heard that question before, and I was now distracting him from his mission. With the wave of his hand, another nearby trooper pointed at me and gave me the, "Come 'ere, you," gesture. I got up and followed him out to the lobby, right near the front doors, half wondering if he was going to escort me out to the street!

The trooper simply said, "Look, we don't have special accommodations for military personnel, but I'll call over to HQ and ask." Which, at the time, I thought was accommodating. I stood at parade rest, while he spoke briefly with someone across the street. The call didn't take long. He turned to me and said, "The Director of Personnel says...,'If you want this job, have your ass back here in three weeks for the Psych.'"

"Roger that," I said.

CHAPTER 3

ESTABLISHING COMMAND

Racing north, I realized the odds were quickly stacking up against us, and we faced a truly daunting task. Two desperate men, with nothing to lose, were now on the run in the Adirondacks.

Twenty miles to the north was the U.S.-Canadian border, with New York State, and relative freedom, if they managed to reach it.

Fifteen miles to the east, Lake Champlain, with its various ferries and innumerable small craft ripe for the taking, would lead them to Vermont, where law enforcement would have nowhere near the resources to deal with New York's problem.

Along the southeastern exposure lay miles of interstate highway and active train tracks affording high-speed avenues of egress, if they could reach them. Not to mention, a surge in the vehicle traffic on the highways and waterways due to the increasing summer tourist population, ready to be exploited. These routes were obvious and well-known. All you had to do was look at a map, and you'd recognize that a pathway to civilization by way of Plattsburgh, the state capital in Albany, and eventually…New York City, lay before you. Furthermore, if you'd arranged to be picked up by an associate, hijack or steal a car, or reach the transportation hub of a major city by any means, that would open the rest of the nation and Mexico to the south.

Due south was the heart of the Adirondack Mountains, an area known as the High Peaks. An improbable, and extremely rugged cluster of 46 mountains all rising over 4,000-5,000 feet.

Last, but not least, was the area to the west of the prison. In short order, given a stolen vehicle, ATV, or even on foot, one would only have to travel a very short distance outside the Village of Dannemora before being able to recede into thick wilderness. This westward territory was devoid of most major thoroughfares, but replete with thousands of remote hunting cabins, or "camps," as they are typically referred to in the Adirondacks, well off the beaten path, or grid. Most, well-stocked and suitably armed for the task, are only visited seasonally. To complicate matters, the proliferation of these camps throughout the region, many owned by correction officers themselves, was well-known by most inmates. While there is no reason, whatsoever, to believe information was intentionally passed, what is known, is that inmates surreptitiously eaves drop on the conversations between C.O.s, for even the smallest bits of information, which can later be exploited in a variety of ways.

So, it was this western quadrant, that while least likely or desirable as a route of travel, worried me the most. For it was here, that a man, or in this case two men, could lose themselves and avoid apprehension, if they played their cards right. I also recognized this region, as they all were to varying degrees, would quickly become a resource vacuum. No matter what numbers we assembled, and how technologically savvy we would become, our assets stood the chance of being quickly swallowed up and rendered ineffective, without efficient deployment and effective supervision.

In addition to the sheer vastness of the region, was the raw environment. For starters, the terrain was mountainous and rugged. Significant swaths of the entire area are dedicated wilderness, in its many forms, laced with swamps, bogs, lakes, ponds, creeks, and rivers. Bear, moose, deer, coyotes, turkey, racoons, beavers, mosquitos, and black flies populate the region in high numbers. Movement, while difficult, would favor two men travelling lightly on foot and tend to confound the hundreds of searchers, who could, at times, see no farther than two feet in front of themselves. Likewise, the thickness of the vegetation would afford the inmates immense overhead concealment, denying the visual observation efforts of our skilled pilots throughout most of the search sector, and routinely thwarting the infrared reconnaissance systems on board our fleet of aircraft. To make the search even more difficult, the summer of June 2015 wrought uncharacteristically inclement weather; it seemed that every other day we experienced torrential rain, wind, and ground fog.

As I made my way off the Adirondack Northway, near Plattsburgh, NY, I was within 15 miles of Clinton Correctional Facility, which is located within the Village of Dannemora. A village of approximately 5,000, just 20 miles south of the Canadian border, where most folks work, or have friends or relatives that work in, or retired from, the prison. Dannemora's existence coincided with a plan to construct a prison in the wilderness of Northern New York in the mid-1800s. Construction of Dannemora prison, today officially known as Clinton Correctional Facility, commenced in 1845. It is New York State's third oldest prison, behind Auburn and Sing Sing, and was originally conceived as a result of a legislative commission formed to develop the use of New York State's natural resources; specifically, the mining of iron ore by convict labor. In fact, Dannemora took its name from an iron-mining region in Sweden, a reflection of its original charter and purpose.

The landscape is harsh and remote, but included massive ore deposits within Lyon Mountain, just west of the prison. Applied convict labor spurred both mining development and the simultaneous construction of the prison outpost itself. At the onset, the prison was little more than a 25-foot-tall stockade, cut from the wilderness, encompassing an area of about 15 acres, but this morphed over past 170 years into a fortress in the heart of the village, with multiple guard towers overlooking imposing walls that are 30 feet tall, and at least 7 feet thick at the base.

Historically speaking, Dannemora's past is largely defined by the purported conditions within those walls. Numerous governmental commissions, inquests, investigations, and legal challenges on behalf of inmates, depict a facility historically marred by accusations of torture, violence, and brutality. Despite decades of reforms, modifications to the penal code and the outright prohibition of corporal punishment, Dannemora continued its vexing reputation as a "Den of Horrors" into the beginning of the 20th century.

Over the years, vast, sweeping transformational improvements have been made, modernizing the entire prison system. However, as in years past, the correction officers are all that stand between society and the convicted, often violent offenders, who perpetrate heinous crimes. Notably, Clinton Correctional Facility is known to house the "worst of the worst" of those offenders, and managing this population remains a daunting task.

On any given day, C.O.s are subjected to the daily stresses of threats of violence, fights, risk of injury, gang assaults, and the intentional exposure to communicable diseases from thrown urine and feces.

It is precisely within this backdrop that the 1,005-member staff of Clinton Correctional Facility, the clear majority of whom are true professionals, found itself attending to the day-to-day affairs of over 2,700 of New York's most hardened criminals, men like Richard Matt and David Sweat.

The first sign I was getting close was the traffic backup. This was the first of several armed check points I would pass through, manned by shotgun- and automatic rifle-toting troopers and correction officers. Even though I was their troop commander, I was driving my assigned, *unmarked* Chevy Impala, and I didn't want to make their jobs any more difficult with any aggressive maneuvering to expedite my way through the road block. Nerves were on a hair trigger, so I waited my turn in line. The closer I got to the facility, the more activity I observed. Now, in addition to road blocks, every 50 yards, less in some cases depending on sight distance, stood a correction officer or trooper on post, lining the roads.

Entering the village, the walls of the facility along Main Street loomed larger than ever. I saw teams of law enforcement officers and C.O.s going door to door interviewing residents, checking garages and out buildings. The Command Post (CP) was located at the Clinton Correctional Facility Training Building, on the campus of the prison, just outside the fence on the south side of the facility, and it was humming with activity. I exited my vehicle and approached the entrance, which was guarded by two C.O.s, to maintain security. I was pleased to see that, according to protocol, they demanded ID. While force protection is a concern at any mass gathering of law enforcement, in this instance, it was more a matter of denying access to unauthorized personnel: the media, well-meaning civilians, and the occasional bounty hunter. Over time, abundant sensitive material, and numerous confidential briefings would occur here, which would best be safeguarded and presented to those in law enforcement with a "need to know."

I entered the building and was immediately greeted by a Corrections Emergency Response Team (CERT) member, who was going about the business of briefing his people, handing out maps, updating a white board and issuing firearms. This encouraged me, because there was some semblance of order, but I did not see any of my people, or any member of outside law enforcement. "Is this the CP?" I asked.

"No, Sir," the officer replied. "Down at the end of the hall."

I walked to the last open door at the end of the hall and found three more DOCCS staff members, just sitting there, in what looked like stunned disbelief at the situation; still I saw no troopers. "CP?" I said.

"Uh, no," came the reply. "End of the hall."

As it was, the Command Post was apparently located at the other end of the building. Nothing had been placarded yet, and some folks just seemed to be doing their own thing. I quickly reversed course, walking past where I'd come in, in the middle of the building's first floor, and set my sights on the opposite end of the hall. Arriving momentarily, I immediately saw the local Zone Commander, Captain Brent Gillam, the officer who had called me earlier that morning, plus a handful of troopers, deputies, police officers, and NYS Forest Rangers huddled around a chalkboard. Although there was no one from DOCCS (Corrections), I knew I was in the right place.

"Brent," I called out. "What do we have so far?" To say Gillam was relieved to see me, would be an understatement, and who could blame him. He looked like he was up to his ass in alligators and could use the help.

"Major," he exhaled, "…we have ALL of the check points established, most of the major roads staffed with Corrections personnel, our roving troop cars are mobile, and we're starting to check houses. Oh, and Aviation is up!"

"What about the border?" I asked. He assured me, once again, that U.S. Customs and Border Protection (USCBP) had been notified once the escape was confirmed and that they were on high-alert.

"Good," I replied. Captain Gillam had, in fact, initiated the entire response plan, as directed. [There were numerous other elements that shall remain confidential.] He was attempting to lock down the village and had boots on the ground searching aggressively, in an effort to prevent their escape from the village. Things were getting done…important things, but judging by the lack of maps, photos, communications, staff deployment numbers, post assignment sectors, and agency representation in the Command Post, we had a long way to go. Basically, other than a handful of uniformed personnel at the CP, mostly troopers, there was no infrastructure, just a chalkboard, a couple of folding chairs and tables. Not even mug shots of our two escapees.

"Where's the DOCCS rep?" I asked.

"They've been in and out," came the response.

"That's UNSAT," I said. "They need to have someone in here at <u>all</u> times to affect coordination."

For that matter, "Where's the BCI (NYSP Bureau of Criminal Investigation)?!" I asked, although I did not care for the response.

"They've set up shop off site," someone said. Adding, "They needed Internet access, and there's none here."

WTF? I thought. *How do you run an investigation without <u>investigators</u> on hand?* This was *not* Gillam's problem, but it *was* mine. "That's got to change," I said. "How do I get there?"

An officer replied, "Not sure, I think you go down two blocks, make a right, go up the hill and…" *blah, blah, blah.*

"Are you kidding me?" I said, noting the separation and convoluted directions.

By this time, my entire staff, ten Troop "B" Commissioned Officers, had been alerted. An exceptional bunch, they were either coming in, or now planning to come in, for the night shift; a couple of them automatically postponing vacation plans. Additionally, we were standing up a Troop-wide response, in addition to that which had already been supplied by Zone One, Gillam's zone. Clearly, the two escapees could be anywhere by this time. And while we had already put out a statewide APB, our folks had to be ready, and at the top of their game. At any time, a trooper 100 miles away could stop a speeding car containing our subjects, and…I couldn't bear to think of the implications.

"Brent, how many people do we have on post here and now?" I asked.

He looked at a lieutenant, who had been assisting him with the deployment. The lieutenant said, "You mean altogether, 'cause I have no way of knowing. Agencies have been kind of self-deploying."

"OK," I said. "How about just troopers? Where are they, and what are they doing?"

At this point, both the captain and the lieutenant looked at a sergeant who stated, "I think we have about..."

"Look," I said, cutting him off, "...you guys have done a great job. I'm actually pleased with what I saw on the ground coming in, but now it's up to us to get this thing squared away. I'll be talking to the superintendent soon, and we must know *exactly* how many troopers we have here. On the operational side, he's going to ask me what I have deployed and what I'll need going forward. So, I need you guys to figure out our current numbers *definitively*. Lieutenant Boyea, I'm assigning that responsibility to you. In the meantime, Brent, get DOCCS in here and a representative from each agency that's assisting. When I come back, I want to see a map depicting the search area, photos and pedigrees of the inmates, a staffing and resource plan on the board, enhanced communications, and an update on computer access," I directed.

"In other words, turn this office into a Command Post. I'm going to find the BCI. I have plenty of questions for them as well," I said, eager to get some answers.

"Aye, aye," Gillam replied.

"Thanks, brother. See you soon," I said.

Heading out of the building, I still knew little more than the identity of these two men, let alone who their associates are, who saw them last, who they're talking to on the outside, if there are any stolen vehicles, did they receive assistance from prison staff, etc. All questions for my BCI. I had to find Captain LaFountain, the officer-in-charge (OIC) of Troop "B" BCI, ASAP. I stepped out of the building and called Bob.

"Major," he answered, "I was just about to call you. The superintendent (warden) of Clinton wants to meet with us in his office, inside the prison. The Commissioner of DOCCS is here too. I'll meet you at the front entrance."

"I'm just leaving the CP," I said. "Be there momentarily."

As I exited my vehicle, my phone rang. It was my boss, Superintendent D'Amico.

"Chuck, Joe D'Amico. How's it going up there?" I filled him in with what I had, advising him that my BCI Captain and I were about to head into the facility to meet with the Commissioner of DOCCS, along with the Clinton superintendent and his staff. He said, "Anything you need, let me or Patricia (NYSP Field Commander Colonel Patricia Groeber) know, and you got it."

I thanked him and advised that we were still wrapping our heads around the number of resources engaging in the search effort, and that I would have a definitive report for him shortly. That assessment, and the situation on the ground, would determine my additional requests.

Over the years, I'd had significant dealings with Superintendent D'Amico, from my time as the detail commander of the Aviation Unit, up to and including granting my request to command at the troop level. A former standout deputy chief from the New York Police Department (NYPD), I knew him to be a straight shooter, level-headed, and true to his word. Solid, a "cop's cop." As for Colonel Groeber, I had known her even longer. A consummate professional, who had risen through the ranks of the State Police, serving in virtually every significant assignment along the way, to ultimately command all Uniform and Investigative (BCI) assets for the agency. There was no one better. I was indeed fortunate to have these two at the helm of the NYSP during this hour of need.

"One more thing," added the superintendent, "the Governor's on his way."

Perfect, I thought. "ETA?" I said.

"He's flying into Plattsburgh and driving from there," he said. "Probably will be in Dannemora around 1:00 PM to 1:15 PM."

I said, "Boss, I've got to tell you…the right things are happening on the ground right now, but the Command Post is a fucking disaster! I've already given instructions to rectify that, but we're not ready for him yet."

The superintendent did not get excited, "Well, he's on his way. Just do your best, Chuck. If there's anyone we have that can pull this off, it's you."

I said, "Thanks, Boss. I'm on it."

Before meeting LaFountain, and entering the facility, I contacted Gillam back at the CP. "Brent, the Governor's on his way."

"You're shitting me!" he said.

"No, I am not," I replied. Get that place squared away! Prepare for a briefing for when he gets here around 1:00 PM. I'll deliver it, but you'll need to bring me up to speed, when I return from meeting with the commissioner inside the prison."

Captain LaFountain arrived and I advised him of my recent conversation with the superintendent. "Bob, where are your guys located?" I asked.

"Right up the hill there," he said, pointing past the western perimeter of the facility, "...At the OSI (Office of Special Investigations, aka Internal Affairs) Building." We're working with their investigators, and they have Internet," he said.

"We'll stop there next," I said. "Let's head in."

The prison was in complete lockdown, but the front gate was expecting us. After securing our firearms, we were escorted up to the superintendent's office. An antiquated facility, the small office was crammed with DOCCS personnel. At the head of the conference table sat "Acting" Commissioner Anthony Annucci. To his right sat, First Deputy Commissioner Joseph Bellnier, and other headquarters staff from Central Office in Albany, including Colonel Dennis Bradford, commander of the statewide Corrections Emergency Response Team (CERT). At the opposite end of the room stood Clinton Correctional Facility Superintendent Steven Racette, his first deputy superintendent, the deputy superintendent in charge of security, along with other ranking Clinton staff.

Over the next 23 days, I would work closely with Commissioner Annucci, Deputy Commissioner Bellnier, and hand in glove with Colonel Bradford; there would prove to be no finer partners in this effort. But, for now, after introductions, I was listening to the superintendent of Clinton, and his deputies, rehash how they thought Matt and Sweat escaped. On the wall and table in front of us, they had hastily assembled schematics and photographs of key areas along the route of escape. A captain or lieutenant, who had just walked the route, assisted in providing a description.

As we took it all in, I leaned across the table and asked the commissioner if he'd gotten word that Governor Cuomo was en route. He had and advised me that it was his understanding that the Governor would be stopping first, at the Command Post for a briefing, and then he <u>may</u> wish to enter the facility himself.

This came as no surprise to me. Governor Andrew Cuomo is a very "hands on" chief executive. I had worked closely with him and his staff over the years as the major- in-charge of the State Police Aviation Unit, and knew that he preferred to make his own, personal, on-scene assessments, of natural or man-made disasters. Just his leadership style and hard to disagree with. Invariably, massive state assets would be brought to bear, and what better way to understand and orchestrate a response leading to a successful outcome, than to see for yourself?

With the clock ticking, an escape on our hands, and the impending arrival of Governor Cuomo, all of us had tasks to attend to. Consequently, we wrapped up our meeting and agreed to reconvene at the Command Post, in advance of the Governor's arrival. Before my departure, I met briefly with the CERT commander, reiterating the obvious, "Colonel our operation must be in sync. I just came from the Command Post and people are headed in different directions. There was not even a rep from DOCCS stationed with the troopers. That needs to change forthwith, and I would appreciate whatever you can do to address that." Fortunately, I was talking to the right guy, because Colonel Bradford made it happen and ensured that DOCCS and the State Police remained *unified* in our command, control, and operational efforts from that moment forward.

LaFountain and I exited the facility, but before returning to assess the level of improvements at the CP, we headed up the hill to visit the remote BCI lead desk. Characterizing it as remote, does not mean it was ineffectual or that it was not buzzing with activity; it was. The Troop "B" Major Crimes Unit, a superlative group of investigators responsible for solving many heinous crimes throughout the region, had commandeered the entire garage adjoining the Office of Special Investigations (OSI) offices and set up tables, run phone lines, and positioned Wi-Fi modems near the garage door. Perhaps most significantly, they had established direct contact with the DOCCS OSI regional investigators; this relationship would prove fruitful.

Right off the bat, Captain LaFountain described how Major Crimes was tying in to DOCCS, <u>plus</u> other troops and specialized units within the

NYSP. Additionally, our local law enforcement partners were being further dialed in and outreach had commenced to the Vermont State Police (VSP), our federal colleagues in the FBI, U.S. Marshals Service (USMS), U.S. Customs and Border Protection and the Royal Canadian Mounted Police. One thing about being a "border" Troop, after decades of interagency cooperation, Troop "B", had deeply rooted connections, arguably the best in the NYSP.

Part of the briefing I received entailed a noteworthy development. It seems that in 2014, an allegation had been made that a Civilian Employee, Joyce Mitchell, an Industrial Training Supervisor in Tailor Shop 1, had been accused of having an "inappropriate relationship" with Inmate David Sweat. At the request of Superintendent Racette, OSI had conducted an internal investigation, regarding such conduct, closing it as "unfounded"; clearly, there was more to investigate here.

Mitchell became a person of interest, and State Police Investigators were looking for her. Relatively quickly, they'd learned the location of Mitchell and verified that she had checked into Alice Hyde Medical Center in Malone, NY, the previous evening (June 5), complaining of chest pain. Efforts were now underway to interview her.

While satisfied with how the Bureau (BCI) was progressing, they were "connected," gathering intel, and issuing assignments to field investigators, they were still undeniably segregated from the Uniformed operational folks at the CP. In fact, during my quick visit, computer access was briefly severed, when someone inadvertently lowered the garage door. I knew this had to change, but we would have to create a suitable working space for the BCI at the Training Building before pulling the plug here and ordering them to relocate. I advised Captain LaFountain of my concerns and intention, so that he and his staff could adequately prepare.

This was my responsibility, and through experience, I had a definitive vision of what an adequate Command Post should look like for the growing multi-agency response. It would take time and coordination to establish the organizational structure *and* infrastructure for such a mission, but time was measured in hours, not days. And, the change-over had to occur *seamlessly*.

Two hours later, I returned to the Command Post, where Captain Gillam ushered me in, and I almost didn't recognize the place. On the chalkboard, Lieutenant Boyea had outlined our total staffing strength by agency and assignment. Two large photos of the escapees and several facility schematics and aerial photographs had been mounted. Additional desks and chairs had been added, along with a couple of phone lines, and some rudimentary placarding, identifying responsibilities. Perhaps the greatest achievement, was the fact that a representative from _every_ agency, currently on the ground, was now located at the CP. They were physically present, which afforded me my first opportunity to address the Unified Command staff, as the Incident Commander (IC). Brent gave me a brief update on our external search and patrol activity, and coupled with what I had learned during my visit to our BCI lead desk, and the prison itself, I felt as prepared as I could be in that amount of time for the Governor's arrival. Gillam and company had indeed been busy!

By now, I was plugged into the SP Protective Services Unit (PSU) our version of the Secret Service, and was tracking the Governor's movement. I had friends in the unit who, knowing what I was dealing with, were keeping me well-informed. Minutes before his arrival, Commissioner Annucci and his entourage arrived in anticipation. As the Governor's motorcade pulled up alongside the Training Building, the commissioner and I walked out to meet Andrew Cuomo. The Governor, who earlier in the day had been on his way to the Belmont Raceway, intending on watching what turned out to be the first Triple Crown winning horse, American Pharaoh, in the last 37 years, before the situation compelled him to redirect to Dannemora, stepped out of his Suburban in a blue blazer and khaki pants. The commissioner went first, greeting the Governor, and then Cuomo turned to me. I extended my hand, as he looked quizzically at me, as if to say _something's out of place here_, and I said, "Good afternoon, Governor. Major Guess… the 'new' troop commander of Troop "B". Now it was clear to him.

He made the connection and replied, "Hello, Major. You may wish you had stayed in Aviation." That helped to break the ice, and we headed inside.

As we proceeded down the hall to the Command Post, I noticed we were being preceded by a member of the Governor's staff, who arrived at the room before we did. Apparently, as became clear later, the well-meaning staff member, had made a comment before we walked in directing, in sum and substance, "Anyone not assigned to a State Agency should leave the room, while the Governor gets a secure briefing." Unbeknownst to me, that was all it took to lose the initial coalition of outside agency reps Gillam had worked so hard to get in the room. As Governor Cuomo entered and began shaking hands, one by one, several individuals representing the Sheriff's Department, DA's Office, and local police slipped out. By the time we worked our way to the front of the small room and turned around, <u>only</u> the State Police, DOCCS, and Forest Rangers remained. The room was still quite full, so, the changeover largely went unnoticed. I would understandably hear from those disenfranchised partners later, and I had additional work ahead of me – getting them all back to the table.

At the front of the room, the Governor, as calm and collected as one could be, looked at the DOCCS Commissioner and asked, "Just how did this happen?"

Commissioner Annucci provided a thorough overview and then turned to Superintendent Racette to describe the mechanics of the escape. After all, it was his prison. Racette, a 37-year veteran, an experienced, and by all accounts admired, DOCCS employee, stepped forward and described to the Governor the purported escape route.

In summary, Inmates Matt and Sweat, after leaving bundles of material (clothes, etc.) in their bunks to appear as though they were sleeping, had both cut rectangular holes through steel walls in the back of their adjacent Honor Block cells, in an area behind their respective bunks, gained access to the catwalks behind the cellblock, shinnied down some three stories to the bowels of the prison, broke through a brick wall near a 18-inch steam pipe, cut their way *in* to the steel pipe, snaked some 14 feet through the base of the prison's 30-foot-tall wall, then cut *out* of the steam pipe, exiting into the sewer system under the street outside the wall, and continued another 400 feet south, in the direction of the power plant. Finally, they cut their way out of a chained and locked manhole cover, in the heart of the village, climbing to freedom and emerging at the intersection of Bouck Street and Barker Street, one block south of the prison.

As improbable as that sounded, the route of egress had been "confirmed" by a team of C.O.s accompanied by a State Police K9. Adding insult to injury, Matt and Sweat had mockingly left a sketch/calling card behind, a derogatory "Asian" caricature, attached to the pipe by a magnet, admonishing the C.O.s to "Have a Nice Day!"

Governor Cuomo had questions: Did they have help from or the knowledge of other inmates? When were they last seen? How long had they been gone? What tools did they use, and where did they get them? How could all the cutting and noise have been overlooked? How could routine cell searches and head counts have missed what must have been going on for weeks? How did they orient themselves to find their way out? Had they received assistance by staff? *DOCCS had none of those answers at that time.* [The mechanics of the escape, will be broken down in significant detail in Chapter 18.]

The Governor then turned to me and said, "Major, what are your thoughts about how we're set up, and what are we doing right now?" I gave him a thorough overview, based on the efforts of Captain Gillam and his staff. The Governor seemed satisfied, for the moment, and it was clear his thoughts turned back to simply, *How could this have happened?* [I must admit, we in the State Police were immediately thinking accomplices, but would hold off on voicing that notion until we had better indication.]

Despite DOCCS official's description and reference to building schematics and several photos of key portions of the route, the Governor had just too many unanswered questions, and who could blame him. He had to see for himself.

Resultantly, and in short order, DOCCS and PSU transported the Governor of the State of New York into a maximum-security prison under full lockdown. Accompanied by a core of key people from DOCCS and the State Police, Commissioner Annucci and me among them, Governor Cuomo was escorted onto the Honor Block, and taken right to the third-floor of A-Block, adjoining cells A6-22 and A6-23, where Matt and Sweat had resided until the previous night. During the walk along the tier, we passed within arm's reach of cell after cell of inmates under lockdown.

To my surprise, it was extraordinarily quiet. I had half expected jeers and raucous behavior, but you could've heard a pin drop. More surprising still, was the conditions of the cells. As a State Trooper, I'd toured many facilities, as part of our joint-security planning visits, and although I do not claim to have a great deal of familiarity of conditions within the walls, I was stunned to observe that this so-called Honor Block, which apparently permits the housing of convicted "cop killers" and multiple-murderers, appeared to allow a very lax living standard. Within the cells, I observed inmates able to wear (certain) articles of civilian clothing, possess hot plates, electronics (not cell phones or computers) and allow a plethora of items to be hung from every available surface within the cell. Aside from the associated "reform" value, this, in my opinion, created the net effect of individual enclaves, where the occupants *and* their activities, were largely shrouded from view by blankets, clothing, towels, hooded sweatshirts, and the like. Now, I do not profess to speak for the prison system, but I will offer the following layman's observation. *No wonder these guys weren't observed cutting through their cell walls or spending nights over many weeks OUT of their respective cells, down the catwalks and catacombs, tunneling to freedom.* I couldn't even clearly see the back wall of many of the cells, or some of the occupants, as I walked by with the Governor.

"Somebody must have heard something," I heard the Governor exclaim, as he peered into the cells observing the holes cut through steel. From there we proceeded to the catwalk behind the tiers, where Sweat had gained access during the preceding weeks, and commenced rummaging around, reconnoitering the underground labyrinth of the prison, crafting a way out. Ultimately, this led us to the area where Sweat had been engaged in digging and cutting, which had been processed by my crime scene technicians in the Forensic Identification Unit (FIU).

Proceeding back outside to the courtyard near the Administration building, we were then able to view, from street level, a gated access shaft to a portion of the subterranean route, as it made its way under the asphalt leading towards the outer wall. From here, we headed outside the prison, and proceeded by vehicle to the now infamous manhole on Bouck Street; which had led Matt and Sweat to freedom, albeit temporary.

Upon arrival, we observed the manhole, taped off and guarded by C.O.s. There wasn't much to say, as we stared down into the sewer, some 400 feet south of the prison wall. My investigators were already conducting neighborhood interviews and looking for any possible CCTV (closed circuit television) from the scant commercial establishments in the area, all of which would be evaluated as soon as practicable. But for now, the Governor just shook his head. He had seen what he'd come to see. The "impossible" had occurred. Initial media reports claimed that in 170 years, no one had *ever* escaped from Dannemora. While that's not entirely accurate, there were a number of escapes and walk offs in the early days, remarkably no one had escaped from the main section of the prison since 1912.[1] It was thought "unthinkable." And, that was part of the problem.

Throughout the "tour," the Clinton staff had authoritatively described "how" they believe two dangerous killers escaped from their control. Now, they appeared spent, and could not begin to account for "why" it happened, on their watch. Good men. You couldn't help but feel for them. As I looked at the superintendent of the facility, I couldn't imagine a scenario where he could survive this professionally. And, now it was _my_ turn. I had to do everything within my power to protect the public, find these two, and bring this nightmare successfully to a close.

After what seemed like eternity, staring at the final breach point, and with my mind racing, the Governor said, "Let's head back. Major, you hop in with me." In the vehicle, he asked directly, "Where do we go from here?" I provided a brief recap of what we had done to date, what additional assets were en route, my projection of future resource requests, an overview of uniformed search and containment tactics, and investigative strategy such as: interview priorities, phone/wire taps, prospective surveillance targets, accomplices, contractors, missing tools (if any), *and* our connectivity and compacts for assistance with other federal, state, and local agencies.

I wrapped up by assuring the Governor of my personal commitment to "follow every lead," no matter where it takes us, and "leave no stone unturned."

As we rolled back into the parking lot of the Training Building, the Governor turned around in his seat, looked me straight in the eye and said, "The State Police are in charge. Anything you need, you let me or your superintendent know." I could not have received a clearer expression of support.

Outside the truck, the Governor resumed his dialogue with the key players. Acknowledging the growing national media coverage, including the throngs of journalists, and media trucks descending on Dannemora, the next responsible step was a press conference. Governor Cuomo set the schedule, and we all agreed to rendezvous at the front of the Training Building, at the agreed upon time.

In front of a battery of mics and cameras, the Governor himself led off. He confirmed, for the world, what many in the press were already speculating, there had been an escape from Clinton Correctional Facility of two convicted murderers. The Governor provided a brief overview of the escape, leaving the details to the DOCCS Commissioner, but added "It was an elaborate plot. When you look at how it was done, it was extraordinary."

In fact, this was the first escape from the maximum-security portion of the prison, since the establishment and creation of the 30-foot wall raised in 1887. Furthermore, statewide, before this day, the last escape from <u>any</u> maximum-security prison in New York State was from the Elmira Correctional Facility in 2003. Thereafter, the Governor turned the podium over to Commissioner Annucci, who would then turn the podium over to me.

Accordingly, I described, without disclosing operational tactics, techniques, and procedures, our current resources on hand, acknowledging the multiple agencies currently assisting us in the ongoing search effort and those pledging cooperation going forward. I acknowledged the difficult task ahead, and the fact that the inmates may have as much as a six-hour head start on us, and that they could literally be *"anywhere."* As such, I reminded local members of the community that we had no evidence that the two had, in fact, made it out of the area. I implored them to remain vigilant and to call us with any bit of information or concern, something I would do countless times in the weeks ahead. I closed by saying, "We have over 200 law enforcement officers in the area with a variety of specialized units and equipment at their disposal. No stone is being left unturned."

After each of us took a few questions, the Governor closed by expressing confidence in law enforcement and pledging his direct support and involvement at this crucial time, reminding the world, "These are dangerous people, and they're nothing to be trifled with, and we want the help of the public." After the conference, the Governor pulled me and the commissioner aside, issued additional instructions, including the need for frequent status reports, and reasserted his support.

Although I hadn't let them "out," thank God, it was crystal clear I was responsible to catch them. Most importantly, I felt profoundly responsible for the safety of every man, woman, and child in the community, not to mention the ever-growing number of first responders. I'll admit to saying more than a few prayers for their safety and well-being in the coming days.

Turning to Commissioner Annucci, I said, "We've got work to do. What do you need from me right now?"

He said, I'm returning to the superintendent's office inside the facility and would appreciate it if you could assign a member of your staff to the office."

"Consider it done," I responded. From that point forward, a ranking member of my staff remained inside Clinton to act as a liaison to the commissioner. This proved invaluable. In addition to regular meetings at the CP, anytime DOCCS had a priority question or concern, the State Police liaison was on hand to get or facilitate the answer.

Before entering the Command Post, I took the opportunity to call Field Commander Patricia Groeber and Superintendent D'Amico to provide an update based on the Governor's visit. I told them the Command Post was taking shape, just in time for the Governor's visit, and he seemed pleased overall with the State Police response thus far. In short order, Colonel Groeber advised me that a member of her staff would contact me to set up a conference call between me, the superintendent, key members of his executive staff, and my fellow troop commanders statewide. This was necessary, to ensure our organization was dialed in for the burgeoning statewide response, but was more added to an already overflowing plate. I began to feel as though I was juggling chainsaws, and there is only one way to deal effectively with that...*delegate.*

Inside the CP I sought out the two individuals, I knew would become instrumental in building the successful fabric of a sustainable operation: First, my Troop Emergency Management NCO (EMNCO) Sergeant Chad Niles, an expert in all things pertaining to State Police response to emerging incidents, both natural and man-made. Second, Captain John Streiff of the Forest Rangers, a longtime friend and colleague, who had both the expertise to integrate the federally recognized Incident Command System (ICS) into the Command Post, *and* the subject matter experts (SMEs) among his rangers, to staff many of the key functional areas. As it turns out, Chad and John knew each other from years of working on a variety of incidents in the North Country, and <u>both</u> were fluent in the language and concept of the Incident Command System; in fact, Niles was an ICS Instructor.

The system, long utilized by firefighters and rangers, as a method of organizing an effective response against wilderness wildfires, had been fine-tuned, and became the national standard of response after 9/11, as part of President G.W. Bush's Homeland Security Presidential Directive – 5, to ensure federal, state, and local assets are properly organized to: *prepare for, prevent, respond to, and recover from* domestic incidents, in accordance with a universally recognized and systematic approach, designed to save lives and manage scarce resources. Although, law enforcement is trained, and depending on who you talk to, well-versed in the system, we didn't use it every day as part of routine patrol operations. As a former captain in the Office of State Police Emergency Management, I understood the advantages of ICS, if properly implemented, and the looming, multi-agency disaster, if ignored. In fact, I had seen ignorance or neglect of the system bite others in the ass before. Not on my watch. As the Incident Commander, I considered the inbound federal, state, and local assets a necessary force-multiplier, and ICS was the tool to manage them.

So, I corralled my two associates for a heart to heart. Both had already been working the escape throughout the day, and recognized, perhaps even more deeply than I, as I had been tied up with high-level meetings and the press, what challenges and limitations we were currently experiencing. I got right to it, "Men, I've got a conference call with NYSP execs coming up. At that time, I'll be making additional personnel and equipment requests. We have the beginnings of a Command Post established, but this thing is about to explode as we try to integrate the FBI, USMS, USCBP, and additional SP personnel. As specialized units from around the state arrive and we increase our aviation and tactical assets, we'll need enhanced coordination to make our ground search truly productive. And, you both know, at the end of the day, I'll have to account for each acre covered and every building searched; and I'll have to do so with confidence. With that in mind, the only way to do this effectively and <u>safely</u>, is to fully implement and embrace ICS. I turned to the Forest Ranger captain and said, "John, can I ask you to handle that?"

John immediately said, "Yes, Sir."

This was a Herculean task, and he knew it. It involved setting up the structure, manning key positions, especially in twice-daily operational planning sessions, managing logistics, facilitating daily briefings, and recording the operational progress of the search. As a member of another state agency, not within my daily SP chain of command, he could have waffled and given me a song and dance about being happy to assist, but needing someone else to be in charge, but not Captain Streiff. He readily accepted the responsibility and took on the challenge of applying structure to what turned out to be the largest manhunt in New York State history. I needed a partner with his expertise and commitment, and John didn't blink.

I then turned back to State Police Sergeant Niles. "Chad, I'd like you to assist John with whatever he needs, *but* I need you to specifically focus on incident-wide SAFETY, across all levels and agencies, *and* facilitate the infrastructure expansion of this Command Post to accommodate <u>all</u> agencies; including taking over the second floor of this building for BCI relocation. I was blunt, "I don't have time to worry about this, you know what needs to be done to build this out, including future field locations if necessary. Let me know if you need anything, or if you can't break through some layer of BS, and I need to get involved. As my Safety Officer, you have my full support and authority to speak on my behalf when necessary.

Next step was a long-overdue conversation with Troop "B's" senior NCO, my friend and colleague, First Sergeant Steve Lacey. Steve, a seasoned professional and 30-year SP veteran, had busied himself throughout the day managing resources, deploying troopers, checking the perimeter and check points for post integrity, and ensuring what needed to be happening on the ground and in the field was indeed occurring. Additionally, he and his closest subordinates, the Troop "B" zone sergeants, were already knee deep in meal acquisitions and lodging requests to take care of our inbound troopers. This, the seamless feeding, lodging, and rotation of what would become over a thousand troopers and investigators, was critical to sustainment.

In addition, Steve supervised key functional area members of the command, who had crucial roles, such as: EMNCO Niles, Communications Supervisor Sergeant Chris Giovazzino, who was responsible for perhaps the most *critical*, if not most *difficult* tasks of keeping all agencies talking, by virtue of an ad hoc system of phones, computers, communications vehicles, etc., and Senior Firearms Instructor Mike Pena, who was responsible for a small group of Troop "B" patrol riflemen, responding to virtually every key sighting, affording command tactical feedback and continuity of operations. All self-starters, who required little oversight, but Steve recognized if *any* of these SMEs missed their targets, the operation would collapse under its own weight and cease to be effective.

First Sergeant Lacey made sure that did not happen.

Finally, before focusing on the upcoming conference call, I took an opportunity to brief the assembled Command Post staff. It had taken us a while to recall the agency reps, and while we didn't have all the initial players back yet, who had unfortunately been asked to step out of the previous briefing, we did have a representative from every agency on the ground at the time. Thus, it was time to introduce myself to those I had not previously addressed.

From past experience, I knew it was essential that we set a collaborative tone from the start. Yes, it was important to have a chain of command

and I was the Incident Commander, but more importantly, it was critical that we established the **unified** nature of this command from the onset. While I would assume full responsibility, the team would make collective decisions with the best interest of safety and success of the search effort in mind. To that end, it was imperative we embrace ICS, and efforts were currently underway to transition into a viable *Unified Command* structure, led by the Forest Rangers. Additionally, we sought to establish the commensurate infrastructure to accommodate growth and efficiency.

I asked for and acknowledged input regarding closing existing gaps, and Captain Streiff posted a future planning and meeting schedule, confirming an Incident Action Plan was under construction. I reiterated ALL operations would be coordinated out of the CP, with special consideration given to preventing *Blue vs. Blue* (friendly fire) incidents. Additionally, all future tactical (SWAT) and aviation operations would now be coordinated through a special operations branch director. Additionally, I acknowledged the essential requirement that past, current, and future search efforts be cataloged and recorded to ensure our efforts are meaningful, productive, and defensible.

Furthermore, it was stated that we would have open communications, recognizing the vitality of input and candor required for productive, safe operations. In furtherance of this objective, it was not simply requested that every agency have a seat at the table, regardless of size, it was *expected*. In this way, and this way only, could each organization have input and access to the latest information driving operations. True, from time to time, specific, *sensitive*, pieces of information may be developed, that only investigators or key decision makers would be privy to, but that was necessary to preserve the integrity of investigative leads and targets. However, that concept should be nothing new, as all law enforcement entities are familiar with these investigative protocols. Again, to ensure the *safety* of all personnel and ensure coordination of effort, ALL agency representatives were afforded *unfettered* access to the Command Post and daily operational briefings. Only the most *sensitive* of information was withheld, under the direction and authority of the Superintendent of the New York State Police.

The mission was straight forward. The expeditious apprehension of two escaped killers, while ensuring the health and safety of members of the community and assigned law enforcement. That remained our mandate throughout the entire operation; on that, there was *unanimous* agreement. I wrapped it up by thanking everyone for their quick response and efforts to date, and introduced the Incident Safety Officer, as safety was of paramount concern. I then excused myself, knowing I had to attend the SP conference call in five minutes.

At approximately 5:00 PM, I, along with my key staff, dialed in from the only working landline speaker phone available to me at the time. Six or seven of us crammed into a one-desk office, like it was "clown car" and listened for Colonel Groeber, the Field Commander, to kick off the meeting. After ensuring the superintendent was on the line and brief introductions, she turned the call over to me. I prepared to bring my colleagues up to speed on what we knew, and where we were, to date. Much had transpired since that 6:06 AM phone call, and while we had made some progress, we had a long way to go.

Of significant interest to all involved, was the timing of the escape, just after midnight early that morning, and the fact that the inmates were *not* discovered missing until 5:30 AM and confirmed escaped until 7:15 AM. That afforded Matt and Sweat a minimum six-hour head start, and the two of them could be headed towards, or passing through, the adjacent territories of my fellow troop commanders as we spoke. Accordingly, each troop had been put on high alert earlier in the day and a corresponding BCI Lead Desk stood up. Effectively, what that meant was, any sighting or information called in regarding this escape would be handled by a dedicated team of investigators in the Troop where reported and then investigated, documented, and forwarded to the Troop "B" Lead Desk in Dannemora, for review and continuity of investigation. For example, a lead was developed in Troop "D", an adjacent troop, regarding an alleged sighting at a McDonald's in Oswego, NY. Information gathered indicated a food service employee had seen the photos of the inmates in the media and claimed two men matching their description had just ordered a meal together at the restaurant. Investigators reviewing in-store closed-circuit camera footage agreed that the grainy, profile stills looked a lot like our two guys. As a result, a brief, but significant undertaking was underway to investigate this development to confirm or deny its efficacy. Ultimately, investigators located the two persons of interest and ruled out any connection. Similar sightings, many from credible, ordinary citizens, would be repeated countless times over the next 23 days. They ran the gambit of individual(s) of similar description reportedly: walking down the road, along railroad tracks, on ferries, on buses, at the border, in NYC, hiking the Adirondack Mountains, occupying camps and cabins throughout the Northeast, even knocking on doors in neighboring states because of a disabled vehicle, etc. And, *each one* of them, had to be investigated and ruled out.

Over all, throughout the entirety of the investigation, over 3,400 leads would be handled by the NYSP, and its law enforcement partners, and cataloged by us in Troop "B".

The conversation wrapped up with an overview provided by my BCI Captain, as to what we had gleaned from interviewing Joyce Mitchell, which wasn't much at that point. Mitchell had checked herself out of the hospital that morning, and came to the State Police barracks in Malone, after learning that we were attempting to locate her. Beginning at about 1:00 PM, she was interviewed. Mitchell was evasive, and we knew she was lying. With little to go on, we left her *"out there,"* so we could surveil her, develop the case, and interview her further.

We also knew from DOCCS: Mitchell, as all employees, had received repetitive training regarding resisting inmate's attempts to find out personal info, exploit, and manipulate prison workers. Essentially, maintain a professional distance and don't reveal personal details that could be used to compromise you, as inmates readily threaten to expose C.O.s, and Civilian Employees, for violating prison rules or protocols.

The conference call then concluded, with several of my fellow troop commanders later contacting me to wish me luck and pledge their support.

Later that evening, Captain LaFountain and I returned to the Clinton superintendent's office inside the prison. The purpose was as much a recap, between DOCCS and the State Police, as it was to generate the first joint update to the Governor's office. Commissioner Annucci dictated several tenets of Corrections developments. As of close of business: The lockdown was still in place, key staff and inmates were being interviewed, some moved from their respective assignments or cells, a facility-wide search (frisk) of all critical infrastructure and cells was being completed, and a comprehensive tool inventory underway. A lot of work. Then, I and Captain LaFountain, contributed bullets regarding the numbers of officers and assets on hand and deployed, the results of initial door-to-door searches, a description of the "perimeter," anticipated challenges going forward, the results of joint staff and inmate interviews with OSI…, etc.

We kept the message brief, agreed on its contents and DOCCS fired it off to the Governor's office at about 1:00 AM. I forwarded a duplicate to Superintendent D'Amico and Colonel Groeber almost simultaneously. Acknowledging the ongoing, 24/7 nature of the search, it was wisely concluded at this point, that each of us needed to get a few hours of rest, to be able to maintain this pace.

I got in my car, under a combination of the very bright lights of the prison and the additional construction lights we had erected lining the village streets, and headed out of town. Compared to the morning, the perimeter staffing appeared to have doubled since my ride in. Dannemora appeared "under siege" by law enforcement, and for good reason…the safety of those working the escape, and all residing in the area.

As I headed back to Ray Brook, for what I hoped would be a couple of hours of sleep, I began to wonder, *Am I truly prepared for the task ahead?* For most of the hour-long drive back to my room at Troop HQ, there is no cell coverage. So, like it or not, this afforded me ample opportunity to be alone with my thoughts. My mind was racing, as I assessed the training, professional development, and *skill set* I had developed over the last 25 years with the New York State Police.

JOINING THE NEW YORK
STATE POLICE

CHAPTER 4

ROAD TROOPER

On October 1, 1990, I entered the NYSP Academy as a Member of the 168th Session. Raw recruits at the time, the class would develop over the years as arguably one of the most impactful groups in State Police history. In addition to the outstanding troopers, sergeants, investigators, and senior investigators conducting important work in public safety within their communities, there are numerous, seasoned Commissioned Officers, running zones, special details, sections, and stations. The 168th's influence is felt statewide, and the Division of State Police is, in my opinion, better for it. Remarkably, the class has also produced three majors, responsible for leading troops and specialized units in the field and assisting with the development of organizational policy.

The New York State Police traces its proud, 100-year, lineage back to 1917. In short, in 1913, a construction foreman named Sam Howell was murdered during a payroll robbery in Westchester County. Because Westchester County was a very rural area then, there was no local police department, and Mr. Howell's murderers escaped, even though he identified them before he died. This vicious crime spurred Mr. Howell's employer, Moyca Newell and her friend, Katherine Mayo, to initiate a movement to form a State Police department to provide police protection to rural areas. Because of their efforts, the State Legislature established the New York State Police as a full-service police agency on April 11, 1917. Since the first 232 men rode out of their training camp on horseback to begin patrolling rural areas, troopers have been there to fulfill the law enforcement needs of the people of New York State with the highest degree of fairness, professionalism, and integrity.[2]

Over the decades, the force has expanded to 11 troops and numerous Special Details covering New York State. At an approximate strength of 4,750 sworn and non-sworn civilian personnel, the agency is the third-largest State Police organization in the country. Troopers are assigned to every corner of New York State, from the tip of Eastern Long Island, to the Canadian border in the north, to Niagara Falls in the west. Even NYC, with its vaunted Police Department of 35,000 officers, enjoys a close working relationship with nearly 150 troopers assigned to the City of New York, assisting with counter-terror, narcotics, and commercial vehicle enforcement.

Upstate, where the clear majority of their work is done, troopers patrol the highways, neighborhoods, small towns, villages, and cities (when requested by mayors) to great effect. In some areas of the state, troopers are virtually the only show in town. In many other locales, where robust law enforcement services are provided by local agencies, which may include the county sheriff, troopers are available to provide invaluable assistance upon request. And, every agency will avail itself of an opportunity to interact with the State Police by virtue of vital, post 9/11 intelligence sharing compacts, or the engagement of a multitude of highly trained special services such as: Aviation assets, crime scene technicians, electronic surveillance experts, the NYSP Forensic Investigation Center (lab), collision reconstructionists, Commercial Vehicle Enforcement Unit, Community Narcotics Enforcement Team investigators, hazardous materials experts, SCUBA divers, Marine Patrol, snowmobile patrols, SWAT team operators; all units available to assist or compliment any agency's investigation, or response, to a critical incident.

After completing 24 intensive weeks of training in the Penal Law, Criminal Procedure Law, Vehicle and Traffic Law, Firearms, Defensive Tactics, Emergency Vehicle Operations, Criminal Investigations, Traffic Enforcement, Physical Fitness, and more, I stood at the podium in 1991, at graduation on my 30th birthday, as the Class Representative of the 168th Session. Selected by my peers, I delivered a graduation address, following remarks rendered by then-Governor Mario Cuomo, to the nearly 2,000 invited family and friends of New York's newest troopers. What an honor! Then, after a brief period of well-deserved leave, in which many of us moved our families around the state to our new duty assignments, we each got down to the very serious business of our Field Training on the road.

The New York State Police is blessed with great people, and some of the best are selected to become Field Training Officers (FTO), a group I would later have the honor of joining. Their task as experienced road troopers, is to take freshly minted recruits, straight out of the Academy, and prepare them for life in the real world. In other words, turn six months of book learning and scenario-based training into practical street application. This was the final, and perhaps, most important step in the crucible. FTOs, of which each recruit had two, spaced roughly six-weeks apart during the 12-week program, taught us how to do the job and stay alive! No easy task.

I was fortunate to be assigned, right out of the Academy, to Trooper Gary Kelly, of Troop "G", Zone One, my Primary FTO. As the member-in-charge of the SP Sand Lake satellite office in Rensselaer County, just east of Albany, NY, Gary was the quintessential FTO. A sharp, seasoned trooper, who had been assigned to the satellite due to his record as a self-motivated and tenacious investigator. It was immediately apparent to me, as a 30-year-old former Army captain, that I was in the right place, and that I stood to learn a lot from Trooper Kelly, and he did not disappoint. By the time my training was complete, we had experienced, in real time, just about every aspect of road patrol: burglaries, sexual assaults, property crimes, larceny arrests, DWI arrests, traffic enforcement, barricaded subjects, and the like. Perhaps Gary's most lasting lesson for me, was thoroughness of investigation and interviewing techniques. If a perpetrator was guilty of committing a crime, Gary could lawfully get them to admit it. He was smooth, effective, and respectful, all at the same time. Virtually nothing went unsolved. [Post script, although our careers would take entirely different directions, it was gratifying to observe from afar, as Trooper Kelly continued to ascend the ranks of the Investigative side of the organization (BCI) and is now considered, both within and outside the agency, as a SME in Crimes Against Children.]

Upon completion of Field Training, I was certified to "Ride Alone" and re-assigned to Troop "F", Zone Two, SP Middletown, the busiest station in the NYSP. After quickly relocating my family, I reported to Middletown for my first day of work. Having been trained 150 miles away in

Troop "G", the tradition is for a "new" guy to ride with another trooper for a few days, to get the lay of the land locally. I walked into my new station for the B-line (7:00 AM to 3:00 PM shift) bright eyed and bushy tailed, expecting to follow that protocol. I reported, patrol bag in hand, and was met immediately by the Middletown line sergeant (first line supervisor) who said, "You're Guess...you got a map, Kid?"

"Yes, Sergeant," I said.

"Good!" he replied. "Grab your keys and get going. You have complaints already backed up from the previous shift. Cars are out back. Don't come back till 3:00 PM."

"Roger that, Sergeant," I replied. And off I went. And, so it goes to this day in SP Middletown, always among the busiest stations in the state, typically sharing that "honor" with Troop "B's" SP Plattsburgh.

Fortunately, I had three things going for me. First, the Army had taught me how to read a map. Second, my FTO had taught me how to take care of business, and third, a few of the junior troopers at SP Middletown had graduated just six months earlier, and had gone through the same thing, so they knew what it was like. Guys like Mike Mc Darby, who caught up with me on the road (our posts overlapped) between complaints (calls for service) and let me know that if I needed *anything*, I could count on him – back up, a map check, a question about local protocol, anything. A real gentleman and a big help.

Additionally, a classmate of mine, Bob Leary, was also assigned to SP Middletown. However, unlike me, he was from the area and had trained in Middletown, so, although he was in a different platoon, and we didn't overlap all that often, he was a tremendous help. Bob, five years younger, but as sharp as they come, had things pretty-well figured out down there, and had already gained respect of the other troopers and investigators. Fortunately for me, Bob and I were already good friends from the 168th Session, and we would become close friends over the years, our career paths crossing many times. No one had a bigger heart and nose for the job than Leary.

This may ruffle a few feathers, but back in the day, many of us assigned to Troop "F", particularly Zone Two, likened the whirlwind work experience to "dog years." In other words, a year on the road in "F", was we thought, the experience-wise equivalence of seven years in many of the upstate troops. Now, based upon my extensive travel and experience, I realize that may have been a bit of an exaggeration. However, what wasn't an exaggeration, was that we went from the frying pan into the fire on day one, handling a dozen or more complaints a day. You had to swim or sink. The take away was that it was good for the professional development and confidence of a young trooper.

Months went by, but the drive from my residence in Kingston at the time (one hour north), never got any shorter. So, I transferred to SP Newburgh, still in Troop "F", Zone Two, but right off the NYS Thruway, cutting nearly twenty-five minutes off my commute. I spent the next several years working patrol out of Newburgh, which provided a great mix of rural, suburban, and small city law enforcement opportunities. While we did not patrol the city per se, unless we were invited in by the mayor as part of Operation Impact, a joint city/SP anti-crime patrol offered frequently throughout New York, we certainly benefitted from our proximity to the city. Newburgh, a small 28,000-person city, in the lower Hudson Valley, was replete with drug and property crime at the time. In fact, although violent crime trends rise and fall across the nation, Newburgh was at one time ranked among the most dangerous places to live in the United States, according to *neighborhoodscout.com's* interpretation of FBI crime statistics.[3] So, there was no shortage of work out of the SP Newburgh Barracks. You could literally be as busy as you wanted to be, and I liked to remain busy. I joined the State Police to make a difference, and wanted the law abiding public to get their money's worth.

My 10 years in Troop "F", especially Newburgh, were formative. Over time, I was involved in several significant cases and had the good fortune of applying to, and being selected for, a variety of assignments and elite special details. There was always something noteworthy going on in Troop "F". In fact, many of the agencies top executives and a few superintendents had spent some time assigned there, often referring to it as the highlight of their careers. So, with that kind of talent, it could be a challenge to stand out. For the bulk of my time in Newburgh, we were led by terrific station sergeants, who expected us to work hard. If you were self-motivated, productive, and took care of business, they took care of you in return. You can't ask for more than that. As one of the station leaders in activity, I was selected early to become a FTO, and approached my responsibilities seriously. My philosophy was, I planned to expose my recruits to as much as humanly possible. Gary Kelly had done that for me, and I wanted to pay it forward.

Early on, I was wrapping up what had turned out to be a quiet summer Sunday night in 1993, in a rural part of my patrol area. I was aware of a larceny of a purse, from a church, which having occurred earlier in the day, the Village of Walden Police had been actively investigating. The extent of State Police involvement, up to that point, had been to BOLO (be on the lookout) for a Caucasian male, approximately 20-25 years old, wearing shorts and a tank top. That description, I thought, could fit half the population of the village on that hot August night. So, while I kept my eyes open, I hadn't given it a lot of thought, since I was patrolling in the next town over. That was about to change with a single radio transmission. At about 10:30 PM, an area-wide radio broadcast for assistance was made by a Village of Walden Police Officer. Apparently, while on patrol, he and his partner, spotted an individual walking down a road within their jurisdiction matching the suspect's description. They stopped to question him on the side of the road, got out of the cruiser quickly, and approached the suspect near the trunk of the car. Upon engaging him in conversation, the suspect was evasive and appeared to possess a woman's wallet, that he claimed belonged to him. Well, that didn't sit right, and the officers wanted to take him back to the station for further questioning. The subject was then told to put his hands on the back of the cruiser and was about to be patted down and placed in the car for the short ride back to the department. Suddenly, he became combative, shoving one officer to the ground and diving for the open front door of the running squad car. The officer quickly recovered, but the suspect had control of the vehicle from the driver's seat and threw it into reverse. With the officer hanging on, trying to prevent the theft of his cruiser, the suspect dropped the rear wheels into a shallow drainage ditch, throwing the officer to the ground, both injuring and dislodging him. The suspect then sped off. With the suspect now barreling down the road in a Crown Victoria Police Interceptor, the officers reached for their portable radio and called for assistance.

In the immediate area was State Police Investigator Phil Wolfburg from my station, SP Newburgh, and he reached me on the car-to-car radio. "Chuck, did you copy that transmission? What's your location?"

I responded, "Affirmative." And told Phil I was already heading that way. Phil said he was en route from a nearby location; he had been conducting follow up interviews for a case, and in no time, we both jumped on the tail of a pursuit-in-progress. Both Phil and I called in to Troop HQ in Middletown that we were engaged in pursuit of the stolen police car and requested a road block be set up at the county line. Middletown responded and coordinated the establishment of the requested road block. Problem was, the suspect driving the police cruiser had access to the police radio within the vehicle and monitored our request. *What are you going to do?* We did not have secure channels, spike strips, or a helicopter at the time, and had little choice but to communicate with fellow police officers. The suspect was hauling ass, and as we were fast approaching the designated intersection, I hoped for the best. Despite our efforts, the suspect blew right through the hastily established two-car road block. The only good thing was, that when the suspect nearly lost control of his vehicle at the road block, he did not hit another officer. However, that momentary hiccup allowed Investigator Wolfburg to try to pass the suspect, in an attempt to get in front of him to slow him down from the lead. At the time, I was right behind Phil, and as he started to overtake the vehicle on the right, the suspect ran him off the road. Last thing I recall seeing, at high-speed, was Phil headed off the road into an open field.

Now, it was just me. I had lost Phil, and the other cars were too far behind to catch up. I radioed to SP Middletown, requesting authority to initiate Vehicle Contact Action, or Pit-style Maneuver, with the other vehicle. It was obvious he wasn't stopping. He had injured a village officer, stole a police car, which undoubtedly contained a weapon on board (most likely a shotgun), almost hit two others running a road block, and ran a fellow trooper (investigator) off the road. He needed to be stopped.

Middletown acknowledged my message, but time was running out. I was now heading north in another county, in the dark, by myself, in unfamiliar territory. With no visible back up, I would have to be very selective in choosing the time and place for the maneuver. Just then, we approached a bridge over the Wallkill River, in Ulster County. The good thing was, there was a guiderail leading up to the bridge, the railing of the bridge itself, and a guiderail exiting the bridge. This was the spot. As we crossed the bridge, I accelerated like a sling shot up the passenger side and drove him into the guiderail on his left. As we exited the bridge, I recall a shower of sparks. I kept the pressure on, and although his car was beginning to decelerate, we were nearing the end of the guiderail, an intersection, and the open road. Just as the guiderail and friction ended, he punched it, and our cars began to disengage. He was again gaining the advantage. Realizing it was now or never, I floored it, ramming into the passenger side of his car, literally pushing his vehicle sideways across the rural intersection and into a ditch on the far side. Our cars came to rest in a "T-bone" fashion, and before you could blink, the suspect opened the driver's side door and bolted from the scene.

Not one to be deterred, I exited my car and set off in foot pursuit. As we ran through the dark, although I was unfamiliar with the area, I knew we had just crossed a river, there was a farmhouse on the other side of the road in the direction we were headed, and I was closing in on him. Passing the house, we proceeded through the backyard as he ignored my commands to stop. Just as I drew within reach, running at full speed, he "disappeared." For a split second, I couldn't understand what had happened, then upon my next step, I too "disappeared," falling down a steep river bank to the bottom, landing on him and a piece of deadfall log, from a downed tree. But, he wasn't going down easily, and a fight ensued near the water's edge of the river. He struggled to get away in the pitch black, and I struggled to hold onto him. He was slippery from sweat, and grabbing at his tank top in an attempt to gain control only resulted in ripping it to shreds. Enough was enough, I hit him…hard! That planted him among the weeds, momentarily disorienting him, but as I drew my cuffs out, I wondered, *Where the hell are those other guys?!*

Just then, as I tried to get the second cuff on him, I heard a voice from the top of the bank, "Chuck?!"

"Down here!" I shouted.

Just that fast, Phil Wolfburg came scrambling down the bank to my aid. "What the hell?!" Phil said. "Are you OK?"

"Yeah," came my reply. My adrenaline was pumping, and I was damn glad to have Phil with me, *and* see that *he* was OK, after that wild ride.

We stood the suspect up and started trying to drag him up the bank. I hadn't noticed it on my unexpected way down, but it was a *steep* slope, roughly a 12-foot drop. Finally, we managed to drag his slimy carcass to the top of the slope and into the backyard of the farmhouse. Upon reaching a line of site at road level, I heard an explosion and saw the Village of Walden Police car totally engulfed in flames. *WTF,* I thought! "My troop car!" I yelled.

"It's OK!" Phil said, "I moved it when I got here because the other car was on fire."

Thank God, I thought. I wouldn't want to have to explain that to my sergeant. Just then, a small posse of flashlights came running towards us across the backyard. The welcomed sight was a couple of additional troopers who'd raced to the scene from Ulster County and a couple of local agency officers who had been involved during the earlier pursuit.

Then, almost immediately, my leg gave out. It felt like someone had hit me in the hamstring with a sledgehammer. "Phil," I said, "...something's wrong with my leg?!"

"Here," he said, "I've got him." Then, he instructed another trooper to help me to a patrol car, as I could barely walk, and get me to a hospital. On the ride to the hospital, I couldn't find a comfortable position. My leg was cramping big time, and while I knew it was nothing life-threatening, the pain was excruciating.

Upon arrival at the E.R., the staff took me right in, and it didn't take the doctor long to diagnose I had torn my hamstring during the pursuit. Probably, a result of the fall and striking the back (posterior side) of my outstretched leg with all my weight, landing on the downed tree near the river bank. He said, "You have a great deal of blood pooling in the area of the injury, and you're going to be out for a while." He wasn't kidding, rehab seemed to take forever, and it brought my fitness level back to square one, something I would work hard at resolving.

Regarding the suspect, he was our guy. The thief who had taken a little old lady's purse right out of church. During his statement, he said when he exited the patrol car after the crash, being from the area, he knew the Wallkill River was just across the road. His intention was to outrun me, jump into the river and swim across to freedom. He never thought the trooper would follow him, let alone catch him. Obviously, he'd underestimated my dedication to do my job.

Thankfully, the village police officer's injuries were non-life threatening. In fact, I would speak to him weeks later, after I had returned to duty, while he was still recovering.

Later that year, I received a Christmas card at the barracks addressed to me personally, which was a rarity. I opened the card, one of those cards from back in the day with the slits in it, into which you could insert a photograph, before card companies started offering photo cards on the Internet. The photo attached to the front of the card was a Polaroid picture of the police cruiser engulfed in flames, and the greeting read, "Warm Wishes! From the Village of Walden P.D."

It was around this time that my wife, Elinor, and I, welcomed our second beautiful daughter, Rebecca, into the world, completing our young family. She and her older sister, Jennifer, are the light of my life!

One night on patrol, I was working a post in the Town of New Windsor, a suburb of Newburgh. At the time, New Windsor had an indoor skate park in a plaza, that became the favorite hangout of local kids. On weekends, you could expect parents and their children attending birthday parties and the like, but during most weekend nights, particularly in the summer, the crowd, many wannabe gang bangers from the City of Newburgh, became decisively more mischievous. The shift in clientele, and their penchant for disorderly conduct, fights, larcenies, and drug sales, drew a significant amount of warranted police attention.

During my shift, a C-line (3:00 PM to 11:00 PM) all units received a BOLO regarding an armed robbery that recently occurred near an apartment complex, close to the plaza. The description was a Hispanic male, late teens, with baggie blue jeans and a white "wife beater" tank top, with a female accomplice. Again, not much to go on, until the dispatcher added that the suspect had a tattoo of a "tear drop" on his face, below the eye.

Now, we had a specific identifying mark to go on. I, along with other units of the State Police and Town of New Windsor Police Department, headed to the scene of the crime, on the lookout for anyone matching the description. Almost immediately, I rolled up on several individuals just hanging around parked cars in the parking lot of the plaza, directly in front of the skate park. Loitering in the parking lot itself raised my antenna, because the lot had been plagued with frequent thefts from vehicles, mostly smash and grabs, anytime the skate park catered to the late-night crowd. So, as I headed in their direction and got closer, the group, which had been "eyeballing" me, now turned their backs towards me in unison.

I pulled my troop car up tight to the parked cars adjacent to them, blocking at least one avenue of egress, and advised my station I would be "out" with three suspicious subjects at the skate park regarding the ongoing investigation. As I approached, the three of them sized me up and stood their ground. Behind them, approximately 30 yards away, was a long line of teenagers, waiting to get into the skating rink, but my presence caught their attention, and I received more than a few unsavory comments. Just as I was taking a position before them, a motorcycle officer from the Town of New Windsor rolled up. I didn't know his name, but recognized him from the road and was grateful to have back up. I quickly nodded to him and went to work as he remained mounted.

The radio report had mentioned the male perpetrator, allegedly armed with a knife at the time of the robbery, had a female accomplice, but enough time had elapsed that I could not dismiss anyone, simply because they were now standing in an all-male group. In fact, their actions upon seeing me enter the lot and their accompanying body language, gave me cause for concern. As I begin to interview them, two of them voluntarily removed their hands from their pockets, appeared forthcoming and answered my questions. The third guy, dressed in baggy pants and a white tank top, kept his hands concealed and wouldn't look squarely in my direction. He was acting "shady," and the second he looked up briefly, to protest the fact that I was holding him up with my questions, I saw why...the *tear-drop* shaped tattoo on his cheek, below the eye. *Bingo!* I thought, now I focused on him and his protestations grew louder. This drew even more attention from the crowd on the sidewalk, but by this time, other units were beginning to arrive as back up.

Now, with another trooper by my side, I asked my partner to watch him, while I made a radio transmission to one of our investigators who had the "victim" from the robbery in the car with him. My objective was to arrange a "show up," which meant the victim was brought back to the scene of the crime, or vicinity thereof, to get a look at the person or persons being detained by the police, based upon founded suspicion that the person(s) may be the perpetrator(s). The investigator acknowledged the transmission, still had the "victim" with him and told me to "Standby," as he would be there in minutes.

At this point, I returned to the subject and reiterated a couple of earlier questions that I believed he had answered evasively. He did no better this time, in fact he changed up a couple of his responses, adding confusion rather than clarity. Everything pointed to him, but the "show up" would be conclusive. That said, the increased police presence was generating additional friction with the crowd and I didn't need this guy taking off, so I advised him to have a seat in the back of my vehicle for a minute while we waited. His eyes darted around, but he complied. Before seating him in the back of my cruiser, I did a cursory pat down of his exterior body and clothing simply feeling for bulky, hard items, such as weapons. While this type of pat down was cursory at best, it was necessary for officer safety. No knife.

Several minutes passed, and the investigator finally entered the lot in his unmarked car, with the victim riding up front in the passenger's seat. Stepping out of his car he said, "Where is he?"

"He's acting squirrelly, so I put him in the back seat of the troop car," I said.

"Well, get him out and bring him up to my car," he said.

I cautioned, "Can't we just do it from here? 'Ya know, have your guy take a look. I'll roll the window down..."

"No, get him out," came the response.

Now, remember, the subject is not in custody. He's not wearing cuffs and we're not restraining him, beyond sitting in the back of my car, at this point, so...

Upon exiting the troop car, the subject was escorted by us towards the investigator's car, but upon seeing the victim looking out the passenger window, he darted off between two parked cars. *Motherf-er!* I thought. Expecting the worst, I was out of the blocks as quickly as he was and figured this would be over in a flash, but in less than three steps, he dodged between another car, and as I tried to follow, I rammed my knee straight into the grill. This brought all kinds of hooting and hollering out of the sidewalk crowd...all of it at my expense. Now, I was pissed.

I shook it off and chased this dude for all I was worth. Once through the maze of parked cars, we ran straight past his fans on the sidewalk who were urging him on and haranguing me with cat calls. Across the lot, I could see the motorcycle officer approaching on his Kawasaki, vectoring in to cut him off, but I knew the perp would have to be taken down on foot. Before too long, we rounded the corner of the plaza, heading through the side lot and toward an adjacent residential area. Even with a banged-up knee and 12 pounds of gear, there was *no way* I was letting this guy get away. So, having recently been issued an expandable baton, as a member of our agency's SWAT team, in one motion, and on a dead run, I drew the baton from its scabbard, extended it and cracked him across the right triceps. This dropped him like a bag of rocks, and I was cuffing him, just as the motorcycle officer rolled up to assist.

I will tell you right now, one of my proudest moments as a road trooper was when I led that mutt in handcuffs back around the front of the plaza to my waiting troop car, much to the surprise and chagrin of his cheering section.

For every memorable and sometimes humorous arrest situation, there are countless, painful instances and reminders of responding to, or participating in, serious investigations pertaining to fatal motor vehicle accidents, domestic assaults, arsons, sexual assault cases, homicides and worst of all, cases of child abuse. While many of these cases are so severe that they become BCI cases, it is the uniformed trooper that is the very first responder. It is the trooper who is privy to the initial, unspeakable horror, and who is often in position, as the first police officer on scene, to comfort the victim or arrest the perpetrator.

At this dark moment in our nation's history, while it has become unfashionable and even unpopular to be a police officer, keep them in your thoughts and prayers, as they are men and women with families, like you and me. Does *any* personal antipathy or political viewpoint, justify their ambush, while they sit in their patrol car ready to respond to their next case, be it a lost child, gruesome highway fatality, or even to deliver a baby? Our uniformed first responders in this country deserve our highest praise, support, and in most cases, adulation. God bless them.

As for doing this job, clearly, the risk level goes up exponentially, when you're riding alone. Troopers normally operate independently, when not training a recruit, or paired up out of operational necessity. There's even an old axiom, "One Trooper, One Riot." But I'm here to tell you, that two is always better than one, because frequently, it is while you are *alone*, that things seem to go sideways.

Another unforgettable experience…

December 1996, I was on "routine" patrol, working a C-line (3:00 PM to 11:00 PM) out of the Newburgh Barracks. It was a cold, snowy night, just three weeks before Christmas. At approximately 10:40 PM, around the time most patrols would be headed back to the station to gas up and sign out for the night, I found myself in a rural part of the Town of New Windsor, well off the beaten path, keeping my eyes open for a DWI. Drunk drivers claim nearly 10,000 innocent lives in United States each year, and it is an important part of the mission of the NYSP. As I cruised down the unlit country road, rounding a bend, I observed the tail lights of a pick-up truck bombing down the center of the road up ahead. I accelerated smoothly, closing the short gap and settled in behind it to observe. The vehicle slowed its perceived rate of speed slightly, but was clearly weaving, and, failing to keep right within its own designated lane. On a two-lane, unlit country road, this could spell disaster for oncoming traffic. I activated my overhead emergency lights indicating the universal signal to pull over. No response. Next, I tapped my siren, just to ensure that the driver knew I meant for him to pull over *today*, but he rolled to a long, slow stop, right near the end of a driveway leading to a residence along a remote section of roadway. I pulled in behind the truck, leaving a small gap between our two vehicles, off-set my troop car slightly to the left, directed my driver's side spotlight into his side view mirror, and activated my overhead "take down" lights (very bright white lights), to provide enhanced visibility and at least some buffer and tactical advantage.

The lights were on inside the adjacent residence, but other than that, no activity, that I could immediately detect. Today, before exiting the vehicle, most police officers would be expected to "call in" or enter the license plate into the in-car mobile data terminal, to receive the status of the registration (valid, suspended, surrendered, stolen, etc.) and a file check of the registered owner (valid or suspended license, wanted person, etc.), always bearing in mind that someone else may be operating the vehicle, before getting out of the car. However, in 1996, mobile data terminals (computers) were very rare in the NYSP (as were portable radios at the time, but I had one), and as a result of our antiquated system, the preferred protocol was for the trooper to first engage the driver, obtain license and registration, return to the car and then call it in on the radio. The reasoning at the time, saved valuable time for the dispatchers and did not overload the system; that policy has since been amended.

So, at approximately 10:45 PM on that Friday night, I, like so many of my brothers and sisters in law enforcement, stepped out of my patrol car alone and uncertain as to who or what I was about to encounter. With my flashlight in my left hand, resting high up on my shoulder, scanning the cab, I approached the driver's side window, which was still rolled up. I bladed my body, standing back near the door post, and with a swirling hand gesture, motioned the driver to roll the window down. When he did, a strong odor of alcoholic beverage, mixed with marijuana, wafted from the vehicle into the cold December air. Carried by the rising heat from the cab of the vehicle, it blasted me in the face. "License and registration, Sir," I requested.

As he began to fumble around, the passenger, a big, heavy-set dude, inserted himself into the conversation. "Why are you stopping us?"

I advised him, "Sir, I'm speaking with the driver right now, and as soon as he provides his license and registration I'll tell him." "Sir, do you have your license with you?" I said to driver.

Before he could answer, the passenger said, "This is bull shit."

I'd seen this routine before, two or more assholes up to no good, and one of them, the one you're NOT talking to at the time, gets loud and mouthy, invariably to distract you from your task and overload your senses. I said, "Passenger, I'm not talking to you right now. Be quiet." By the time, I looked back at the driver, after momentarily being diverted, he had his license in his hand.

"This is my girlfriend's truck," he said. I don't have the registration." Knowing where most people keep the vehicle registration, I pointed at the glove box and he reiterated, "Don't have it," as he handed me his license.

"Where are you coming from tonight?" I asked the driver.

"What business is it of yours?" said the passenger.

"Again, I'm not talking to you!" I said. "If you want to get on your way, you'll let me finish my business with the driver," I warned.

"My Place," the driver interjected.

I recognized that as a local bar in my patrol area. "Where are you headed now?"

"Jesus Christ" I heard the passenger mumble, but ignored him.

"Loughran's," the driver said.

While on the fringe of my patrol area, I knew where the tavern was, and his route of travel between the two made sense. "Have you had anything to drink tonight? I asked the driver.

"Two beers," came his response.

I thought, *I don't know that I've ever arrested a drunk who didn't say they had just "two beers."* "Sir," I said, "I stopped you for weaving...At times you were in the middle of the road."

"Here we go," said his partner.

The passenger was becoming a huge pain in the ass. "I'm going to need you to step out of the car," I said to the driver.

"Why?" he asked. I advised him that I was getting a strong odor of alcohol, and in order to know whether it was coming from him, the vehicle, or his passenger, I needed him to step out.

"C'mon," his passenger retorted.

Shining my flashlight right on the passenger, getting a better look at him, I could tell he was a big boy, 250 pounds easily, and I knew I'd have my hands full with both of them. "You, stay in the vehicle," I directed.

The driver said, "Look, my friend's expecting us, and you're making us late."

I said, "Sir, step out of the vehicle. I'm going to ask you to perform a Field Sobriety Test, and if you've only had "two beers," you'll be on your way. With that, he reluctantly opened the door and got out. This was the first time I was able to adequately size him up…about 5'10" and a solid 210 pounds. He was wearing some type of OD green, nylon, hooded, military flight jacket, with his hands firmly implanted in his pockets. As we proceeded to the rear of his vehicle, I was hyper-alert, and upon reaching the back bumper, I asked him to take his hands out of his pockets.

"It's cold out here," he said.

"Do you have any weapons on you?" I asked.

"No," he replied.

"Take your hands out of your pockets, you're going to need them out to perform the sobriety tests anyway." He complied, and I quickly patted him down for a gun, standard operating procedure *before* you begin any sort of lengthy interaction with a person under suspicion of committing a crime, in this case DWI. As I was doing that, I heard the vehicle door open and jackass getting out, louder than ever.

"This is fucking bull shit!" he said.

"YOU, get back in the truck, and shut the fuck up!" I said. Much to my surprise, he did.

Now, I know what you're thinking, *Why didn't he call for back up?* In hind sight, I probably should have, but as a six-year trooper, I was quite accustomed to working alone, having made numerous DWI arrests unassisted. But, this one would be different; and one's all it takes.

Believing, based upon my training and experience, that due to his erratic driving, glassy eyes, slurred speech, fumbling mannerisms, and the odor of alcoholic beverage emanating from him, the driver was likely either under the influence of alcohol, and/or, impaired by drugs; I still wanted to conduct Field Sobriety Testing to definitively establish the case for arrest.

As I began to put the driver through his paces, in the lighted gap I had prepared between our vehicles at the end of the driveway, I noticed out of the corner of my eye that someone was backing a car down the driveway. In between tests, I looked over at the driver of that car and held my index finger up signifying, "Give me a minute," as I was almost done. Upon completing the tests, there was no doubt in my military mind that the driver I had pulled out of the pickup was hammered.

I told him, "Sir, I am placing you under arrest for DWI. What I need you to do is turn around, face away from me, and interlace your fingers behind your head. Do it now."

With that, he just sort of looked at me, sizing me up, as best as I could tell by reading his body language, began to turn, raising his hands up over his head and said, "Yeah…Nope!" and bolted down along the driver's side of the pickup truck.

Well, now it was on. I followed, immediately commanding him to "Stop!" multiple times. As he reached the end of the truck, he hung a right, passing by the hood, continuing off-road and into darkness. I switched into pursuit mode. Right on his heels, I got the sense that we were at once running up a very short slope (later confirmed to be a drainage ditch leading to a front yard). Having just graduated from the NYSP Defensive Tactics (DT) Instructors course weeks earlier, it occurred to me that by switching my flashlight from my left hand to my right hand, I would have an impact weapon at my disposal. I could lawfully utilize my flashlight to strike his peroneal nerve, running down the side of his right leg, ideally creating a parasympathetic response from the impact, which would cause him to fall to the ground. So, faster than it took me to explain it, I swung my Maglite, striking his right leg. No effect. My assessment after the fact, is that I likely struck his quad or hamstring muscle, missing the nerve altogether, because it didn't faze him, and he kept on running.

With the lights of the troop car now in the distance, shaded by trees and a hedge row, I remember it was very dark. Combined with my adrenaline rush and associated tunnel vision, I couldn't see anything, but the guy I was chasing. As I closed to within arm's reach, I reached out, grabbing his jacket by the collar, when we suddenly both crashed into a brick wall - literally. This wall would later be confirmed to be the brick front of a ranch house, located among the pines, whose elderly owners had gone to bed for the night without leaving any interior, or exterior, lights illuminated. As abrupt as hitting the wall at full speed was, I remember thinking, *OK, I've got him,* but he spun away from me, and his hood ripped off in my hand. *SHIT!* I thought. He broke right, running down the front of the house, and I followed.

Upon reaching the end of the house, in front of us appeared a dark, solid hedge row, and he suddenly took a 90-degree left turn at the corner. He was now headed for the backyard, with me right behind. We reached the back of the house in a matter of steps, where we both fell flat on our faces, tripped up in the dark by some unforeseen obstacle (later determined to be a 2 1/2-foot-tall chicken-wire fence stretched between the corner of the ranch house and the hedges running parallel to our right). The good news, or so I figured at the time, was that he was face first in the snow and that I, falling on his back, now had the upper hand. I commanded him to "Stay down!" as I tried to pin his arms for cuffing, but I was too high up on his back, actually near his shoulders, enabling him to quickly regain his feet.

There we were, face to face in some backyard, slugging it out. This was for real. I had long ago lost my Stetson, my prized possession, and my flashlight. There was minimal ambient light coming from the glow of a neighboring porch light, beyond the hedge row, and we were holding onto each other trading blows; and let me tell you, he was giving as good as he was taking. Neither of us able to claim an advantage. Suddenly, I felt my legs tangled in some ground-level obstruction (later determined to be a landscaping bush staked out with metal stakes), and I began to lose my balance. My adversary sensed this immediately, grabbed me by the throat, and shoved me backwards into the hedgerow. *OK,* I thought going in; *I'll punch through the other side of this hedge, roll out of it, and regain my footing.* But that's not what happened. Unfortunately, the same chicken-wire fencing that had partitioned off the backyard at the corner of the house, was apparently running all along the hedge row, standing about five-feet tall (apparently to keep the owners dog in the yard), and I was now hung up on it!

My situation was dire. I had been shoved backwards onto my heals, held completely off balance by the flexible chicken-wire fencing which both supported my weight at about a 30-degree angle and prevented my escape. To make matters worse, my opponent was squarely over me, holding me down with one hand on my throat, while continuing to rain blows down upon my head with the other. The pressure placed on my wind pipe cut off my air supply.

All throughout the pursuit, my mind had been keeping up with the events, providing me options. In stressful situations, it's easy to become OBE, or overcome by events, and fall helplessly behind. Thankfully, in this case, I hadn't, which I credited to my recent training as a DT instructor and my commitment to fitness – but this was becoming life-threatening. Resultantly, my mind presented me the next appropriate option: it was time to escalate. The NYSP had recently trained and outfitted its members with OC Pepper Spray, and I reasoned this would be the perfect time to deploy it. While attempting to fend off my assailant with my left hand, and trying to lessen his grip on my throat, I reached across my body with my right hand to access the pepper spray from the carrier on my left hip, in a cross-draw motion.

But, before I could reach the canister, I felt something sharply probing my abdominal area and right hip. I realized immediately, it was my opponent's hand. He was reaching for my gun! We had been taught in the Academy, and I had recently taught recruits as a newly certified instructor that you never let anyone place a hand on your weapon; from there, you are likely moments away from death. I instantaneously ceased reaching for pepper spray, knowing I had to keep that gun from being withdrawn from its holster. With my right hand, I clamped down on the back strap of my Glock Model 17 9mm pistol, attempting to "lock it down" and prevent losing it to my assailant. Success. My hand was the first hand on the handle of my gun, and I felt a momentary twinge of relief. But that was short lived; as now, I could feel my opponents hand on my wrist pulling, trying to rip my hand off my own gun.

By this time, the situation was desperate. It had been some time since I'd taken a breath, and the "bad guy" was still going for my gun. How much longer could I hold out? To this day, I recall the clarity with which I made the necessary decision. I was in a fight for my life, and I had to respond accordingly.

During the early weeks of the Academy, an elderly clergyman affiliated with the State Police named Brother Gregory, had made a point of telling us: "There may come a day on this job, where you may have to use Deadly Physical Force to save someone. That someone may be an innocent civilian, your partner, or yourself. You may have to "Shoot to Live!" he said emphatically. "Do you have what it takes?" he asked us collectively.

For me, that day was at hand. Still fighting on my last breath, with one of his hands on my throat and the other prying for my gun, I made the decision that if the gun was going to come out, it would come out on my terms. With my head back in the brush, suspended by *this fucking fence*, I drew my Glock, rotated it at the hip, and fired one round…point blank. I remember the affect like it was yesterday. My assailant immediately stood upright, released his grip on my throat, allowing me to gulp in air, rotated slightly away from me, and collapsed face first into the snow, not even extending his arms in front of himself as he fell. There it was.

I quickly extricated myself from the hedge row, separating myself from my assailant, but continued to "cover" with my firearm. "Put your hands behind your back!" I shouted. No movement. I repeated the order; still no response.

I looked briefly over the hedge row, that had nearly become my final resting place and observed a face peering out from the side window of the sunporch on the adjacent residence, back lit by a light. "Call the State Police!" I shouted.

The voice replied, "My wife's on the phone with the Town Police!"

I repeated, "No! Call the State Police!"

My mind was racing; I had to get a radio call out for an ambulance, _and_ I still had that big bastard in the truck to worry about! *Where the fuck is he!* I wondered.

Still covering the driver, I got on my portable radio and called my barracks, "2F33 to Newburgh…"

"Newburgh's on 33," came the dispatchers reply.

"2F33 to Newburgh, SIGNAL 30! (our request for emergency assistance) I have shots fired; one suspect down. I need an ambulance at my location. Advise responding patrols there's another guy at the scene too…a passenger, whose whereabouts are unknown." The dispatcher at my station expertly handled the call and proceeded to coordinate all available resources to assist me. All of this happened in seconds. Now that I had medical assistance en route, I reached down and handcuffed my assailant. This was protocol, especially since I may have go "hands on" with his partner.

In short order, I heard familiar voices…, "Chuck, Chuck, where are you?"

I replied, "I'm back here." It was Troopers Dave Lennon and Pat Beyea. "Watch out, there's another guy out there somewhere!" I shouted.

"I don't see anybody," Pat replied. "The truck's empty!" Both members proceeded to my location and linked up. Clearly, this was the best course of action. They could both check on me, *and* help me defend myself, if the other turd was lurking in the woods somewhere. "Man, you look like shit," Pat said. "Are you OK?"

"Yeah, I think so…," but I had taken a pretty good beating; I was bleeding from the head and face, shirt ripped wide open, but happy to be alive!

Relatively quickly, it seemed, the cavalry converged on my location. I was never so happy to see my brothers and sisters in gray! I knew they had a lot of work to do, not the least of which was attempting to locate the other dirt bag. Upon interviewing the neighbor, who had started out that night simply backing down the driveway to pick up his daughter from an extracurricular event, it was reported in sum and substance that: When the trooper took off chasing the driver, the passenger got out of the truck and headed down the driveway, towards the backyard as well. When he heard the gunshot, he paused momentarily, then kept coming; until he saw the face of the neighbor (witness) in the window. He then turned, ran down the driveway and off down the road.

A hasty perimeter was set up to intercept the passenger. Unfortunately, he'd made a quick getaway, stopped at a friend's house down the road to use the phone, and called his girlfriend for a ride out of the area. When the BCI caught up with him the next day, they took his statement, after which he was in for a rude awakening. Seems the passenger thought that the driver had actually gotten the better of *me* in the fight; when he heard the gun shot, he figured his friend had killed me. The passenger had apparently spent the rest of the night, following the traffic stop, and next morning, calling around to local bars and associates looking for his buddy. Ultimately, he was not arrested, as there's no crime on the books in New York for just being a shithead.

Following the incident, I was taken to the Emergency Room for assessment, where it was determined I had multiple lacerations and contusions on my face, neck, and back, in addition to a broken hand, a separated shoulder, and associated torn rotator cuff, which would require surgery.

The investigation proceeded, and according to protocol, my actions were vetted. The Orange County Grand Jury was presented the case in January 1997, as is customary, in accordance with their policy for all police-involved shootings resulting in the use of deadly physical force. It was determined, without hesitation, or condition, that I was fully justified in my actions, and I was appropriately cleared.

As for my assailant…investigators determined that he was a local drug dealer. Allegedly, he had a habit of going bar to bar, pedaling his wares, usually marijuana, sometimes cocaine, and whenever it suited him, getting into bar fights. Apparently, he had spent some time in the service, where my fellow veteran had trained and fought as boxer, officially or unofficially, I don't know; however, he fancied himself as a bit of a bad ass, now that he had returned to polite society. Investigators also found that he had baggies of marijuana on his person, was intoxicated by alcohol (.15% BAC), and had cocaine and marijuana in his system. Significantly, he had an open lock-blade knife in his jacket pocket. Speculation is that the subject carried the knife regularly and opened the blade during the time he was in the car, or while he exited the vehicle with his hands stuffed in his pockets. I had not detected the knife through his winter clothes, during my cursory pat down while getting him out of the car, as law enforcement is generally not allowed to become too intrusive in a search, until you have elevated, justifiable circumstances, such as probable cause to place someone under arrest. Investigators would ultimately speculate that the assailant simply didn't have a chance to pull the knife later during the close foot pursuit and constant, ensuing struggle…fortunately for me.

As a post script, any life lost is a waste. At <u>any</u> given moment, my assailant could have complied with my multiple instructions to cease and desist, as verified by independent witnesses. The bottom line, he was under arrest, and proceeded to resist, flee, assault, and attempt to take my firearm from me, despite my lawful orders and efforts to the contrary. He, and he alone, escalated this event. As a result, he determined his own fate; another of Brother Gregory's salient points to my Academy class. But, my experiences as a uniformed trooper in Special Operations, would ultimately far surpass what I had experienced on the road.

CHAPTER 5

SPECIAL OPERATIONS: SCUBA

In 1994, I applied to be on the SCUBA Unit. Traditionally it's considered among the most elite assignments within the State Police, because so few people actually have the desire to endure the hardships that go along with doing the type of work the team does, and fewer still are capable of making it onto the unit. Many have earned their SCUBA certification in warm, tropical waters, or a high school pool from the various recreational dive programs that cater to civilians, but only a select few attain the level of skill, training, and courage necessary to become a public safety diver.

The NYSP Dive Team, established in 1932, received its first training from the U.S. Navy. The troopers initially trained brought the basic program, consisting of hard hat, surface-supplied air, recovery, and salvage diving knowledge back to the State Police. The program continued to evolve and expand over time, including transition to the use of SCUBA in 1957, developing into today's capabilities for all manner of underwater search, recovery, investigation, and on rare occasion, rescue.

Today, the unit consists of an authorized strength of 65 divers: eight, 8-man teams in Troops A, B, C, D, E, F, G, and K and one Division Diving Officer, a technical sergeant at Division Headquarters, who runs the show. It is outfitted with the latest equipment including: a variety of organic dive vessels, air boats, SCUBA wet and dry suits, diver-to-diver or surface-tender communications, surface-supplied air systems for wreck and confined spaces, handheld and side-scan sonar, remotely operated vehicles (ROVs), and the like. Members are trained on all systems and are certified in basic and advanced open water, ice diving, rescue diving, and specialty programs operating in New York State's many creeks, rivers, lakes, streams, swamps, cow ponds, or even the open ocean. All divers are certified to a deep dive depth of 132 feet (5 atmospheres), and certain specialists now go farther on mixed-gas rigs. Additionally, the members are trained to helicast from hovering helicopters, conduct ice and swift water rescue, operate airboats during floods, and performing rescues during natural disasters.

So, with four years on the job, and at the earliest possible opportunity, I applied and competed for one of a few open spots on SCUBA. At the time, basic training lasted seven-weeks, including winter ice diving, which is essential given the number of instances each year snowmobilers, ice fisherman, or wayward trekkers go plunging through the ice. Even though I was already a certified Advance Recreational diver, I found the school to be demanding. It didn't matter if you already had your C-card (certification card), from a certifying body, you started from scratch. In fact, the unit preferred to take on people with no experience, so they wouldn't have to waste valuable time breaking bad habits. You either performed to their standards, or you were sent home.

The course was designed to test candidates physically and mentally, with the hope of weeding out those individuals potentially unfit for extreme depths, temperatures, climactic, and claustrophobic conditions, to which SP divers were routinely exposed. As a result of the two-day tryouts and Novice SCUBA Course, there is an approximate 80 percent washout rate. In fact, it is extremely difficult to fill all the vacancies on the roster. Tryouts are typically only held every three to four years, and at the end of the process, due to attrition, some troops are left with no net gain in manpower. Fortunately, the unit operates without boundaries, and members travel frequently from troop to troop, to accomplish the mission. Spots are hard to earn, but once a member of the team, divers tend to stay put, typically leaving only for promotion to higher rank or retirement. In fact, many divers choose to forgo promotional opportunities, spending the balance of their careers on the unit until retirement. That speaks volumes about the integrity and camaraderie of such a group.

In October 1994, I graduated at the top of my class as the "Best Overall Diver" and was presented a commemorative dive knife by the instructors. We learned from the best! Men like Division Diving Officer, Technical Sergeant John Knoetgen, his assistant, Sergeant Gary Barlow, and Senior Divers, Troopers Bob Caridi, Karl Bloom, Joe Benziger, and Steve Posada, to name a few. As a new Troop "F" diver, under Caridi, I spent countless hours diving in the Hudson River and the lakes and streams of the surrounding Catskill Mountains. Frequently partnering with our fellow troopers across the river on the Troop "K" team, we remained busy for days and weeks at a time, searching for: bodies, homicide weapons, proceeds from burglaries, missing persons, etc. The best thing about it was, although sergeants and Commissioned Officers showed up to monitor the progress of the search from shore, they <u>never</u> tried to tell us how to do our jobs! After all, what the hell did they know about law enforcement diving. So, as troopers, we were left to strategize and execute our own plans; and boy, were we successful!

Our unit functioned at such a high level, collectively averaging over 1,300-1,500 dives per year, that the NYC Police Department Dive Team, one the world's best, sought us out for training on deep-dive fundamentals, joining us several years running during the 90's at Lake George, NY, for their certification. And, that relationship would prove to be extremely fortuitous.

On July 17, 1996, TWA Flight 800 had been sitting on the tarmac for nearly two hours, awaiting approval for departure to Paris, France. On board were 230 passengers and crew. Upon take off, at 8:19 PM, FLT 800 was climbing through 13,000 feet, en route to cruising altitude, when it exploded over the Atlantic Ocean twelve minutes later, 11 miles off the coast of Eastern Long Island. Flaming debris rained down creating a search area of some 400 square miles. The USCG and civilian fishing vessels in the area launched an immediate search, but there would be no survivors. Dozens of independent witnesses observed the explosion and aftermath. Many claiming they thought they saw a "missile" streaking toward the aircraft immediately before impact. *If* this were true, then terrorists had attacked the United States. The largest joint investigation of law enforcement, NTSB, and FAA, had just commenced.

At the time of the crash, I was a uniformed trooper on temporary assignment at the Orange County Fair detail in Upstate New York. When I bumped into my Senior Diver, Trooper Caridi, on the midway, I said, "Bob, did you hear about the crash that just occurred off Long Island?"

"Yeah," he replied, "but, it's 11 miles out to sea, it's got to be way too deep for us. That's the Navy's territory."

Good point, I thought. Still, what a tragedy. What's worse, I wondered, *Who the hell was responsible for bringing it down?*

The next day, after arriving home late from the previous night's assignment, I turned on CNN to see the latest on the investigation. While they played an endless reel of video tape over the crash site depicting burning jet fuel and floating debris as far as the eye could see, I noticed at the bottom of the screen a ticker message stating, "...crash site 11 miles out to sea, in 126 feet of water." *Holy shit,* I thought. *That's just within our limit!* We were all trained and certified to 132 feet, and I wondered if anyone else had picked up on that detail yet. Just then, my phone rang.

It was Bob Caridi, "Chuck, grab your shit, and meet me at Stewart Airport, we're going to Long Island."

"You got it, Bob," I said. "See you there."

An hour later, Bob and I met at the State Police Aviation office at the airport. They had a small Bell Jet Ranger helicopter located there, similar to the last model I flew in the Air Cav. "Who's joining us?" I asked.

"Just us," Bob said. "The rest of the guys are meeting in Albany and getting picked up by a National Guard Blackhawk."

Good, I thought, because that Jet Ranger would not carry more than the two of us by the time we loaded our dive gear on board. We met the pilot, Technical Sergeant John Harrington, a fellow Army aviator and trooper inside. John had already completed his pre-flight and checked the weather. We were good to go. All we had to do was get our stuff strapped in.

"Chuck," he said, "I want you to sit up front with me. I put the co-pilot's controls back in (cyclic and collective). You know how busy flying through NYC airspace gets. I plan on letting you do some flying while I talk on the radios for clearance. You up for that?"

"Hell yes." I said. *Who's got it better than me?* I thought. I hadn't flown since leaving the Army in 1990 and was happy to assist. Tragedy notwithstanding, here I was deploying to the biggest dive mission in history, and I get to fly part of the way!

We strapped in and John received expedited clearance from the tower for take-off. As we cleared Newburgh, he brought us up to our cruising altitude over West Point and handed me the controls. "You have the controls," he said.

"I have the controls," I repeated, in accordance with Army Standard Operating Procedure (SOP).

He went on to say, "I want you to get comfortable flying again, before I turn my attention to the radios, and we transit the busy airspace around the city."

"Sounds good!" I said.

Near the end of the Academy, six years earlier, the chief pilot-in-charge of the Aviation Detail, a State Police captain, came to pay three of us recruit troopers a visit before graduation. One of my classmates, Ralph Pineda, was an Army OH-58 pilot like me, and the other was a Marine Corps CH-46 pilot named Scott Oseback; both of them came on the job with a fervent desire to join the Aviation Unit. Many would jump at this opportunity, but such was not the case with me. I had joined the State Police to become a *trooper*, not a pilot. Furthermore, here I was, having just been unexpectedly called out of class, meeting the captain for an impromptu interview, and finding myself in the unenviable position of telling this guy I was not interested in his unit, at this time. I might be later, but not now. *How do you do that without pissing him off?*

The interview was brief and went kind of like this, "Recruit, I see by your records that you're a Jet Ranger pilot."

"Yes, Sir," I said.

He subsequently asked specifics about my flying experience in Hawaii, Korea, and Japan, all pertinent to the mission of the NYSP, because I had flown in a mountainous environment overseas, similar to that of the Adirondack and Catskill mountains. After this brief Q&A, he went on to say that, "The Aviation Unit has several openings, and I'm also interviewing two of your fellow classmates, but you all look promising due to your military training. Of course, if selected, and there are no guarantees, you'd have to complete your 12-week FTO program before coming on the unit."

"Captain," I said, "…with all due respect, I'm not interested in joining the unit at this time. If I only wanted to fly helicopters, I never would have left the Army. I joined the State Police to become a trooper, first and foremost. Truthfully, I believe I would be of more value to the guys on the road as a pilot "*someday*," if I learned to be good at my primary mission first. I hope you understand and that I haven't burned any bridges..."

He just sat back in his chair and looked at me like I had two heads. "OK," he said simply. "Go back to class."

Now, here I was, six years later, flying myself, albeit under the watchful eye of Pilot-in-Command Harrington, down to Long Island. It was surreal. As we approached the East Moriches Coast Guard Station for landing, it was buzzing with activity. I had the landing pad in sight, and from a distance I could see a lot of SP brass standing off to the side intently watching our helicopter approach. *For that matter, who doesn't like to stop and watch a helicopter landing?* Anyway, I had the before-landing check completed and approach angle worked out, as I started to lower the collective to descend.

"Not so fast, Chuck," John said. "With all that brass down there, if they see a SCUBA diver land the freaking helicopter, I'm out of a job...I have the controls!"

Damned if he wasn't right. Here I was, dressed in the bright gold T-shirt and black BDU pants of a NYSP diver, sitting up front in the plexiglass cockpit of a Division helicopter with the Troop "L" Commander and national media looking on. "You have the controls," I responded. I appreciated the pilot's generosity and the opportunity to partake in the flight, more than he would ever know.

Now it was time to go to work!

Upon landing, Caridi and I quickly learned we were the first State Police divers on site, so we set about the business of "advancing" the arrival of the rest of the unit. Regardless of the cause of the crash, mechanical, pilot error, or terrorism, this was a disaster of immense proportions, and it wouldn't change the way in which we approached the task of recovery all that much. As always, safety and inter-agency coordination would be the key. Right away, we noted that although the NYPD, Suffolk County PD, and FDNY divers were in the area, no one was in the water yet. The reason was twofold: a) the surface of the ocean within much of the target area was still covered with jet fuel. Fourteen hours of wind, currents, and sporadic burning had not adequately diminished the hazard, and b) the sea state (wave action) was rocking, prohibiting safe diving conditions. Also, the depth and potential for undersea hazards presented by the twisted wreckage of a Boeing 747 would be immense. Pre-dive safety briefings highlighted the danger and the existence of: twisted metal, the potential of danger in confined spaces, and reportedly nearly 30 miles of wires and cables potentially splayed across the ocean floor.

Resultantly, on the first day, SCUBA divers searching off-shore were relegated to assisting with the surface search, first for survivors (which proved fruitless), and then for victims and debris, which was evidence that *must* be collected, each and every piece. In fact, given the possibility of terrorism, each dive boat operating in the area after the first day had both an FBI Special Agent *and* a member of the NTSB on board, to ensure what was brought up from the ocean floor was carefully segregated, documented, and triaged for investigative value, even before returning to shore.

Right from the start, Senior Diver Caridi and I recognized that the existing, organic vessels of the NYSP SCUBA Unit would be insufficient for operating on the open ocean. What we needed, and fast, was access to an ocean-going launch. A boat large enough to handle the seas 12 miles off the coast *and* capable of safely carrying the requisite number of divers and gear, while functioning as a suitable dive platform. This was a monumental ask. Thankfully, our dive leaders had spent the last couple of years providing joint, deep-water training to our colleagues in the NYPD. Not only did this pre-existing relationship solidify a strong bond between our two units, but the training previously provided by the NYSP at Lake George, literally provided the NYPD divers the required five-atmosphere (132-foot), deep dive certification necessary to qualify to operate in the search area environment. As it turned out, throughout much of target area, the depth was a fairly uniform 110-130 feet, just within our limits. Given that the NYPD SCUBA Team typically operated in water depths of 30-60 feet within New York Harbor and the surrounding rivers, no matter how experienced they were, had they not qualified with us previously, they would not have been able to dive to the depth required during the search. This fact was not lost on the leaders of the NYPD SCUBA Team. Accordingly, our Dive Team Supervisor, Sergeant Knoetgen, along with Troop "F" Senior Diver Caridi, set about resolving the "boat" issue forthwith.

From the start, the NYSP was welcomed into the fold. In fact, we were essentially provided our own vessel, which was captained by a crew from the NYPD Harbor Unit. These were specially trained police officers and expert mariners, who, as members of the full-time NYPD marine patrol, owed their first allegiance to their craft, but once given the nod of approval by the NYPD SCUBA Team, worked with us, on a daily basis, taking troopers on board and under their wing for the next four months. Unsung heroes, for without them, the SP would never have left the dock.

As the task of finding transportation to the "job site" was being nailed down by our supervisors, the rest of the team began to arrive by air and vehicle, and set about readying ourselves for deployment. Truth be known, our first foray into action was a disappointment. Out at sea, and away from the hustle and bustle of optimism and activity at the Coast Guard Station, it was immediately evident that no one could have survived this. To make matters worse, initially, we had no definitive targets to prosecute and couldn't get into the water if we wanted to, and we desperately did, due to existing environmental concerns. So, bobbing around like a cork, we were directed by overhead Coast Guard helicopters to proceed here and there, across the surface of the ocean, recovering debris. Clearly, this was a necessary part of the job, and none of us would rather have been anywhere else, but the enormity of the challenge was becoming evident, and no more so than when we got our first call regarding a "victim..."

A 37-foot vessel is an intimate work environment, and as soon as a helicopter hailed us, claiming they were hovering over a body, and requested our assistance, all hands became immediately attentive. The aircraft proceeded to vector us into position. At first, we approached expeditiously, then the captain slowed us rapidly, to ensure we would not overshoot our intended target. From the bow, we could just make out a body floating face down. Our divers sprang into action, extending a rescue pole out to the body in an effort to arrest the victim and position the body for recovery. Just as contact was made, however, the immense reality of the entire mission took hold...We quickly realized, it wasn't a body, in the conventional sense of the word, it was the paper-thin remains, just the skin of a victim, floating on the waves, after a 13,000-foot freefall from an airliner. At that moment, everyone on board swallowed hard; I know I did. On the positive side, and you couldn't lose sight of it, we had just recovered some of the first remains that ultimately would be positively identified and returned to loved ones, bringing some measure of closure.

The next day, as I recall, and every day thereafter (weather permitting), we got wet. Seemingly overnight, we had linked up with our fellow divers, the FBI, and the NTSB. We then organized into teams, sorted out who was heading out to sea and on what vessels, and received search assignments based upon GPS coordinates. The FBI provided additional assistance to us, in the form of redundant air cylinders (pony bottles) and hand-held sonars, to make our diving safer and more productive. Dive team leaders attended detailed daily briefings, orchestrated by the U.S. Navy SUPSALV (Supervisor of Salvage), designed to assure our safety and coordination.

Briefly, daily operations were predicated upon several factors and conditions. During overnight hours, research and salvage vessels from the Navy and NOAA sailed the search area, charting the ocean floor, attempting to identify and pinpoint anomalies representing potential pieces of wreckage. Within the limits of technology at the time, using sonar and other mapping methods, they developed a target list, which was then turned over to the Navy for dissemination and prosecution. Chiefly, targets of significant size, or beyond the capabilities of SCUBA, generally due to depth or structural constraints, were turned over to Navy Salvage Divers. These trained professionals, then deployed primarily from their vessels moored above the site, utilizing surface-supplied air to conduct extensive decompression dives, which greatly extended their bottom time and productivity.

Peripheral "targets" were provided to the dozens of highly trained public safety divers from the NYPD, NYSP, and FDNY for prosecution. These targets were no less important and were often harder to locate. Divers utilized hand-held sonar, to hone in on clusters of debris and single objects on the ocean floor, such as: airplane wreckage, components, seats which had separated from the fuselage (some still with passengers strapped in), luggage, and the assorted remains of passengers. This was an enormous task, taking months to complete.

On my second or third dive, my partner and I descended 127 feet to the floor of the Atlantic. Because of the depth, near our operating limit, our dive tables directed we had about 10 minutes of bottom time to conduct our search activities. After that, another crew would descend, and then another…Good thing; this was a hot spot. The coordinates proved to be so accurate, that as we neared the ocean floor, we saw that our hand-held sonar was unnecessary, as the sand was littered with debris. We worked our way along the bottom, filling our mesh recovery bags with what we could. When we ran out of room, we stuffed a few items in the pockets of our BCs (buoyancy compensators), where my dive partner secured a human foot, and then proceeded to cut sections of wire, as I continued to swim forward. (Wire was everywhere, and we had been told bring samplings up every chance we could, because every two feet or so, a serial number is imprinted, and it would help engineers determine what part of the plane we were working on.)

As I propelled myself forward, I subsequently observed, laid out on the sand in front of me, a large section of the aircraft coming into view. This was, by far, the largest piece I had yet come across. It appeared to be a side section of the fuselage, judging from the portal-type windows and "wrinkled" aluminum skin of the aircraft. Protruding from a break in the aircraft's skin was the body of a man. I recall his arms were outstretched, as if he was "reaching" for *help*. I looked at my watch and observed it was nearly time to wrap it up and head for the surface, but there was no way I was leaving without this guy. I grasped his arms by the wrists, thinking I could simply guide him away from the aircraft, but he did not move. Working my way in closer, I wrapped my arms around him and kicked my fins for all I was worth. Nothing. Now, taking a closer look, I could see that his lower body was pinned in the wreckage. I enveloped the victim in a "bear hug," and bracing my feet against the skin of the aircraft, leaned back with all my weight; he finally broke free, literally tearing loose at the knees.

I had him, and it was time to head for the surface. Looking over my shoulder, I noted my dive partner had just swum up behind me, his recovery bag clipped to a D-ring on his vest and one hand full of recovered items. Looking at is watch, he first pointed at my victim and then gave me the "OK?" sign. I replied in the affirmative, and he then gave me the "thumbs up," indicating it's time to ascend. Both of us had to manipulate the controls of our BCs in order to add compressed air from the tank and establish positive buoyancy for our rise to the surface. This "controlled ascent" is a maneuver every diver must master. Do it properly, and you gradually ascend, while off-gassing potentially dangerous compressed air and nitrogen as you go. Go too fast, and you risk an air embolism, ruptured lung, or decompression sickness, also known as "the bends," any of which is guaranteed to ruin your day. Facing each other, victim locked between us, we both began to add air into our vests, I could feel myself getting positively buoyant as my BC began to fill with air. My partner was doing the same, and we simultaneously began kicking. Thing was, it didn't feel like we were going anywhere. In fact, when I stopped kicking, we immediately settled back onto the bottom; no good. We looked at each other, "thumbs up," once more. *Let's go!* Same result, only this time we both observed a stream of bubbles rushing from his BC.

For whatever reason, his BC was not inflating properly; the air was just dumping overboard. At this depth, and upon reaching our time limit, this was decidedly not good. We had to make ourselves positively buoyant, and in a hurry, but leaving the victim behind was not an option. In SCUBA school, they told us, "Don't panic. Fix your problems on the bottom." Indeed, the training we'd endured was generally so arduous, introducing one challenge after another, that we had developed a high degree of confidence in the water. We both knew what to do, but there would be an element of risk, especially from this depth. My partner pointed at his weight belt, designed to afford you the negative buoyancy required to descend, by off-setting the buoyancy of the neoprene wetsuit and other specific items of gear, indicating he was about to execute the Emergency Procedure of ditching his weight belt. This would render him *immediately* positively buoyant and he *would*, in short order, reach the surface. The challenge now would be to retard his rate of ascent sufficiently, so he would arrive topside safely, without incurring one of the previously mentioned dive injuries. Instinctively, we knew what had to be done. He removed his belt, a good 40 pounder as I recall, and held it at arm's length out to the side. With the victim still pinned between us, we grasped a strap on each other's vest, reasoning two divers can create more drag than one, thus slowing his rate of ascent. With one last eye contact, he dropped the belt. We lifted off the bottom immediately, gaining speed with each passing second. Continuing to breath, we were sure to *exhale* on the way up so as not to rupture a lung from over pressurization, and spread eagled, to create more friction in the water slowing our rate of ascent. The last thing we wanted was to break the surface of the ocean like a couple of Polaris missiles! Fortunately, our teamwork paid off. We broke the surface in a controlled fashion, with our victim in tow. In fact, the first indication to our dive supervisor that anything had gone awry, was when he was taking our gear from us into the boat, and my partner didn't have a weight belt to hand up to him. "Long story," he said, to the supervisor.

Upon toweling off and breaking down our gear, it didn't take him long to figure out what had happened. Apparently, during a previous mission, he was removing his BC from a boat and caught one of the emergency CO2 inflator cords on the gunwale. Just that tug of pressure had caused it to go off, inflating his BC on the dock. At the time, he admitted, he removed and discarded the spent cylinder, deflating the vest, but did not have a fresh one on hand with which to replace it, figuring he would get one later from stock. Apparently, that replacement never happened, leaving nothing but an open port in the vest. No wonder air being introduced, moments earlier, was just rushing out into the sea. "No shit!" I said, looking at the hole. "That explains it." I've got to hand it to him. He was a very experienced diver, and admitting this oversight was more than a bit embarrassing, but to his credit, he didn't think twice. During that evening's After Action Review, he disclosed his "lesson learned" to every SP Diver present. A true professional! I was proud to be a member of a team with men of that caliber.

After diving in the initial wave, I was rotated out, to attend scheduled training and allow fresh divers, from around the state, an opportunity to work the site. But, being away, and watching the recovery effort on TV, was difficult. I coordinated with my supervisor and returned to Long Island briefly for another dive rotation. Then, I headed to the Academy, where I attended the Defensive Tactics Instructor Course. In all, 48 State Police divers participated in the mission.

By the end of the detail, on November 2, 1996, the State Police had safely conducted 646 dives, under the expert supervision of Technical Sergeant John Knoetgen, and played a significant role in the massive investigation and recovery effort. Overall, the combined efforts of ALL divers and crew, regardless of organization, is said to have recovered nearly 95% of the aircraft, and most significantly, at least the partial remains of *all* 230 passengers and crew, representing 13 different countries.

As a post script, "officially", the FBI and NTSB ruled out terrorism as a cause of the crash, finding "no evidence" of foreign, explosive residue or material. Instead, they attributed the crash to an explosion caused by a malfunctioning component which resulted in a spark in the main fuel tank within the belly of the aircraft. Exhaustive review has been conducted, and while this theory remains heavily disputed by eyewitnesses to this day, aviation and investigative professionals stand by their finding.

Following Flight 800, all was relatively quiet the rest of the decade. In all, I would spend 10 of the best years of my career serving with the SCUBA Unit, the last three of which were as the unit's leader, having been appointed the division diving officer (DDO). While there were unquestionably more tenured divers on the unit, by this point in my career I had been promoted to sergeant, and running the team required more than just time under water. Supervision of the statewide unit required capabilities beyond basic organizational, administrative, and supervisory skills; it necessitated interfacing with members of the Division Headquarters staff, procurement specialists, outside agencies, specialty equipment vendors, and SCUBA certifying organizations. As "dry" as all that sounds (pun intended, because the Dive Team Supervisor spends a lot more time coordinating resources than diving) there was a fair amount of operational work to do, including running the 2001 Novice SCUBA School. In addition to providing basic training, the unit spec'd out and issued a complete set of new dive gear for each student including: new dry suits, laser depth finders, chain saws for cutting ice, underwater 35mm cameras, underwater video cameras, new lift bags, etc. We also made significant advances in the acquisition of an ROV. It was truly a high-water mark of Division-level support.

On September 11, 2001, tragedy struck New Yorkers and the nation, as terrorists attacked the World Trade Center and Pentagon. The U.S. was experiencing its darkest hour. Immediately, at the direction of then-Governor George Pataki, the NYSP made any and all of its resources available to NYC, in an effort to assist. Ultimately, while hundreds of troopers would "serve in a support and assist roll" at Ground Zero, two units in particular, the SCUBA Unit I was leading and our Mobile Response Team (MRT), a tactical unit of which I was the operations NCO, were called up immediately. Divers from Troops "F" and "K" deployed immediately to Ground Zero and partnered with NYPD to evaluate and conduct port security, screening piers for possible IED's. This assignment, I delegated to top-notch senior divers in those respective troops, as I was then coordinating a multi-team response from the MRT.

As all Americans know, in addition to the massive loss of life of innocent civilian employees at the World Trade Center, hundreds of first responders died rushing into harm's way to aid their fellow citizens, including the 343 members of the FDNY. Among that group of brave New Yorkers, were the highly trained men and women of the Department's Rescue Companies. In addition to their basic skill set, these experienced firefighters, also possessed additional specialized training, including certification as department public safety divers.

Arguably, no agency was harder hit than the FDNY, particularly their Rescue Company firefighters. As a result of grievous loss of life, the department lost most of their rescue divers in one tragic blow. At the time, due to my heavy involvement and work on the "Pile" with my fellow members of the MRT, the scale and scope of their specific loss may have gone unnoticed. That is, if not for our Special Services Commanding Officer at the time, Captain Steve Nevins, whose brother, Gerry Nevins, was a Rescue One firefighter and diver tragically lost on 9/11.

Months into the response, Steve brought to my attention the prospect of aiding FDNY in reconstituting their dive team. "Chuck," he began, "as you know, FDNY's Rescue Companies were devastated. What you may not know is, that they lost virtually all their SCUBA divers and most of their instructors; I think they may have one left." "What can you do to help them?" Steve, an accomplished, former SP diver himself, knew that this was a big lift, proposing the training of dozens of new divers, while simultaneously attempting to develop and certify additional instructors to replenish their cadre, a significant undertaking. He also knew, he had come to the right guy. There was no way I would balk or turn him down. Helping the Rescue Companies would be an honor!

So, gathering up my best senior divers, we proceeded with a sense of purpose. The captain arranged my first meeting with a representative from the Rescue Battalion, a training lieutenant, and we discussed their highly specific needs. It became instantly clear that we did not have a training program "on the shelf," that would meet those needs. So, we spent many hours identifying the tasks, conditions, and standards necessary to certify new fire department divers, including developing a syllabus and reaching out to our governing body, to ensure the new program would be recognized and certified. The results would be a top-notch program, tailored especially for their needs. I also directed my team of senior divers who were fine tuning the curriculum, there would be no short cuts; we were putting our names and reputation on it. And, I knew the FDNY didn't want it any other way!

By the summer of 2002, we were ready to go. We had created a unique, certified, FDNY Rescue/Municipal Diver Certification program, aimed at not only qualifying new divers, but also elevating several existing qualified divers to dive master and open water instructor status. Over a two-year period, the State Police conducted four, two-week SCUBA training sessions, held entirely in and around New York City, resulting in the certification of nearly 80 divers, reconstituting the unit, and returning the FDNY to a fully operational and self-sufficient status.

Finally, prior to the end of my time as division diving officer, as a result of my impending promotion to lieutenant, I had an opportunity to coordinate a relatively high-profile response to a maritime disaster occurring right in the figurative backyard of Division Headquarters, in Albany, NY. The pressure was on, especially due to the location within virtual sight of the State Capitol, but our divers, armed with their experience at Flight 800, and advances in equipment, were more than up to the challenge.

In December of 2003, the oceangoing, 289-foot Dutch freighter, Stellamare, capsized at the Port of Albany. As cranes loaded the second of two huge (308-ton) generators destined for overseas into the hold of the vessel, the load shifted affecting the ship's center of gravity, causing it to roll over in its berth at the dock, killing three Russian crew members. State Police divers, along with City of Albany divers, responded immediately and launched one of the most hazardous search efforts in Division history. Divers braved confined spaces, frigid temperatures, tidal currents, and a mix of ice and diesel fuel, in addition to shifting cables, chains, and materials, in near-zero visibility conditions. Over the course of the three-week detail, SP divers from around the state participated, ultimately resulting in, or contributing to, the recovery of all three victims.

Culminating my tenure as division diving officer, I look back with pride on what we accomplished, particularly assisting the FDNY in their hour of need.

CHAPTER 6

SPECIAL OPERATIONS: SWAT

In 1996, I achieved what had been a career objective of mine since entering the State Police six years earlier, selection to the Mobile Response Team (MRT), Division's version of SWAT. I knew both getting on the team and serving as a member wouldn't be easy, but given my military background and specialty training, I felt I'd be a good fit. So, when the announcement came out that the tryouts would be held, I seized the opportunity. I had been waiting for this since day one in the Academy and had rigorously maintained top-physical condition. I knew I had to hit a home run, because it would be years before this opportunity would present itself again.

At the 1972 Summer Olympics in Munich, Germany, eight members of the Palestinian terrorist organization Black September had taken nine Israeli athletes hostage, and the resulting carnage played out on world television. All nine hostages were either intentionally murdered by their captors, or inadvertently killed by their rescuers, during a siege at the airport, as German authorities attempted to affect a hostage rescue. The failure reverberated among law enforcement agencies and military units around the world, guaranteeing security at a major event would never be approached quite the same way again.

Because of the events in Munich, the NYSP, being the lead agency providing security at the 1980 Winter Olympics in Lake Placid, NY, formed the MRT, a team of highly trained troopers, who received additional training in tactics, firearms, hostage situations, barricaded subjects, sharpshooting, helicopter assault, rappelling, skiing, etc., and integrated them into the massive security plan. The problem as I see it was, once the Olympics had wrapped up without incident, Division disbanded the team. Rather shortsighted, in my opinion. It wouldn't be until 1984, when the country observed LAPD prepare for the Summer Olympics in Los Angeles, stepping up training for their SWAT teams, that Division took note and rekindled the MRT. Fortunately, the "blue print," if not all the players, was still in place.

So, the MRT that I was applying for in 1996 had nearly 12 years of experience and operational seasoning under its belt, albeit part-time experience. The unit had many stated capabilities and expectations placed upon it: high-risk entries, expertise in multiple firearms, sharpshooters, defensive tactics, search and rescue, woodland searches for fugitives, dignitary protection, high-risk transports, high-angle rescue, helicopter rappelling, cold weather operations, night-vision assisted operations, etc.

Unfortunately, at the time and for years to come, even with all that on their plate, the NYSP, an agency of thousands, elected not to dedicate the 30-40 full-time line numbers (troopers) to the task, with a singular commitment to train and respond to the worst of the worst in New York State. Figuratively, it has often been said, "When the public calls 911, they need the police to respond to an emergency, and when a police officer calls 911, he needs a SWAT team." Perhaps an oversimplification, but accurate nonetheless. Where was the sense of urgency? [Today, and since 2009, that is no longer the case, but it took years of effort, tragedy, and reflection to get there.]

Upon graduation from the 10-week basic school in '96 (Today it's 28-weeks long, to reflect how far they've come.), I was assigned to the eight-man South Team. At the time, there were only three teams, North, South, and West; the South Team covered the lower Hudson Valley, Long Island, and part of New York's Southern Tier, an immense geographic area of responsibility. Fortunately, like the SCUBA Unit, we really didn't have to adhere to regional boundaries and frequently assembled additional unit members from other regions of the state to conduct meaningful operations. However, the team was only allowed to train quarterly, and the jobs came sporadically. To put it bluntly, our operational tempo at the time was deplorable, and at times, it appeared that Division was reluctant to use us.

From the troops, we'd heard every excuse in the book: "You guys are never available...You take too long to get anywhere...Who's going to pay the OT (overtime)...You're a bunch of prima donnas...Who needs you?" *Blah, blah, blah.* Remember, the old *"One Trooper, One Riot"* mentality?

Painful as it was, some of the criticism was justified. We *were* spread way too thin. We did *not* have our own cars, which delayed our response; we had to stop at our respective stations to pick up a troop car, which just pissed the sergeant off. To be honest, we *were* overly parochial, rarely collaborating with other teams on substantive training matters. Although we weren't "prima donnas," I could see why other troopers might think so. Finally, for whatever reason, perhaps all of the above, plus institutional animus, Division did *not* universally promote our utilization. For example, back in the day, it was not unheard of for a handful of uniformed troopers and investigators to handle an armed standoff with a barricaded gunman, while hiding behind trees and bushes, in sub-zero temperatures, equipped with only standard police uniforms, and ballistic vests, and armed with only handguns and a megaphone. Troopers may have been armed with a shotgun, if they had signed one out of the station armory. All this, while a trained, fully equipped tactical team sat at home on their asses! Imagine the officer safety issues and organizational liability!

Still, I felt very fortunate to be on the team. The majority of the guys were extremely dedicated, *and you've got to be part of something, to help improve it,* I reasoned. Almost immediately, and much to my delight, I was sent to DT Instructor School, Firearms Instructor School, and promoted to South Team leader, an NCO billet, when a vacancy occurred. In early 2000, I was promoted to sergeant, based on a Division-wide competitive exam, which necessitated a transfer from my beloved SP Newburgh, back to SP Middletown. *Thought it was tough being a trooper in Middletown?* You had to learn the ropes and get your shit together quickly, to survive there as a sergeant.

At that time, I had just completed running the 2000 MRT Basic School as the lead instructor, under our new Special Services commander, Captain Steve Nevins. Steve, a hardcore, no-nonsense man of uncompromising integrity, would not settle for the status quo, and was more than willing to discuss and implement substantive changes to the program. With his support, we revised and extended the length of the course to 16 weeks, developing a comprehensive curriculum to address significant gaps in training. I regularly rotated assistant instructors in from around the state, and together we spent countless hours preparing for, and delivering, training in an attempt to take the program to the next level. By all accounts, we were successful. By the end of four months, we graduated 16 new operators, who were just chomping at the bit to make a difference.

As a part-time team, we did the best we could. When we got together for a week of training every three months, invariably we would shoot our asses off at the range, because the job expected us to be experts, and we demanded the same of ourselves. Given the myriad of highly perishable skills and capabilities listed in our repertoire, we tried to focus on what we perceived to be our "bread and butter" skill set: firearms and dynamic entries (raids). There was precious little time to train, and we deemed those to be very high-risk pursuits. As the Marines like to say: *"Improvise, Adapt and Overcome."*

Make no mistake, all of us, incumbents and new guys alike, wanted to vastly improve the team. However, while hearts may have been in the right place, the concept of improvement, often means different things to different people. Correspondingly, the pace and degree of change can become a source of contention. Talk to any tactical team member, and they will confirm that that *leading* a bunch of Type-A SWAT operators can be challenging, especially when they're not busy! Kind of like "herding cats!" However, it was a new decade, and the MRT had to evolve to keep pace with the changing scope of law enforcement. Although, the process itself would prove challenging. My view was, this was a team of unlimited potential, and we owed it to the Division, and ourselves, to push hard to get to the next level. As any metallurgist will tell you, a finely honed blade can't be created without a lot of work, including experiencing a chip or two along the way. However, by applying the right vision, technique and perseverance, a razor-sharp edge results. As far as the MRT was concerned, we were working on no less than the tip of the spear.

It was in this environment, that 9/11 occurred.

September 11, 2001, began like any other day. One of those iconic starts; the sun was shining, and there was not a cloud in the sky. That all changed at 8:47 AM, when American Airlines Flight 11, travelling at a speed of nearly 500 MPH, with 87 innocent passengers and crew on board, struck Tower One of the World Trade Center in New York City. The plane went in dead on, banked steeply, slashing through floors 90-100, leaving a jagged hole in the structure. Though mortally damaged, Tower One would manage to remain standing for approximately one hour.

Then, at 9:02 AM, while cameras focused on the burning first tower, a glimpse of another passenger jet entered the television screen. This one, United Airlines Flight 175, travelling at a speed of approximately 600 MPH, with 60 innocent souls on board, blasted into floors 78-87 of the Trade Center's South Tower. Tower Two, the South Tower, remained standing for only 56 minutes, before it succumbed at 10:00 AM. The North Tower collapsed at 10:28 AM.

America was under attack.

At 9:37 AM, a hijacked American Airlines Flight 77, with 59 innocent passengers on board, was intentionally flown into the Pentagon, the very symbol of our National Defense, killing an additional 125 victims at that location. Almost simultaneously, the 40 courageous passengers and crew of United Airlines Flight 93 took matters into their own hands, violently wrestling control away from their Al Qaeda hijackers, presumably headed for the U.S. Capitol. Instead the aircraft slammed into a field in Shanksville, PA, heroically preventing untold loss of life at the intended target in Washington, D.C.

Resultantly, 2,977 innocent lives were lost that day, between the World Trade Center, the Pentagon, and Shanksville. This included 414 first responders who perished in New York City, rushing in to aid the victims and save lives by evacuating an estimated 25,000, before the collapse.

Against this act of barbarism, as the operations sergeant for the NYSP MRT, I received a call to assemble team members and prepare for inevitable deployment to what would come to be known as "Ground Zero."

By 1:00 PM, MRT members from around the state had arrived at Stewart International Airport, in New Windsor, NY, as ordered, preparing for what we believed would be a short flight to lower Manhattan. Despite five or six State Police helicopters assembled for this task, it became immediately apparent we weren't going anywhere. For the first time in U.S. history, all non-military, unauthorized flights, had been grounded by order of the president. It stood to reason, that if our own commercial aviation assets were being successfully used against us as implements of war, until we knew the attack was over, and exactly what we were dealing with, the sky was off limits.

No problem, our contingency travel plan was to convoy south, as the airport was merely one hour from our intended destination, but before we could get on the road, a stand down order was received from Headquarters. Understandably, the scene on the ground in NYC was chaotic. The NYSP was amid coordinating with, and through, the Office of the Governor, NYC Mayor, and NYPD Commissioner, to determine exactly what resources were required. Clearly, the folks on the ground had their hands full, and we did not want to add to the chaos. Subsequently, like all Americans on 9/11, we were relegated to watching events unfold on TV that day and wanted desperately to help our fellow citizens. Unlike most Americans, we knew we had the training and tools at our disposal to make a difference. Still, we would just have to remain patient; and it wasn't easy. We waited on the tarmac till 10:00 PM that night, only to be told we would depart with special clearance first thing the next morning, September 12.

By 5:00 AM, we had checked out of our hastily reserved hotel and headed back to the airport. We checked on our gear, which we had loaded on the aircraft the day before, and verified our roster with the pilots, who were still working on obtaining the necessary clearance to fly. Half the group departed by convoy, heading south, as we would need those vehicles and the bulky equipment they carried in the city, in the days and weeks ahead. Although, it would be two days before commercial air travel, under tight restrictions was reestablished, we were given the "green light" and boarded our helicopters for the short flight south. Ironically, it was another beautiful day, much like 9/11. It was clear and sunny, and you could see forever; but the mood was somber and there wasn't another aircraft in the sky.

Flying south, in a formation of three State Police helicopters, we began to observe, from a point well north of the landmark George Washington Bridge, a huge plume of smoke rising from the tip of lower of Manhattan, where the WTC had stood just the day before. As we drew closer, we got a sense of the enormity of the devastation. Something not readily perceivable on television. Ultimately, we landed at the 30th Street Heliport, along the west side of the island and checked in at the State Police Command Post in the Jacob Javits Convention Center. For years, the SP had maintained a primarily uniformed presence at the convention center, and now it paid off in spades. Over the course of the detail, the Javits Center would function as the State Police Command Post and key portal for nearly 1,000 troopers who would cycle through to assist with traffic control, port, terminal, train, and subway security, and assist with securing the WTC perimeter itself. Specialized units like ours (MRT), and our top-flight K9 Unit, would see many months of uninterrupted service, right up until the closing memorial ceremony in May of 2002.

Upon checking in at the Javits CP, we found we were essentially on our own. SP bosses in NYC didn't have a specific assignment for us yet, so I advised a Commissioned Officer that we would attempt to establish contact with our counterparts in the NYPD Emergency Services Unit (ESU). That was fine with him, as he had his hands full with other matters. As the operations NCO for the entire team, I was fortunate to be accompanied by my close friend and colleague, Sergeant John Gomez, who had taken over for me as South Team leader, upon my move up to Headquarters. John was a loyal, highly effective leader, and we shared many of the same progressive views. Returning to the group that had accompanied us by helo, we said, "Stand by here and coordinate for the arrival of our convoy. John and I plan to scout ahead and link up with ESU. We'll be back for you."

We then exited Javits, and headed south on foot, toward lower Manhattan, passing dozens of waiting ambulances lined up, without any patients. Walking further down West Street became surreal, the closer we got to the site. As I recall, the final 10-15 blocks north of the WTC was increasingly covered with debris and dust, several inches thick. Approaching nearer still, the landscape took on an unbelievable appearance. What had once been a thriving, towering, financial district, and source of pride, had been turned into a smoldering mass grave. Once-impressive towers reduced to a pile of rubble five or six stories high, just spilling out into the streets in all directions. Attempting to navigate, we couldn't round the corner of any block without it taking on the appearance of a Hollywood Sci-Fi movie, only this wasn't fiction. As we pressed on, looking for the elusive ESU Command Post, we penetrated deeply into the scene, passing police officers and firefighters looking completely disheveled, covered with dirt, ash, and sweat. Many them, looking like they'd been up for the last 24 hours, milled about in an apparent state of shock.

Running out of options, we grabbed the first ESU officer we saw, as identified by the patch on the back of his uniform, and asked, "Where's your CP?"

He simply replied, "Stuyvesant High School," and kept on walking. Unbeknownst to us, we had passed it on the way down and now had to back track. Locating the high school, we entered the main doors to the lobby and observed what could best be described as a medical triage site. Doctors, nurses, medics, etc., were attending to responders, many getting their eyes and nasal passages flushed out, a service we would require later that same day, and for days to come. Passing the tables and stretchers, we proceeded through the double doors of the auditorium to the ESU Command Post.

Looking out over the "audience," all you could see was NYC cops waiting for an assignment. Centered up on the stage itself, was a couple of folding tables and a handful of ESU Commissioned Officers, pouring over maps. During what we perceived to be a break in the action, John and I neared the steps of the stage and grabbed a lieutenant who was on his way up. "Excuse me, Sir," I said, "We're with the NYSP Mobile Response Team. We have about 25 men with us here today and more that will be on their way shortly. We're here to help."

The lieutenant just stared at us, as if we'd just told him one more thing than his mind was capable of processing. It was clear he was completely overwhelmed. "Take a seat," he said, pointing to the bucket seats in the auditorium holding the other 200 guys, and up the steps he went.

That went well, I thought. *If our names don't get passed to the officer doling out the assignments, we'll be no closer now than we were 12 hours ago.*

Gomez, who had a relative who'd retired from the NYPD, said, "Let me give it a try." He poached the next guy passing by, dropped his relative's name, and seemed to get some recognition. This individual then headed up the steps, stopped by the assignment desk and whispered something in the lieutenant's ear. The LT looked up at us briefly, over his glasses, and went right back to work. No surprise. These guys were up to their asses in alligators, and we were a relative unknown to them. *Remember, I said earlier, that the MRT had not done much outreach to other units over the years? We, the relatively new supervisors, were paying for it now.*

John's "contact" looked our way and mouthed the words, "Have a seat."

OK, we didn't need to be told twice. At least they didn't kick us the hell out!

So, we took up a position in the front row and discussed our strategy. "John," I said, "…let's get the guys down here, seated in the auditorium. At least then, if something comes up, we're ready to roll."

"You got it, Chuck," he said, and stepped out briefly to make it happen. That chore, communicating with our people, would prove challenging in and of itself, as the city's cell phone service had been significantly disrupted as a result of the attack. That said, John took care of it, and before long, we had approximately 25 men, the convoy having arrived during our absence, seated in the auditorium. During the time it took us to coalesce in this area, we had observed ESU supervisors being called upon, one by one to the front desk, and handed assignments. With that, a group of 8 or 10 men would stand up and head out. *"That's where we need to be,"* I thought.

It had been well over an hour and a half, since anybody had so much as looked our way. Then, as if on cue, I noticed someone that I knew. Someone with rank, and he was headed right for the stage! Jumping to my feet, I plotted an intercept angle with the intention of catching him before he mounted those steps and getting us some business.

"Doctor Martinez!" I said. The Deputy Chief looked at me hard, before recognizing me.

"Oh, Sergeant Guess! What are you doing here?"

A year earlier, I had met Dr. Martinez, a physician at Jacobi Medical Center, during a visit we conducted for our novice SCUBA divers to their recompression chamber. It was a required block of instruction for our troopers, and Martinez was not only the physician conducting the tour, but also, an NYPD Surgeon. A great guy, who told me at the time, "Let me know if you ever need anything." We'd struck up a long conversation back then, and I hoped that it was about to pay off now.

"Doc," I said, "In addition to being a SCUBA diver, you may recall that I'm also on our SWAT team, actually the operations sergeant. We're here to help."

"How many people do you have?" he asked.

"Twenty-five" I told him. With another ten or so standing by."

"Come with me," he said. We walked up the stairs, crossed the stage, bypassing the lieutenants at the assignment table, and stopped directly in front of the Inspector-in-charge of ESU, Yu, I think his name was. "Inspector, this is Sergeant Guess with the NYSP Mobile Response Team," the Chief said. "He's a good man, and I'm sure we can find work for his unit."

"Yes, Sir," said the inspector. "We'll attach him to one of our Truck crews right away."

"Thank you, Sir!" I said. The inspector headed immediately over to the lieutenant at the assignment desk and pointed my way. "Thanks again, Doc," I said.

"Careful out there," he replied. I returned to our spot in the auditorium, and the next ESU team that went out, had our guys attached to it. We were on our way.

The ESU sergeant and I introduced ourselves and got to work. "What are you qualified to do?" he asked. "Ever do any high-angle rope stuff, bridge work, etc.?"

"Yes," I said. "Our gear's out in our trucks."

"Good. Get it and meet us outside on the side of the building," he said.

Our first assignment had us proceeding to a residential high-rise on the periphery of the Trade Center's footprint. The mission was to check the building, top to bottom, for trapped individuals, as the power had gone out, searching for any victims and/or evidence, which may have been projected onto the roof top by the crashes. John and I rounded up the men, grabbed our gear, and met the ESU Truck squad outside. From there we proceeded on a circuitous route, because of the massive obstructions in the street, to our first intended structure.

Entering the lobby of the building, the salty ESU sergeant said, "This building's got something like 35 floors. You Troopers look like you're in shape," he added with a wry grin, "so…, you take the top half, including the roof, and we'll take the bottom half, including the basement. Meet back here in the lobby."

"Roger that," I said, and we did just that.

The search of the upper floors was uneventful, just a lot of stair climbing and knocking on doors, but when we stepped out on the roof, we were awe struck. In addition to the expected dust and debris, we had a bird's eye view of the site. It was overwhelming. All of us stood there for a moment, holding our breath. Where once stood two magnificent towers, an adjacent hotel, and office buildings, was a gnarly pile of twisted, smoking steel and concrete. The multiple lines of "rescuers" visible below, manning the "bucket brigades," looked woefully insufficient for the task at hand. You couldn't look away. Yet again, another kick in the gut.

After completing this assignment, we searched another building with our ESU colleagues, checking off the two structures we had been assigned, and headed over to the "Pile." I use that term, which became synonymous with the final resting place of thousands of Americans, with all due respect and reverence. According to the media, the towers were places for employment for upwards of 50,000 people. At that time, how many had died in the collapse, or remained trapped, was unknown. Early estimates speculated by the media put the number as high as perhaps 10,000. Although no one knew for sure this early on. Consequently, there was a palpable sense of urgency and activity at the Pile.

Initially, everyone's prayer was that survivors would be found, as is common in the aftermath of a building collapse caused by an earthquake or construction accident, but this was no average scenario. In fact, nothing on this scale had ever occurred. Years of investigation and scientific study later revealed the cause and nature of the structural collapse and why it was non-survivable. In layman's terms: the towers whose construction began in 1968, were completed and opened in 1973. They had not been designed to withstand intentional attacks by terrorists utilizing enormous passenger planes filled with jet fuel as flying missiles. Planners had accounted for a potential, accidental strike by a 707, the largest commercial airliner at the time, but not Al Qaeda's deviant scenario. In fact, the ability of the 1,400-foot-tall towers to initially remain standing is a testament to its design and construction. As studied and widely reported, the unique, redundant, tube-within-a-tube design, allowed the tower to absorb the impact like a net and its weight to be redistributed. During this critical period, more than 25,000 people were able to escape, with the corresponding assistance of WTC staff, firefighters, and police.

However, structural damage was not all the building had to withstand. The Boeing 767s had an enormous fuel capacity. A fact not lost upon the terrorists, who chose these planes because they were westbound flights and known to be carrying a full load of fuel. Upon impact, the planes blew the fireproof coating off the steel trusses and exploded into flames. The resulting fire reached temperatures nearing 1,800 degrees Celsius. Because the melting temperature of the exposed steel trusses was approximately 1,500 degrees Celsius, the structural integrity was rapidly compromised. The supporting trusses gave way, and horizontal support for the floors was lost. Correspondingly, the weight of the upper floors caused the external steel frame to fail, resulting in a cascade effect of 110 floors plummeting to the ground.

Complete structural collapse of the Twin Towers and several collateral surrounding buildings resulted, surpassing Osama Bin Laden's wildest dreams.

On the Pile, the mood was just indescribable. Anger, shock, sadness, helplessness, and the thirst for revenge lingered in the air.

Searching for survivors was paramount! The effort, underway by the time we arrived, had started out with merely the tools on hand: buckets, shovels, pry bars, head lamps, etc. The lines of the bucket brigade included hundreds of people, initially including citizen volunteers, such as construction workers and area residents, standing side by side with New York City Police, Port Authority Police, New York City Firefighters, New York State Troopers, federal agents, etc.

The low-tech practice initially involved filling buckets by hand or shoveling buckets full of debris. The buckets were handed down a line and upon reaching the end, the debris was deposited onto a cleared portion of the street where, after inspection, a dump truck would later come and remove it. In the early days, individuals, from all occupations, worked as a team, and were literally doing everything they could, by hand, to excavate the site and reach their fellow citizens.

While people were digging and filling buckets of debris, we were also listening for any sign that someone possibly trapped beneath, was calling, tapping, or signaling for help. Occasionally, a well-meaning "rescuer" would shout, "Quiet!" and hundreds of workers would stop moving and hold their breaths, hoping to hear a sign that someone was alive, only to realize that was not the case, again and again. Ultimately, the search included crawling into an endless variety of structural voids, and underground areas, a hazard beyond parallel, as the six-story pile of debris was shifting, burning and flooding in pockets for months. However, the search had to continue. There was no place we wouldn't go looking for survivors. Unfortunately, there would be no further rescues after the first 12 hours, in which five people were found in a collapsed stairwell.

Over the next several days, the initial chaos turned into a form of organization. Top members of the recently formed Unified Command eventually got a handle on how to approach the disaster, and the result was an increasingly organized, methodical recovery effort. "Sectors" or "quadrants" were assigned to different rescue teams throughout the site. Our team, initially charged with going into many of the other surrounding buildings, uncovered pieces of the planes and materials from buildings on several of the surrounding rooftops. But it was our time on the Pile itself, over the ensuing months, that our team felt we made our biggest contribution. For men who wanted to make a direct contribution, it didn't get any more up close and personal than that.

One of the major hazards people involved in the recovery effort faced each day was the fact that many of the surrounding buildings had either partially collapsed or received structural damage. The threat of those unstable buildings collapsing was deemed high and was constantly monitored by engineers with laser measuring devices. If any shifting of the structure occurred, engineers sounded an alarm, usually in the form of a blaring horn, signaling the workers to evacuate the site immediately. Considering buildings, including a 70-story skyscraper, were thought to be at risk of toppling, there were several instances during the first days we found ourselves "running for our lives" because of a warning.

A second, more prevalent and insidious concern, later scientifically determined to be a cause of many forms of chronic illnesses and disease, was the overwhelming amount of smoke, dust, and other particulate matter inhaled and ingested due to working at the site. The problem was especially vexing for those individuals directly or subsequently exposed to the myriad of unknown and materially altered contaminants. [Despite early air quality assurances, this would prove to be a growing health crisis in the years to come, eclipsing initial expectations.] Initially, on site, you were fortunate if you could get your hands on a paper dust mask. Even those unsatisfactory "filters" were in short supply, and true respirators, the appropriate protection, just weren't readily available. Early on, we all developed acute headaches and had difficulty breathing in the environment. But no one stopped working, opting simply to have their eyes and noses flushed out daily. Continuing the search unabated simply took priority. Proper respirators became a priority for our unit and those returning to the Pile for daily work, and it was something our commander, Captain Nevins, resolved as his first order of business. Although some on our team have developed some form of chronic, treatable illness as a reminder of our service at Ground Zero, a tribute to Steve Nevins' quick action, along with the absolute insistence by me and our team leaders that respirators were to be worn at all times, has resulted in the markedly low incidence of serious, life-threatening illnesses to MRT members, at least as of this writing.

Days into the recovery effort, machines were brought in to assist rescue workers with the seemingly insurmountable task of moving tons of debris, attempting to minimize the danger to possible survivors and those working to free them. One machine used was the Grappler. This machine used its metal teeth to pry large pieces of steel and debris from the Pile and deposit it directly in front of a group of recovery workers where it would be raked and sifted through. We were looking for any type of recognizable items or remains that would be useful in helping to identify a victim. Workers searched intently for personal effects such as clothing, wallets, purses, uniforms of firefighters or police and their equipment (badges, firearms, turnout gear, etc.), anything that would aid in identification. The focus on representative DNA would become an increasingly important task, as it became obvious to everyone that no additional survivors would be found. Locating and identifying remains became an obsession, as we knew that may be a family's only opportunity for closure.

The task was daunting. The physical reality of the tremendous, crushing forces involved in the collapse, subsurface fires which had been burning for months, and exposure to water and the elements took its toll, leaving very little recognizable, as layer upon layer was removed. Even though excavating the site in this manner was taking months, the process could not be significantly expedited, as the risk of overlooking remains of a victim or failing to identify evidence would increase substantially. When human remains were located while working the Pile, you knew it. A dedicated crew proceeded to the site of the recovery, logged the location with GPS for posterity, and respectfully bagged the remains. Following a specific radio transmission to all team leaders manning the quadrants, work at Ground Zero was brought to a brief, but immediate halt, as an "Honor Guard" paid its respects, and the victims remains were removed from the site.

Most of the time, it was a matter of painstakingly inspecting debris, day after day. Once the debris had been vetted at our location, it was then transported by truck to a waiting barge. Ultimately ending up at a New Jersey landfill called Fresh Kills, where it was again meticulously raked through and sifted by detectives and investigators, in hopes of finding anything that may have been overlooked at Ground Zero.

And so it went; days turned into weeks, and weeks turned into months. Ultimately, we completed the objective of the Unified Command: total, respectful, excavation of the site of the worst terrorist attack in U.S. history. Unlike many agencies and organizations that had to return to matters within their home jurisdictions, I'm proud to say that the SP remained for the duration, eight months, departing only after the ceremony marking the end of the cleanup effort at Ground Zero, on May 30, 2002, commemorating the removal of the last iconic steel beam.

As a result of our deployment to 9/11, the MRT had been operating in a full-time mode for the last eight months. In fact, we had picked up the ancillary mission of augmenting the Governor's protective detail, providing a counter-assault element. In addition to rotating operators to NYC, our operations tempo had also increased, as the troops got used to seeing us around and utilizing us. So busy, that I had submitted a proposal at the end of 2001 requesting to expand, justifying the team's permanent transition and continuation as a full-time unit. The numbers seemed to bear it out; the unit was on fire. In fact, we had put through another Basic School in 2002, adding a fourth, Central Team, and additional personnel. But, by the end of August 2002, just shy of one year operating in a full-time capacity, the team got dealt a crushing blow and was reverted to part-time status.

While we had more personnel than ever (40), would continue to operate at a higher-tempo than before, and carved out additional training time, it was still a morale killer and drastic set back, which effectively derailed our best efforts to truly get to the next level of operations.

In 2004, I was promoted to lieutenant, after another of Division's rigorous, competitive examinations. Since, at that time, the Office of Special Services did not have a lieutenant's slot, this meant it was time to hang up my spurs, after 10 years with the SCUBA Unit and 8 years on the MRT. Subsequently, I was transferred up to Troop "B", in the Adirondacks, where I would begin the next stage of my career as a lieutenant – Uniform Force.

The next two years flashed by, with six months spent working out of the Troop Commander's Office in Ray Brook as an administrative lieutenant. Then, I accepted an opportunity to transfer two hours closer to home, by taking a post as an assistant detail commander of the Executive

Services Detail – Capital, in Albany. Although I didn't realize it at the time, both assignments would be career altering, for different reasons. First, in Troop "B", I would meet many of the officers, NCOs, troopers, and civilians that 10 years later, I would be fortunate to lead as their troop commander. Second, I would have the good fortune of working for one of the most accomplished leaders in the NYSP, then Captain Patricia Groeber, at ESD – Capital. Patricia would later serve as our Field Commander and be counted among my lifelong friends.

But, all that is with the value of hindsight...

THE CRUCIBLE OF TACTICAL LEADERSHIP

CHAPTER – 7

BUILDING THE COALITION AND CAPACITY

Waking from a fitful couple hours of sleep on the morning of **Sunday, June 7, Day 2,** I immediately realized it had not been a dream. Yesterday, Inmates Richard W. Matt and David P. Sweat had escaped from Dannemora, the toughest prison in NYS, and unless someone had recaptured them in the last few hours and failed to notify me, I had a busy day ahead. I checked my BlackBerry…no messages of the kind – time to go to work!

On my way in to the CP, I observed even more had been accomplished to harden the perimeter around Dannemora. During the overnight hours, DOCCS had bused in additional personnel, spelling some much-needed relief for those standing the perimeter posts, and additional troopers had arrived. While that marked progress, I attended the morning's intel briefing, conducted by the BCI, which indicated we still didn't have much to go on. They recapped information gleaned from Mitchell's first interview, the fact that she had been released, and that we believed we still had more to learn from her. Furthermore, the BCI reported that as far as we knew at that point, Matt and Sweat had been observed by two witnesses, who reported seeing two adult males in their backyard on Bouck Street, on June 6, between 12:15 AM and 12:30 AM. When they asked the men what they were doing, one of them replied, "I went the wrong way, sorry." One of the suspicious subjects was carrying a black soft guitar case, and the men continued on their way, walking at a fast pace toward Smith Street. As far as we knew, these were the first, last, and only people, to see individuals matching the description of the inmates. This confirmed they had at least a six-hour head start. Wrapping up the intel brief, investigators stated they were still interviewing Clinton Correctional Facility staff, A-Block inmates, and writing warrants for wire taps.

While, we were only 24 hours in, it continued to disturb me that the BCI was still co-located with CCF's OSI, *separate* from the OPS personnel at the Command Post. In fact, while the necessary investigative staff was present for the morning briefing, including representatives from DOCCS, FBI, USMS, etc., we were missing several of the uniformed staff from the OPS side. *Had word of the meeting not gotten out?* They shouldn't have to travel in the first place. Either way, this was unacceptable. While I understood the relationship with OSI was essential, and the immediacy of investigators coalescing in that space initially, we had to rectify the situation ASAP.

"Bob, you're moving in the next 24-36 hours," I told him. "Just as soon as Chris Giovazzino (Communications Supervisor) finishes building out the required infrastructure at the CP and gives me a "thumbs up."

The BCI Captain, being a true professional, simply said, "We'll make it happen."

Upon conclusion, I headed back to the CP for the OPS briefing (further demonstrating the need for consolidation), where post/assignment charts had been created and maps and aerial photos were affixed to walls, depicting our current deployment. Better yet, where every agency had a representative on hand. Even the BCI was represented here, because I had insisted from Day 1 that an investigator be physically present in the OPS center for continuity, a standard that would be greatly enhanced and maintained throughout the duration of the mission. Ultimately, OPS would also include a member of our New York State Intelligence Center (NYSIC), State Police Investigator Tim Ferris. In addition to the agency reps present from the FBI, USMS, USCBP, DHS, and other state and local agencies, through his higher HQ, Tim had the ability to reach out and touch, Intel channels any place in the world. Ferris would later play an increasingly integral role in the search, by cataloging and reporting past, current, and future operations. This proved to be of great assistance to the case in general, and me personally, as it eventually spared me the responsibility of creating the end-of-day SITREP and projection of future taskings, which I sent to the superintendent and Field Command staff at HQ daily. Ferris, surrounded by the other SMEs in the OPS section, became proficient at producing the message on his terminal at the CP, then forwarding it to me for review, which allowed me to disseminate the report to those with a true need to know.

Within the prison, the lockdown continued, with a deliberate effort to reconfirm the previous day's 100% tool inventory, ordered by the DOCCS Commissioner. Also, prison officials were providing the BCI with lists of construction contractors for the myriad of projects going on within the walls. Each would have to be interviewed and checked, again, for criminal history and associations. Foremost on everyone's mind, was the fact that these two had used tools of some sort, hand or power, we still did not know conclusively; but the question remained, *Where did they get them?* Had tools been smuggled into the prison by staff, by contractors illicitly working with the inmates, or were they merely targets of opportunity, inadvertently left out of locked tool boxes due to complacency. We came to learn, that these tool boxes, known as "gang boxes," were sanctioned and approved by the prison, designed to securely contain necessary tools, which were to have been inventoried daily, to facilitate contractor's work in ongoing projects behind the walls. Understandably, the types and source of the tools was a key question. No one worked harder than DOCCS and the State Police, even calling in FBI tool mark experts from Quantico, VA, to assist in resolving this issue.

Meanwhile, with an ever-expanding perimeter growing outside the walls, I was told by OPS we were wrapping up what searchers described to me as a "cursory" search of the Village of Dannemora.

Cursory?" I said.

"Yes, Sir," came the reply. They continued, "We just didn't have the time or resources to hit everything on Day 1. We're far from covering the surrounding terrain, but the houses are nearly done."

"Understood," I said. "Look, yesterday, we were in *exigent* search mode. Today, we're going into *deliberate* search mode. That means <u>every</u> home, outbuilding, and shed, must be checked...*again*. Interview <u>every</u> resident, and look under every tarp. We cannot move on, and run the risk that these two were right under our noses all along, and find out later that they had taken a local family hostage, murdering them, thus permitting them to steal a car and escape. Sounds dramatic, but these men are certainly capable of anything. So, *do it again.* Document everything, and be able to depict it on a map. If someone wasn't home during the first round, or this time, when we knock on their door, leave a message, and recontact them. *No stone is to be left unturned.*" I knew we still had a lot of ground to cover within the 16-square-mile zone around Dannemora, but we had to be methodical.

Shortly thereafter, Captain Streiff of the Forest Rangers came to me. "Major, I have recalled rangers to the CP who know this area like the back of their hand. Together, we have conducted a map reconnaissance and identified potential avenues of egress, like this abandoned railroad bed and these power lines," he said pointing to the map. "I took the liberty of sending rangers as mounted patrols on ATVs out to search them."

"Perfect, John," I said. His guys knew the terrain better than anyone, and we would come to rely heavily on their expertise in the weeks to come. Additionally, I knew that Streiff's rangers would not just cruise up and down the trails, they would look for any "sign" (man-made indication) that the inmates had passed through the area.

Deploying enough highly specialized law enforcement officers, who were both familiar with the area <u>and</u> experienced woodsmen, would prove to be a challenge. If they weren't utilized on tactical teams, they often found themselves assigned as team leaders, supervising dozens of Corrections and police officers on the ground. Although the majority of assigned officers did not possess an extensive woodland skill set, they certainly exuded heart and were admirably led by the SMEs. These men and women, deployed from around New York State, were routinely exposed to the elements and worked night and day in some of the most arduous and austere conditions. And, when an ever-expanding perimeter needed to be secured after a long day's effort, many of them remained on the line, *long* beyond what would be otherwise desirable, until they could be properly relieved. [These individuals, non-specialized officers, are the unsung heroes of the effort. For it was their sheer will to do the job, to prevent Matt and Sweat from slipping past *their* edge of the perimeter, that would ultimately run these two to ground, containing, and exhausting both inmates, causing them to make the mistakes which would lead to their eventual capture.]

Also, he said, "I heard you're ordering the investigators go door to door again in Dannemora."

"True," I said, without explanation, because I knew John would understand intuitively.

"Well," he said, "I have a suggestion as to how to make our grid searches in the woods and fields more productive."

We had inserted hundreds of CERT and tactical team members into the woods again just that morning, so I said, "Lay it on me."

He offered, "As you know, my rangers are each equipped with GPS devices, that both depict their location and track their course overground for SAR (Search and Rescue). That info can then be downloaded at the end of the day to outline their route on the map."

"I'm aware," I said, as I had worked with the rangers many times on the ground on missing persons' cases.

"Well," he continued, "CERT does not have that capability. I propose teaming up my rangers as search team leaders with CERT, to both guide them through the woods, keeping them both on course and on line (tied into other units on their flanks), through the use of GPS, and download their tracks at the end of the day's assignment; thus, depicting graphically, what was covered."

"Outstanding, John! Find, Colonel Bradford, (Streiff's counterpart as CERT commander) and brief him on the plan. Let's get your folks infused with his people on the ground ASAP." And, so it went. Dennis Bradford and John Streiff formed a crucial bond, vastly improving our field operations. At one time, as they pushed the search area, known as the "box," south of Dannemora, from west to east, they had a search line over 3,000 feet long. The search line consisted of several hundred CERT members, who were aided and guided adeptly by Forest Rangers, through some of the thickest shit in the North Country. Impressive.

Even as our efforts ramped up, we were no closer to finding our quarry. Accordingly, I fielded a phone call from Saranac Central School District (CSD) Superintendent Jonathan Parks, who coordinated with me to conduct a search of all District buildings and buses. Also, in addition to sweeping the woods and swamps around the middle and high schools, outdoor activities were suspended, and troopers were stationed at each school, to ensure the safety and security of the students, school, and community.

Later that day, Sunday, investigators got another crack at Joyce Mitchell. Mitchell, who was under surveillance since the time she was released the day before, contacted the State Police requesting to speak with the investigator she had spoken to previously, and was interviewed again for several hours. During this interview, she admitted she had first met both Inmate Matt and Inmate Sweat in 2008, in her role as the Civilian Industrial Training Supervisor of Tailor Shop 1, where both Matt and Sweat had been employed. Mitchell got closer and closer with the inmates, developing an increasingly inappropriate relationship with both, and even engaging in sexual contact with Matt.

Investigation would subsequently reveal, allegations of an inappropriate relationship between Mitchell and Sweat, resulting in his removal from Tailor Shop 1 in September in 2014. OSI would later deem the claims "unfounded." Although Sweat had been moved, and they were now working in different locations, Matt and Sweat manipulated the system by requesting the assistance of Correction Officer Gene Palmer in Sweat's quest for return to Industry, his preferred area of employment, albeit in Tailor Shop 8. Once a supervisor approved that assignment, it paved the way for Sweat's subsequent move back to Honor Block and, ultimately, his return to his old cell adjacent to Matt. Still it was another C.O. assigned to Tailor Shop 1 on a near-daily basis, that inexplicably did not report anything that specifically concerned him about Mitchell's daily interactions with Inmate Matt.

Mitchell, who developed a fondness for both men, purchased numerous items and provided these items to Inmate Matt, beginning in 2014, through a variety of means. She also developed such an appreciation for artwork he produced back in his cell, that she essentially "commissioned" him, to produce several pieces for her personal use. The pieces were smuggled out of the prison, again, allegedly, with Palmer's assistance, and Mitchell took them home. An extraordinary breach of prison security and protocol.

Beginning in 2015, Mitchell, as admitted in her interview with investigators, had engaged in sexual contact with Inmate Matt several times. As their relationship deepened, Matt confided in Mitchell that he and Sweat planned to escape, and, manipulating her further, said that they wanted to take her with them! However, they would need her help in procuring the necessary tools. Subsequently, Mitchell admitted to purchasing hacksaw blades and other small hand tools for the pair and smuggled them into the prison. During an explosive interview, Mitchell also admitted for the first time that she'd known for months about their intention to escape, _and_ for the last three or four weeks, that Matt and Sweat had cut through their cells and were exploring the tunnels. Mitchell further stated that she was told the date and time of the escape, and she was to meet Inmates Matt and Sweat in Dannemora at midnight, with various items that would assist them on the run.

In the final analysis, Mitchell stated that on the night of the escape, she simply aborted the plan and went to the hospital, Alice Hyde Medical Center in nearby Malone, after experiencing a "panic attack." Mitchell adamantly denied picking them up and along with her husband, Lyle, gave consent for a search of their premises, which was subsequently conducted by State Police.

While this was a bit of a smoking gun, and was beginning to shed more light on _how_ they did it (fully explained in Chapter 18), Mitchell insisted she had no idea where Matt and Sweat could be; and we were no closer to finding them. Accordingly, a decision was again made not to arrest her, but to continue to surveil her, to see if anything in her actions led us to the fugitives.

That afternoon, the State Police held a conference call, in which developments and strategy were discussed. Then, the Governor was cued in, and a conference call was held with the media. Governor Cuomo announced a $100,000 reward for information that led to the arrest of both men stating, "It's an unusual step for the state but, they're killers. This is a crisis for the state. These are dangerous men, and they're capable of committing grave crimes once again."

As the Incident Commander, I added, "We have about 250 law enforcement and correction officers involved in the search as of Sunday. We're processing over 150 leads, and considering every conceivable scenario." Furthermore, I added, "Tools that would allow for limited cutting were found, but no sophisticated implements," and that although the State

Police has recovered and reviewed surveillance tapes of views from outside the prison, the tapes have revealed nothing fruitful.

Commissioner Annucci then added, that he had ordered a comprehensive inventory of tools owned by the prison and reported, as of Sunday's conference call, everything was accounted for.

From the start, a <u>serious</u> question existed about the use of power vs. hand tools, and we were focusing intently on contractors, who performed work for DOCCS. We knew background checks and daily inventories are required, but had gleaned from sources inside the prison, that both are sometimes delayed. However, I was able to add with conviction, "All contractors, currently working in the prison, have been cooperating with the investigation." I concluded my contribution to the conference call by urging the community, "If you see something, say something."

On **Monday, June 8, Day 3**, Mitchell was reinterviewed, which resulted in another stunning admission, that she had been recruited into a plan developed, according to her, by Matt to kill her husband, Lyle.

Mitchell had been told, and believed, that after the escape and the murder, she was going to run off with the fugitives and live happily ever after in Mexico. But, for that plan to come to fruition, it would be necessary to remove the *"glitch,"* as Matt allegedly (and Joyce, according to Sweat) referred to her husband. Prior to leaving the house, she would take the two pills provided to her by Matt, and slip them into Lyle's drink, rendering him unconscious. Then drive to the agreed-upon manhole in Dannemora to pick them up at mid-night. Then, they would return to her residence, take care of the problem by killing Lyle, and flee the area. Mitchell claimed she did not know where they were going, but that it was somewhere six to seven hours away, and a four-wheel drive vehicle was necessary. Later, after things "quieted down," Matt would go off by himself and she and Sweat would be "together."

Ultimately, Mitchell claimed, she couldn't go through with it; the resulting "panic attack" led her to the hospital, in lieu of the rendezvous point. Still, Mitchell insisted, she did <u>not</u> know their current location, plans, or destination, now that things had gone awry. So, we left her out there again, in lieu of arresting her, with the hopes someone may try to contact her for assistance, or she would divulge more information without a lawyer present, <u>prior</u> to her inevitable arrest. A portion of this would be reported upon in the media the next day by the savvy *Press-Republican*, naming Joyce Mitchell of Dickinson Center, an Industrial Training Supervisor, at CCF as a person of interest. Additionally, the reporters had done their homework and revealed that her husband, Lyle Mitchell, also worked at the prison. When queried by the media about this development, I was obliged at the time to say only, "We are questioning employees, both civilian and uniformed, as we have since the beginning."

While the investigation ground on in Dannemora, Monday night at approximately 9:00 PM, two Essex County residents reported a possible sighting of the escaped inmates in Willsboro, NY, approximately 40 miles southeast of Dannemora. Two credible, well-meaning civilian sources reported seeing two white males carrying duffle bags walking on the side of Middle Road. As their vehicle headlights approached the males, both subjects reportedly crossed into a ditch and ran off into the woods. The area was close by comparison, and the sighting warranted a full-scale response. Over the next 36 hours, Monday night and all day Tuesday, troopers, CERT teams, deputies, and federal agents, searched camps, cabins, woods, and swamps in close proximity to railroad tracks, for a sign of the inmates. The intensity of the search effort, generated coordination with the local school district, which resulted in a precautionary lockdown. While temporary, the district appreciated that we were following up on every possible lead and were determined to keep them safe. Accordingly, I disclosed to the media that while searching *simultaneously* in Dannemora, we had expanded the search to the Essex/Willsboro area, and were continuing to work leads developed Monday night.

Ultimately, the sighting was determined to be unfounded, and a portion of our forces, some 440 strong at this point, were recalled from Willsboro. However, it had generated several false news reports that the inmates had been surrounded, "captured," and/or "shot," which we had to spend valuable time correcting. However, our message was clear, as my Public Information Officer (PIO), Trooper Jennifer Fleishman vowed, "We will cover every inch of ground."

On **Tuesday morning, June 9, Day 4,** another positive sign. Even as we pushed into Willsboro, it was both evident and gratifying to see that our message of "Unified Command" was taking root, as evidenced by City of Plattsburgh Police Chief Desmond Rasicot's comments in the *Press-Republican*: *"Having witnessed the regional response firsthand, Rasicot said, he is confident the two escapees will be apprehended. 'With state, county, local and federal agencies involved, the search is under way with an extraordinary level of expertise,' he said. 'We have the best of the best in law enforcement working on this.'"* [4]

Also, by **close of business, Tuesday, Day 4,** my Communications Supervisor, Sergeant Giovazzino, with assistance of the DOCCS TSU (Technical Support Unit), accomplished a small miracle and declared the second floor of the CCF Training Building, where we had established our CP on the first floor on Day 1, now ready for the overnight BCI transfer. Now, both OPS and Intel would be under the same roof! A major accomplishment, streamlining our operation.

On **Wednesday, June 10, Day 5,** we had investigated over 500 leads to date, and the lockdown, in which inmates remained confined to their cells continued inside CCF. In addition to casting a wider net of roving Forest Ranger and State Police patrols north and west, we were at the peak of retracing our steps, in the Village of Dannemora. Simply, we were redoubling efforts that had been ongoing since the escape on Saturday, including going house to house, while maintaining tight road checks out of an abundance of caution. As reported by the *Press-Republican*, an article characterized the level of cooperation between the State Police and our federal partners on the border. It noted that, as a result of our proximity to Canada, we'd worked closely with our partners at the Swanton Border Patrol Sector from the onset. This resulted in assets being assigned from U.S. Customs and Border Protection's: Office of Field Operations, the U.S. Border Patrol, and the Office of Air and Marine, all placed on high-alert, including deployment of sensors and cameras to monitor remote sections of the border. Additionally, State Police PIO messaging remained consistent, reiterating in consecutive press releases: "Unified Command has deployed all available assets in an effort to ensure the safety of the public. We are also requesting the public's continued cooperation and vigilance throughout this investigation – that includes any sign of trespass, burglary or vehicle larceny."

Additionally, on that afternoon, a press conference covered by all media sources was held at the Incident Command Post (CCF Training Building) at Dannemora. Present were: New York Governor Andrew Cuomo, Vermont Governor Peter Shumlin, NYSP Superintendent Joseph D'Amico, VSP Colonel Thomas L'Esperance, Acting DOCCS Commissioner Anthony Annucci, and me as the Incident Commander. Immediately prior to the press conference, those listed above, and key staff, attended a strategy meeting to ensure that New York and Vermont were in sync operationally <u>and</u> to guarantee a <u>coordinated</u> approach to the possibility of the fugitives attempting to flee towards Vermont.

The purpose of the conference was to demonstrate to the public that a spirit of cooperation existed between our neighboring states and offer assurances that leadership was unified from the top down. This stemmed from Vermont's proximity to New York's eastern border, approximately 30 miles from Dannemora, and largely took into account, a revelation in an interview with Mitchell that she and the inmates had conducted "research" on camps in the Green Mountain State. Governor Shumlin (VT) said, if the inmates had concluded New York would be too "*hot*" and Vermont somehow "*cooler,*" they're mistaken. Vermont will be ready. Shumlin also advised, he had directed the VSP to deploy a liaison to the New York Command Post, committed a tactical team, stepped up marine assets on Lake Champlain and road patrols along the borders.

Governor Cuomo simply added, "If they're headed toward Vermont, Vermont is engaged, and Vermont is mobilized."

Superintendent D'Amico was quick to add, however, in spite of the proximity to the border and Champlain Ferry, "We don't know that they have left the state or the area." D'Amico also confirmed Mitchell as a person of interest, saying only, "She befriended the inmates and may have had some sort of role assisting them." Additionally, it was noted, that the statewide intelligence centers in both states, the NYSIC and VCIC, are tied in, and the NYSP had set up 50 digital billboards bearing photos and information pertaining to the fugitives were set up in New York, New Jersey, Pennsylvania, and Massachusetts.

Governor Cuomo concluded the conference by saying: "You follow each and every lead with all the energy and all the vim that you can muster." Adding, he is "confident the fugitives will be found…The only question is when."

By mid-week, the media, who had been searching for answers, like the rest of us, as to what had transpired within the prison leading up to or facilitating the escape, began to report out. The *Press-Republican* summarizing: On June 1, a major fight had broken out between two groups of inmates, about 40 altogether. Apparently, Muslim inmates clashed with inmates suspected of being members of the "Bloods" gang, in which an inmate suffered a broken leg. Correction officers fired chemical agents from the guard towers to end the disturbance. Normally after a serious incident, the prison is placed in lockdown and searched, including inmate cells for weapons and contraband, which *could* have led to discovery of cell wall breaches. Correction officers widely allege that DOCCS Central Office in Albany denied the request for lockdown due to OT (overtime) costs. A claim that is wholly rejected by DOCCS. [This assertion would ultimately be investigated by the NYS Inspector General's Office, as part of their comprehensive year-long review of CCF.] [5]

Additionally, throughout the evening of June 10 and early morning hours of June 11, Mitchell was interviewed for several additional hours, providing her third statement, in which she divulged additional details of the escape plan and how the contraband was introduced into the facility. According to Mitchell, she placed the hacksaw blades, drill bits, and steel punch inside hamburger she had purchased, then froze it, and smuggled it into the prison through lax security at the front gate. This occurred on more than one occasion. Once inside, she placed the frozen hamburger in a freezer, knowing that Clinton Correctional Facility Correction Officer Gene Palmer, a tenured staff member, would take care of getting the hamburger to Matt. Mitchell, also admitted that just this week, following the escape, and since she'd been interviewed, she flushed the two pills Matt had given her down the toilet at her residence.

During the early stages of the investigation, Palmer was identified as a suspect in what would amount to criminal activity at the prison and was interviewed on multiple occasions between June 6 and June 20, 2015. Palmer related he had purchased paint and brushes for the inmates and brought them into the facility, in violation of prison policy. In return, he received numerous works of art from Matt, approximately ten, and several from Sweat. Upon learning of the escape, he destroyed some of the paintings by burning them in a fire pit and secreted several in the woods a couple of miles from his residence. He admits to allowing both Matt and Sweat onto the catwalks, behind the cells, on more than one occasion. Once, he allowed Matt to hide paint there, and at least four times he allowed Sweat to work on wiring behind the cells, to enable their cooking with hot plates without tripping the breaker. Palmer further acknowledges transporting frozen hamburger packages from the freezer in Tailor Shop 1, at Matt's and Mitchell's request, to Matt's cell at the Honor Block, bypassing the metal detectors en route. Palmer adamantly maintained he did _not_ know of the escape plan, did _not_ know any contraband was hidden in the frozen hamburger, and denied knowingly facilitating the transfer of hacksaw blades and tools between Mitchell and Matt. There is _no evidence_ to contradict that statement. Palmer subsequently passed a polygraph to that effect. However, on June 24, 2015, two days before Matt was apprehended and four days before Sweat was captured, the New York State Police arrested Correction Officer Palmer on charges of Promoting Prison Contraband 1st degree, Tampering with Physical Evidence (2 Counts), and Official Misconduct.

On Thursday, June 11, Day 6, as the SP bolstered its task force to more than 500 officers, it was important, and gratifying, to note that even in the face of mounting pressure, we enjoyed outstanding support within the local community. This was made evident by a report in the *Press-Republican* that morning. While residents were rightly concerned, many locking their doors for the first time and keeping their firearms handy, they were confident law enforcement was doing all it could. This sentiment was perhaps best summed up by the owner of a local establishment, Dannemora's Maggy Marketplace, who was quoted as saying, *"No. 1, we feel* *exceptionally safe because each corner has either a New York State prison guard or State Police and a firearm, so they're doing an excellent job of keeping the public safe, while at the same time, looking to apprehend these bad guys. The exceptional training of the law enforcement officers is evident in the way the numerous agencies have been able to flawlessly synchronize their efforts with military precision."* [6]

Additionally, early that same morning, we were wrapping up a "discovery" from the night before by Forest Rangers, a trail leading into woods in the northeast corner of the Dannemora search box, an area characterized by locals as thick and swampy, complete with coyotes, bears, blackflies, and even patches of quick sand. Apparently, the search team located a spot of "matted grass." *Had a man spent the night there; or, more likely, a deer?* We had to find out. Concurrently, the southwestern corner of the box lit up, when a C.O. located "food wrappers" in the Bucks Corners area. Canines scoured both sites, ultimately with negative results. Those are just two examples of the thousands of leads and attention to detail of our search teams. As my Troop "B" PIO, Trooper Jennifer Fleishman, would say to the media summing up the determination of the Detail: *"We're looking behind every tree, underneath every rock, and inside every building until we catch these two."*

On Friday morning, June 12, Day 7, in the adjoining Town of Saranac, where schools were closed for another day, we received a report of "two men jumping over a stone wall" on the outskirts of Dannemora, in the southwestern corner of the box. While the response was instantaneous, including air assets, and was later deemed unfounded, it paled in comparison to the size, scope, and *synergy* demonstrated in the response later that afternoon, in the southeast search sector…

That day, I was out checking the perimeter with Captain Teppo, and Zone Sergeant Mike Trimboli, a hard-as-nails former MRT operator, who I'd worked with in the Tactical Operations Center at the Phillips Manhunt in 2006, when a radio transmission reported a "gunshot" was heard in the wood line, in the vicinity of Trudeau Road and State Route 3, in the southeastern corner of what had come to be known as the Dannemora box. Being out on the road, instead of tied up at the CP, we rolled right up. It was pouring rain when we stepped out of the car on Trudeau Road, but it was immediately apparent that troopers, deputies, and federal agents, already had it under control. As the sergeants and respective supervisors took the bull by the horns, all I had to do was stay out of the way, and marvel at the response that was unfolding in front of me.

At the time, I was located on Trudeau Road itself, on an elevated section of the roadway, affording me a spectacular view of the area of concern, an open field, adjacent wood line, and a farmhouse set back a good distance off the road. Shotgun-toting troopers instantly reinforced the perimeter. The number of roving patrol cars quickly tripled, locking down that quadrant. Sheriff's Department ATVs arrived and our Patrol Rifle Team coordinated a mounted approach to check the farmhouse and outbuildings. K9 handlers also arrived and repositioned, poised to attempt a track. Immediately overhead, a State Police helicopter circled, providing eyes in the sky and coordination throughout the operation. Concurrently, a Bell 412 helo carrying the FBI Hostage Rescue Team (HRT) quickly landed in the adjacent field and off-loaded its operators, who commenced sweeping the tree line. All this, while our own Special Operations Response Team (SORT), previously known as MRT, arrived by vehicle. They expeditiously dismounted and patrolled the nearby streams, culverts, and drainages leading from the target area south, into the nearby Saranac River, to seal off escape.

Although, the reported "gunshot" would prove to be unfounded, the coordination of the response I had just witnessed, steeled my resolve. We didn't have them yet, but I now *knew* we were _ready_! We had developed tactical *synergy*, and in my opinion, could now exploit opportunities. None of that would have been possible without the knowledge, experience, and dedication of SORT NCOIC, Sergeant Ron Pastino, SORT Training NCO, Sergeant Derek Cerza, and Special Operations OIC, Major Chris Fiore, and his Executive Officer (XO), Captain Eric Underhill.

By the end of that day, another significant development occurred, Joyce Mitchell was arrested and committed to jail in lieu of bail or bond. Clearly, none of these developments would have been possible without the persistence and superb case supervision provided by Troop "B" BCI Lieutenants Brent Davison and Shawnda Walbridge, and Senior Investigator Kurt Taylor. Furthermore, the investigative team was significantly fortified early on by the assignment of additional NYSP standouts, expertly led by Major Dave Krause from Division Headquarters. Dave aided me and Captain LaFountain (Troop "B" BCI) in managing the thousands of leads, interviews, and technical evaluations generated during the manhunt. As Division's specialized investigative services were increasingly utilized, Krause and the attached Commissioned Officers and senior investigators (including Mike Drake, Tom Jones, Frank Stabile, John Brooks, et al.) afforded an increased span of control and continuity to our massive undertaking – a true "force multiplier."

As a result of this development, a press conference was scheduled for that Friday night, to be held at Saranac High School gymnasium, indoors due to a torrential downpour. I addressed the breaking news, in sum and substance: "This is one large piece of the puzzle in the search for Matt and Sweat. Our interviews with Joyce Mitchell have been fruitful and productive. Mitchell was arrested today's date, and has been charged with two crimes: Promoting Prison Contraband First Degree (Felony) and Criminal Facilitation Fourth Degree (Misdemeanor). Our investigation has revealed that on May 1st, she'd supplied Matt and Sweat with hacksaw blades, a punch, and drill bits. She has been suspended from her job at the prison, and remanded to Clinton County Jail, in lieu of bail. Additionally, we have interviewed her husband, Lyle Mitchell, also a Civilian Employee at the prison, but found <u>no evidence</u> he had any knowledge of the escape, or his wife's involvement."

I continued, "We have non-conclusive evidence that the two felons are still in the area, and no reason to think they have separated, but are planning for both eventualities." I noted that the terrain is rough and the weather, especially the heavy rains, has been a challenge for the searchers – but also for the escapees. The difficult environment, both hampers, and aids in the investigation. The escapees have had to deal with the same inclement weather. If they have not escaped the area or they have not availed themselves of shelter, you've got to assume they are wet, cold, tired, and hungry. I remind the community, just as I did our officers earlier, that

Matt and Sweat could be even more desperate and dangerous. We are using every available resource at our disposal in New York State, and if we should need more, I have the authority of the Governor and the Superintendent to request more."

As PIO, Trooper Jennifer Fleishman, would say separately, "We're going to get them." She went on to describe the fortitude of the 800 federal, state, and local officers, who were working long shifts, some in excess of 24 hours out of necessity, revealing searchers were reluctant to leave their assignments. Fleishman said, "Despite the arduous environment, attempts to send people home and provide relief have been met with resistance. This is a tribute to the dedication, commitment, and perseverance of our team."

She was right! The dedication was phenomenal! Experience had taught me that when the opportunity presented itself, we had to be prepared, fluid, and responsive enough to take the appropriate action, whatever it may be. In this environment, we may not get a second chance. All we needed was a break, because I *knew* we were ready to capitalize. My overarching strategy was one of **Relentless Pursuit.** Resultantly, as the State Police Troop "B" Commander and IC, I had a message for fugitives Richard Matt and David Sweat: *"**We are coming for you, and will not stop until you are caught.**"*

A bold, some would say foolish, statement to be sure. *But, if I didn't believe, who would?* With what I had witnessed that day during the massive tactical response, and the fact that a federal warrant had been signed calling for the capture and arrest of the inmates, triggering authority of the United States Marshals Service (USMS) and allowing for international extradition, I knew things were coming together. We had achieved synergy of effort!

What, in my background, had prepared me for such an assertion? Earlier in my career, as a member of special operations, I had participated in extraordinary assignments, which had expanded my experience base, taught me valuable lessons, and forever affected the lives and careers of many within the NYSP...

My dad, Ed, and I – off to a great start!

Ranger School graduation, August 1983.

My best friend and fellow SORT team member, Trooper Ross Riley.

The girls and I at the New York State Police Academy.

Off the coast of Long Island during TWA Flight 800 recovery efforts, 1996.

Early during my deployment at Ground Zero.

Special Operations Response Team training with FBI Hostage Rescue Team
at Quantico, VA.

NYSP Aviation Detail Commander after UH1-Huey pontoon training.

NYS Governor Andrew M. Cuomo and I at Clinton Correctional Facility press conference
on Day 1. (Darren McGee, Office of NYS Governor)

Street level view, Village of Dannemora, outside the prison.
(Rob Fountain/Press-Republican)

Press conference outside Command Post at CCF. (Rob Fountain/Press-Republican)

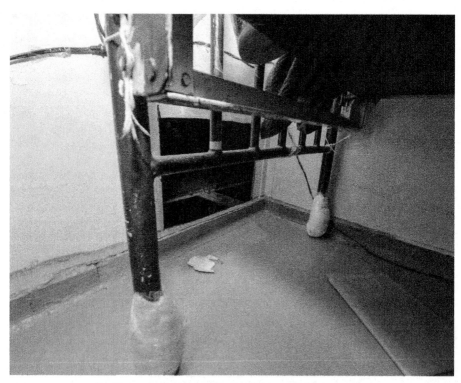

Inside escapee's Honor Block cell, site of initial cut out.
(Darren McGee/Office of NYS Governor)

Honor Block catwalk behind escapees' cells. (Darren McGee/Office of NYS Governor)

Subterranean main steam pipe penetrating base of prison wall. (Note message left by inmates, "Have a Nice Day!") (Darren McGee/Office of NYS Governor)

Confirming the escape route - NYSP K9 team exiting manhole on Bouck Street. (Gabe Dickens/Press-Republican)

Leading off at a joint press conference. (Matthew Turner/Adirondack Daily Enterprise)

The fugitives - Sweat and Matt. (Gabe Dickens/Press-Republican)

Road block on State Route 374, Dannemora, NY. (Rob Fountain/Press-Republican)

Leaving no stone unturned, just one of hundreds of road checks.
(Rob Fountain/Press-Republican)

NYS Corrections (CERT) Officers deploying on search line.
(Rob Fountain/Press-Republican)

NYS Trooper manning a checkpoint as tactical team deploys.
(Rob Fountain/Press-Republican)

CERT officers searching at arm's length. (Rob Fountain/Press-Republican)

Tactical teams were omnipresent, safeguarding the community.
(Rob Fountain/Press-Republican)

BORTAC on one of dozens of aerial quick-reaction flights. (USCBP)

NYSP SORT and K9 during training.

Highly mobile ATV patrols scour the area. (Gabe Dickens/Press-Republican)

Aviation on standby. (Gabe Dickens/Press-Republican)

First Sergeant Steve Lacey and I discussing strategy. (FBI/NYSP)

NYSP SORT on point during training.

Joyce Mitchell in custody. (Rob Fountain/Press-Republican)

Surrounded by media at a multi-agency press conference in Plattsburgh, NY.
(Rob Fountain/Press-Republican)

Matt apprehended by BORTAC and Troopers near State Route 30, Malone, NY. (NYSP)

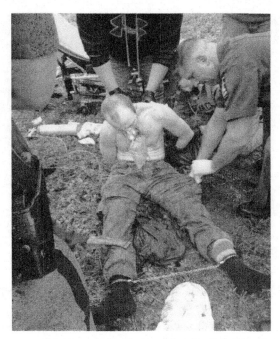

Sweat captured by State Police Sergeant Jay Cook, 2 1/2 miles south of the Canadian border. (NYSP)

Governor Cuomo, Superintendent D'Amico, and I among agency heads at Unified Command press conference shortly after Sweat's apprehension. (Darren McGee/Office of NYS Governor)

Superintendent D'Amico presenting my third Superintendent's Commendation at award ceremony at Headquarters, Albany, NY, May 2016. (NYSP)

Author, NYS Assemblywoman Janet Duprey, and Sergeant Jay Cook, at the Capitol for recognition ceremony in Assembly Chambers, Albany, NY, March 2016. (Jan Duprey/NYS Assembly)

"Living the Dream" – Retirement, August 2016.

Memorial Day Service 2016, Troop "B" Headquarters.

CHAPTER 8

PHILLIPS MANHUNT

On April 2, 2006, convicted burglar Ralph "Bucky" Phillips escaped from the Erie County Correctional Facility in Western New York, near Buffalo, by cutting his way through the corrugated metal roof of the jail's kitchen with a can opener and screw driver, slipping out onto the roof of the jail, ultimately gaining his freedom. Phillips, a lifetime petty criminal, was a local man with a long criminal record who had spent roughly 23 years in prison, mostly for property, burglary, and drug crimes. He had an extensive family network and was initially deemed a relatively low threat by authorities but his escape, nonetheless, warranted a statewide BOLO and warrant for his arrest.

In the early morning hours of June 10, 2006, Trooper Sean Brown and his partner, Trooper Donald Will, were on routine patrol in Troop "C" near Elmira, NY, when they observed a vehicle pull abruptly to the side of the road. This vehicle was either "disabled" or "suspicious," either way, the troopers stopped to render assistance and investigate. Although the State Police had been aware of the escape and were assisting locally in the Buffalo area, the troopers were checking on a vehicle approximately 144 miles from the jail Phillips had escaped from in Erie County. Exiting the troop car, Trooper Brown approached the vehicle. As he neared the window of the car, the driver, Phillips, knowing there was a warrant for his arrest and return to jail, and driving a stolen Ford Mustang, fired his .38 revolver at point-blank range, striking Trooper Brown in the chest. Phillips sped off. Trooper Brown was rushed to the hospital by Trooper Will, where he would later recover from his injuries, having been saved by his ballistic vest. However, the hunt for Phillips took on an entirely new dimension.

At the time of the escape and subsequent shooting, I was still assigned to ESD – Capital, in Albany, as the assistant detail commander, and it had been two years since I had turned in my MRT equipment.

While cognizant of the escape and deeply concerned at the news of the shooting, I presumed, correctly, that I would have no involvement in the search ramping up hundreds of miles away, as my duties at the capital would preclude my assignment. That said, I did contact a few of my closest colleagues on the team, knowing they would now be deployed to assist, offering my thoughts and well wishes.

Weeks went by, as the investigation took one turn and then another. Phillips, aided by a network of family members and former prison associates, knew the area well and used his friends to stay one step ahead of the police. Even as law enforcement interviewed and surveilled family members, he continued to receive assistance. Some individuals afforded him shelter, while others provided transportation or made food and equipment drops to wooded hide sites utilized by Phillips. An avid, experienced outdoorsman, he took to the woods to evade authorities, and his strategy seemed to be working.

On July 13, while at my desk at the Capitol, I received a telephone call from Division Headquarters advising me to report to Lieutenant Colonel James Schepperly, then the Assistant Deputy Superintendent in charge of the Uniform Force. The subject, the Phillips search. I had known Colonel Schepperly throughout my career. As my former captain and zone commander down in Troop "F", I had worked for him for many years. He was a highly capable, no-nonsense officer, with a reputation for getting things done. I figured as a former MRT member, since what was not getting done right now, was the apprehension of a dangerous man, I was about to have a role to play.

I walked into the colonel's office, on the second floor of Division HQ, and saluted smartly. "Good afternoon, Colonel," I said.

Schepperly returned my salute and said, "Chuck, good to see you. Have a seat," pointing to a table in the corner of the office covered by maps. He continued, "You following this Phillips search?"

"Yes, Sir." I replied, "As best as I can from my desk at the capital."

He declared, "That's about to change. This thing's becoming a mess, particularly on the tactical side. I need someone out there who knows what the hell they're doing to coordinate the tactical teams. We currently have the entire MRT assigned, and the FBI's sent a team as well. I want to send you out as the officer-in-charge of that effort. What do you say?"

"Absolutely, Colonel."

"Good!" he said. "Grab a map, take whatever you need. You leave first thing tomorrow."

"Roger that, Sir...Does the troop commander (Troop "A" major) know I'm coming?" I asked.

"I'll take care of that right now," he said. "The major and I went to the Academy together, he'll be happy to have the help. In fact, I'll fly out in the morning and meet you there; it won't be a problem."

I had to ask that question. After 16 years in the State Police, I knew that a lieutenant coming out to an ongoing investigation to "take charge" of the tactical side could be a bit sticky. Even though the Incident Command System (ICS) states that an event of this size and scope should have a Special Operations Branch Director, this was still a relatively new concept for the State Police, and I recognized the word hadn't really made it out to most of the "old school" troop commanders yet.

On the flip side, having been on the team for eight years, I knew all the key players and the vast majority of its members. Those I didn't know, had just graduated from the most recent MRT Basic School that summer, and this was their very first deployment. Furthermore, and perhaps most importantly, I had a good sense going in of where the MRT's operation would need help. Historically, the MRT was strong on field operators and door kickers and short on support staff. So, unless things had miraculously changed over the last two years, I envisioned gaps in planning, the gathering and dissemination of "actionable" intelligence, and acquisition of assets and resources. Additionally, it had been my experience, that often the capabilities of the team, which are definitively <u>subordinate</u> to the Incident Commander, were frequently misunderstood, resulting in unnecessary friction between conventional command staff and team members. Clearly, *anything* I could do to alleviate that friction, and make the assigned tactical teams operate more effectively and <u>safely</u>, would be time well spent.

The next morning, I left my residence at "0-dark-thirty," for the 320-mile trip west, to arrive before the colonel's plane touched down. The previous night, I had poured over the maps I had taken from the colonel's office and spoken with the MRT Coordinator, Sergeant Ron Pastino. Ron had been involved with the incident for the last several weeks and was one of my closest friends. It was essential to get his perspective on the current state of affairs. In a nutshell, Pastino advised me that the MRT and its FBI counterparts were, at times, being <u>both</u>: misutilized <u>and</u> underutilized. Intelligence sharing was insufficient for the task, and most of the Commissioned Officers did *not* have significant prior experience with a manhunt or utilizing the team in this capacity. Additionally, given the fact that Phillips was running around, with increasing support from the community, making law enforcement look silly, frustration was growing exponentially.

Naturally, I respected and appreciated Ron's opinion and later found him to be spot on. But, I also knew that was only part of the equation. In order to be effective, I had to obtain and account for the Incident Commander's perspective, if I had any hope of resolving the rising tensions and making the team impactful. There was much to do.

Upon his arrival, Colonel Schepperly introduced me to the Troop "A" Commander, saying, in sum and substance, "Chuck is a very experienced MRT officer, handpicked by me, to assist you in running the tactical operations. He'll coordinate the activities of all the SWAT teams, and because of his extensive experience in Special Services, he can also assist you with K9 and Aviation."

The major and I shook hands and then proceeded into a meeting with key members of his staff and the FBI, including an element of their Hostage Rescue Team, up from Quantico, VA, who had been handling the night operations. At the meeting, the Troop "A" BCI Captain and an FBI analyst provided an overview and talk soon turned, at the colonel's behest, to future tactical operations. I had some thoughts about the prospect of saturating specific areas (key terrain and last-known locations) with proactive, tactical patrols, which I shared with the group, acknowledging that this would be something that needed to be fleshed out further among the operators. The meeting didn't last long. I think it was primarily a "meet and greet" for the colonel and me, and sensing it had served its purpose, the boss said he had a plane to catch. From my point of view, I had been introduced to the stakeholders and was ready to get to work.

Outside the Command Post, the colonel pulled the major and I aside for one more moment. "Chuck's got the tactical portion of this now. Naturally, he works for you and will run everything by you that he's planning, for *your* approval. I have directed him to report back to me daily on the team's progress. Any questions, either of you?"

"No, Sir," we both replied, almost in unison.

"Good," the colonel said. "Catch that bastard!" With that, Colonel Schepperly jumped in a car for the short ride back to the airport.

The colonel's car door had no sooner closed before the major wheeled around and said, "Listen, I don't know who you are, but nothing goes back to Headquarters without my knowledge, got it? In fact, leave the reporting to me, Lieutenant. I'll handle it!"

"Major, with all due respect," I said. "You're the IC, I work for you. I will keep you abreast of *all* of our operations, and we will *not* execute without your authority, but you heard the colonel, I do not plan on disobeying a direct order, I will report back to him, but no surprises. I will not blindside you."

With that, he said, "Make sure you don't!" and stormed off.

After that encounter, I met with the commander of the HRT. They had already been on the ground for approximately 10 days, integrating with our team and specifically handling the night operations, with their advanced aerial platforms, night observation devices (NODs), and sensors. During the guided tour of his Tactical Operations Center (TOC) I was perhaps most impressed with their support footprint of analysts and operations staff. Clearly, the HRT had their shit together, and we were fortunate to have them!

Later that day, after meeting with all tactical team leaders present, seeking their input, and assessing where we were, I met collectively with the MRT operators upon their return from their assignments. After shaking hands with friends and former teammates, and introducing myself to the new guys, I basically pledged that my objective was to make their time on target more impactful. As I saw it, I would do my best to ensure we closed the intelligence gaps, ensure that missions matched their capabilities, that they had the personnel and support needed to operate *safely,* and obtain or expedite the receipt of additional necessary equipment. I also quietly assured the team leaders that I would act as a buffer between them and the staff, expecting that they lead their men in the field and leave the Command Post primarily to me and the small staff I intended on assembling.

This was a tall order, and I wasted no time in getting started. Now that the intros were over, the first thing I asked to see was the OPLAN, or operations plan, and Intelligence Summary from which we had been operating. Neither document existed. I recall being provided a couple of excuses as to why there was no foundational plan, but it didn't matter; it would have to be resolved, and ASAP. My next order of business, was to test this theory that we weren't receiving adequate intelligence. I did not have to go far, walking right down to the end of the hall at the Command Post to the BCI Lead Desk and finding that there was no protocol to routinely share reports or updates with the MRT. Essentially, if a forward thinking Commissioned Officer or savvy senior investigator felt information was essential for the team to know, they walked it down the hall. Otherwise, there was no consistent "flow," and the tactical guys often didn't get essential information.

Typically, "jobs" or assignments were just handed down from the Operations (OPS) desk, with little more attached than an address or coordinate to check. Even if the lead had been ginned up by the BCI, the complete *reason* for the assignment often didn't accompany the tasking; as anyone with military or tactical experience will tell you, that's a recipe for disaster. Not only are you less effective, reacting instead of acting with intent, but you could be walking into a trap. To make matters worse, in addition to the "certified" tactical teams, the BCI had developed the habit of deploying small units of investigators, with no formal training, deep into the woods, dressed in camouflage, <u>without</u> advising the tactical teams operating in the same area of operations (AO). Can you say, *"friendly fire"* situation? I certainly did *not* want to and brought it to the troop commander's attention forthwith. "Sir, this practice must cease immediately!" I said.

He largely agreed, siding with my concerns of fratricide, and directed the BCI Captain to coordinate through OPS and the MRT anytime investigators would insert deeply into the woods. We would have preferred they stay out of the deep woods, as they were not adequately trained or equipped, but we had to settle for being notified and gave them a <u>wide</u> berth.

By the end of the day, I knew I had my work cut out for me. I would handle developing the OPLAN myself, as I couldn't really spare the manpower by pulling someone out of the field for that task, but I needed assistance with the intelligence package. For that, I turned to Colonel Schepperly. "Sir," I said, "I'd like your permission to contact UNYRIC (Upstate NY Regional Intelligence Center, now known as NYSIC -NYS Intelligence Center) and steal Investigator John Zimmerman. There's a significant gap on the Intel side here for the team, and I could use John to both interface directly with the BCI and to develop the boilerplate of our Intelligence Annex, which will be used to drive future operations." It was my first request of the colonel. I didn't go to the well often, and he granted it immediately.

He said, "Call UNYRIC, and tell them you've got Zimmerman for the next week or so, my authority."

"Thanks, Boss!" I said. I had met Zimmerman when he was earlier assigned to ESD – Capital. John had introduced himself to me, and I quickly learned that he too was an Army Ranger, having served in battalion and that he had expanded his skill set into the field of intelligence, once he'd gotten beaten up enough as a "grunt." The more I heard about his qualifications, the more impressed I became. With his eventual assignment to our Intelligence Center, I knew I had the perfect guy to assist me in formulating the plan and closing the gap. After securing the proper approvals, I called Investigator Zimmerman and told him it was a "Go." He was thrilled, as analyzing and tracking people on the move was right in his wheelhouse.

John arrived the next morning. We had just "jumped" or moved the Command Post overnight to a high school in Randolph, NY, as Phillips had been involved in a burglary and possible sighting in a southern part of the troop. I wasted no time in introducing John to the Incident Commander. "Major, this is Investigator John Zimmerman from UNYRIC," I said. He's here to help the team develop a comprehensive Intel plan…" John saluted.

"You're from where?" the major asked.

"UNYRIC," John said.

"Jesus Christ! Another fucking Headquarters rat!" he exclaimed. "Just what I need!" and walked away.

John, still holding his salute said, "Well that went well."

"C'mon, we've got work to do," I said.

Zimmerman got right to it. I already had the format up and was working on the OPLAN, and I handed the Intel Annex off to John. Fortunately, he was an investigator, and although he wasn't from Troop "A", his fellow investigators accepted him, opening up their shop. John was straight forward. He wasn't there to step on anyone's toes, just provide the MRT with an Intel product and assist with (create actually) a sustainable flow of information, making everyone's life more productive. In a matter of about 48 hours, between the two of us, we'd assembled an OPLAN, with a substantive Intel Annex and prepared to brief the team. Before addressing the team, I provided the TC and his staff with a copy of the document. Assisting us during the briefing were Troopers Jay Curry and Jim Meltz, both experienced, ranking military veterans, who'd compiled and assembled our mapping products.

The guys filed in and took a seat. With operators there from four different teams, some having recently arrived, and some having worked the detail already for weeks, we knew and acknowledged that a portion of what they were about to hear would be redundant, but necessary. In addition to providing a thorough overview, from which to conduct future operations, we also needed to standardize certain operational protocols as the team had no *written* SOP at the time. This included such things as: Rules of Engagement, SITREP requirements and frequency, Lost Commo plans, MEDEVAC extraction criteria, critical debriefing and reporting requirements, etc. The briefing concluded with Zimmerman's Intel Summary, complete with criminal history, family and associate link analysis chart, and corresponding predictive analysis of the subject's behavior, right down to his propensity for three potential courses of action. The information was well-received, particularly John's work product, which brought everyone up to speed. I figured you had to know your adversary in order to capture him.

The search effort intensified and waned multiple times over the ensuing weeks. Troopers and MRT members were kept busy with numerous calls for service, sightings, burglaries, associate interviews, road checks and roving patrols, countless building and woodland searches, proactive woodland patrolling, static surveillance missions, sensor monitoring, helicopter overflights, etc. Massive inter-agency resources were being utilized and searching continued day and night. After weeks of this level of intensity, with very little to show for it, the inevitable draw down of resources came. The FBI tactical teams withdrew and large numbers of uniformed troopers from around the state, began to be sent back to their home troops, this included the MRT.

In August, after weeks of engagement, I found myself reassigned along with the majority of MRT operators. For me, this meant going back to my duties at ESD Capitol in Albany, where I had no further input or responsibility in the search. While we were happy to see our families again, we all, each and every trooper in the NYSP, felt we had unfinished business as long as Phillips roamed free. Even Troop "A", the epicenter of the escape and search, had scaled its Uniform presence back a bit. While the BCI was working the case *hard*, they had nowhere near the resources they had before, *but* the objective had not changed. Phillips still needed to be apprehended. He had shot a NYS Trooper and continued to remain free. That fact was not lost upon the tenacious investigators in the BCI. They doggedly pursued every lead and worked at creating opportunities to get closer to an arrest, turning up the heat on Phillips' family, with the arrest of specific family members for Hindering Prosecution, for allegedly assisting him throughout the summer, helping him to avoid capture.

On August 27, 2006, a report came in of a gun store burglary occurring in Chautauqua County. The proceeds of the burglary included 41 firearms. This burglary was directly attributed to Phillips by an associate, who reportedly gave Phillips a ride following the burglary. Furthermore, the subject informed investigators that Phillips had told him, "he had to protect his family." The BCI believed they now had something current and actionable, indicating that Phillips may be headed to visit his former girlfriend, at Bachelor Hill, in the Town of Pomfret, Chautauqua County, a location familiar to the MRT. Accordingly, they contacted the MRT West Team, the local asset they were accustomed to working with; however, the West Team had recently completed their rotation and was on pass. The responsibility for their tasking was deferred to the North Team, which was in troop to cover a few days off for their local mates. So, early in the morning, a sergeant with the North Team was awoken in his hotel room by a call from the Command Post about setting up surveillance, in the form of a Listening Post/Observation Post (LP/OP) in a wooded area near a relative of Phillips' at Bachelor Hill.

As luck would have it, the North Team had just wrapped it up for the day and was back at the hotel sleeping. During the draw down, MRT had been cut back to 12-hour shifts, no longer having a dedicated team for the night shift, instead relying upon "Recall" for night operations. This was one of those times. So, the sergeant contacted two members of his team by phone in their hotel room and advised them that he was assigning them to an LP/OP at Bachelor Hill. Little is precisely known about the level of detailed intelligence shared in the chain between the BCI member requesting the MRT and the two operators given the assignment, but it appears deficient. Indeed, it is entirely possible, that the two men heading out to Bachler Hill understood they were to gain and maintain eyes on the house at that location, but had no idea Phillips himself was in the AO, *or* had insinuated he meant to do harm to the troopers.

Regardless, what occurred was, after very little rest, the deployment of only two MRT members. Troopers Don Baker and Joe Longobardo, geared up and inserted into the woods in the vicinity of Bachelor Hill, establishing a hide site by 11:00 AM, on August 31, 2006, which they would maintain throughout the entire day, surveilling a residence that Phillips may intend to visit. Initially, they were without immediate tactical support. Their team, for whom they were dependent upon for tactical security and relief, continued their off-duty status and did not report back to duty till later that afternoon.

At around 6:15 PM, Phillips opened fire on the hide site. Investigation reveals that Phillips was aware that troopers had been watching the Bachelor Hill residence off and on for weeks, often secreted in the surrounding woods. So, during his approach, Phillips took a circuitous, overland route through the woods to the property and began stalking his prey. Treading cautiously, Phillips observed the two troopers from behind, as they lay prone in the field facing their objective, the residence. Creeping up to within approximately 50 feet of their position, he opened fire with his high-powered .308 rifle, striking Trooper Baker in the abdomen creating an immediately debilitating wound and Trooper Longobardo in the thigh, rupturing his femoral artery. Heroically, Longobardo, one of the newest members of the team, joining just two months earlier, was a member of the USAF Security Forces Squadron and Marine Corps veteran (of the Gulf War), returned fire with his M4. His actions stopped Phillips' advance and forced his assailant's retreat. Trooper Baker, suffering grievous wounds, contacted the Command Post to advise they had exchanged gunfire with an assailant and requested assistance, before going unconscious. Longobardo, then bleeding profusely, attended to Baker's wound by applying a pressure dressing and is credited with saving his life.

A SP helicopter with four MRT members on board was on scene within minutes. They had recently returned to duty and landed in what they believed to be a "hot" LZ, secured their two wounded operators, immediately applied life-saving measures, and transported them to a local hospital. [Because of the courageous response of his teammates, Trooper Baker, while grievously wounded, would live. Although, despite their best efforts, Trooper Longobardo would ultimately succumb to his injuries.]

The news travelled quickly, and I recall walking into my residence on the other side of the state after a day at the capital, only to take a call from a division communications specialist, who knew I had close ties to the MRT, advising me that two members of the team had just been ambushed, their condition, at the time, grave. I made one phone call to ascertain when I could catch the next flight with the MRT heading west, grabbed my gear, kissed my wife, and headed for the airport. In the 22 years the team had been in existence, no one had ever been shot. Now, two lives were hanging in the balance, and we, the MRT, had to pick ourselves up, dust ourselves off, and get back in the fight.

Within hours, hundreds of troopers and nearly every member of the MRT and K9 in the State Police, plus FBI, USMS, ATF, Border Patrol, and other local agencies descended upon the Fredonia, NY, Command Post. So many personnel responded that they opened up a school for everyone to report to and receive a briefing. Road blocks and road checks went up everywhere. This was the nuclear option, and it was chaotic. For my part, I met immediately with the Incident Commander and his staff. What was known, was that Trooper Longobardo, now in a coma, had gotten off several rounds. It was unclear if he had hit Phillips or not. For all we knew, perhaps he had, and Phillips had crawled off into the weeds wounded, or made his way into the house. Either way, the crime scene was not in State Police control, sensitive items of equipment remained on the ground, and we had to go back in there at first light and secure the area. I knew the hazards involved in such a direct-action mission. Bachelor Hill was a single residence, on a hilltop, with relatively clear, unobstructed fields of fire over 360 degrees. Additionally, the surrounding woods formed a dense perimeter and would easily provide cover and concealment to someone awaiting our return; so the threats were multi-dimensional. We needed numbers, we needed air assets, and we needed armored vehicles.

Fortunately, we had established the federal, state, and local partnerships to establish just such a task force and set about planning our return to Bachelor Hill. We were up most of the night, constructing a viable assault plan. While it would be a long night for the leaders, we ordered as many of our operators as possible to get some rest for the long day to follow. That was likely an impossible task, as we noted the combination of rage and anxiety in the eyes of our people. By 6:00 AM, I was at the State Police Command Post briefing the Incident Commander (the major) and the Superintendent of the New York State Police, Wayne Bennett. After describing our multi-pronged, multi-agency approach, entailing the use of nearly 75 SWAT team members, two armored vehicles, three helicopters, and half a dozen canines, the superintendent nodded his head in agreement and said, "Anything else, Chuck?"

I said, "Yes, Sir. In two of those helicopters, I will have MRT sharpshooters. As you have seen by the aerial photos, we are exposed during much of our approach. The Jet Rangers (helos) will act as our cover, air support if you will." While unstable platform (aerial sniper) operations were common in the military, they were not common in law enforcement, and at the time, our agency had never trained or performed the task. Under the circumstances, for the safety of our personnel, I was willing to take the chance.

To his credit, the superintendent did not even flinch and said, "Do it!"

We briefed the operators, pilots, and drivers and mounted up. It wouldn't be a long drive, so we waited just long enough to ensure our air assets were spooled up and performed a final communications check. "Green light," we launched. With the perimeter covered, and additional snipers inserted, we were making our final approach in Bearcat armored vehicles, when the helicopters streaked overhead, at low level, reporting that the objective "appeared clear." That was from their perspective, we still had work ahead of us as we dismounted on the X (objective), racing to secure the primary residence in a dynamic entry, secure all outbuildings, and gain immediate control of the property out to and including the wood line. This effort occurred simultaneously, to expeditiously establish the most security practical under those conditions. Once secured, deliberate patrols and canines swept the wooded areas surrounding the residence. Negative contact. We called the crime scene techs forward, so they could begin the deliberate task of gathering evidence for later prosecution, and we reported to Headquarters.

While our return to Bachelor Hill proved negative, in that we did not locate Phillips, we did secure gear left behind by the two-man MRT element and collected crime scene evidence. In addition, it proved to our tactical responders that they could immediately get back on the proverbial horse and execute a complex operation. This proved invaluable as our operations tempo (OPTEMPO) for the week continued unabated. With the shooting of these two troopers, in addition to Trooper Brown in June, the stakes couldn't be higher. Superintendent Bennett himself took over the operation, and it was a pleasure to serve under the leadership of a legend within the State Police. He handled the massive press attention expertly, made brisk, logical decisions, and when Trooper Longobardo expired three days after being shot, respectfully lifted the morale of each and every member of the NYSP by his commitment to bringing the perpetrator to justice.

On the early morning of September 8, 2006, I was awakened in my hotel room, with a report that at approximately 1:55 AM, a Warren County, PA, roving patrol had attempted to stop a stolen vehicle along the Pennsylvania border, only to be led on a pursuit. The vehicle, lost control and crashed, the driver fleeing from the scene. Deputies called for backup, and units from both Pennsylvania and New York responded, setting up a hasty perimeter and commencing a search of the wooded area, but the driver had apparently slipped out. Approximately thirty minutes later, a second car was reported stolen in Pennsylvania. Subsequently, the driver later crossed back into New York, and two observant NYS Troopers spotted the vehicle, engaging in a brief pursuit and crossing back into Pennsylvania. The desperate driver, unable to shake the patrol car, decelerated and jumped from the moving vehicle, fleeing again into the woods. This time, articles left behind in the stolen vehicle appeared to belong to the fugitive and would provide recent scent material for our canines. Thus, officers were now attempting to establish a "new" perimeter, bordering a remote golf course.

Scrambling out of bed, I alerted the rest of the team and headed to the CP. I believed the probability was high that the troopers were onto something and ordered our guys to head south, for the one-hour drive, to Akeley, PA. Fortunately, the NYSP had entered a temporary compact with the USMS, "deputizing" select members of the State Police, such as the MRT, so we had seamless authority when it counted most. I knew I had to get on the ground ASAP and commandeered a helicopter for the brief flight. If this was the real deal, we had no time to lose and containment would be the key. Phillips was a formidable foe, and had eluded capture for months.

I exited the aircraft in a field and hustled over to the edge of the road looking for the senior New York State Police member on scene. Police cars from various agencies were all lined up, line of sight, with their respective officers all facing the wood line, guns drawn. "As far as I know," the sergeant said, "He was last seen going into the woods on this side of the road."

"OK," I said, "How far down the road do you have coverage?"

"I'm not exactly sure, but I've been sending everybody down that way, around the bend. There's a Pennsylvania Trooper down there holding the line," he said.

"I've got more MRT en route," I said, "but they're still a ways out. In the meantime, I'm going to head that way and see what we've got."

So, I started walking. After a couple of hundred yards, I rounded the bend and noted that the dense foliage was now transitioning into a large cornfield on my left. It was still a good distance down to the corner, but it was a straight shot and appeared well covered by officers. Although, there was no way they could see him among the corn, it was just too tall and thick, it would be difficult for him to crossover behind them I reasoned; unless he'd done it *before* they set up.

I found a Pennsylvania Trooper and introduced myself, "This is a golf course, I'm told?"

"Yes, Cable Hollow Golf Course," he said.

"How come I'm not seeing any fairways and shit?" I asked him.

"This is the bordering property," he said. "The course is up the road, or through the woods from where you just came from."

"Oh, so anyone entering the woods back there," I pointed behind myself, "can squirt out onto the course?"

"That's right," he said, "but it's not easy. It's thick in there."

"Do we have a perimeter on the other side?" I asked.

"Nope," he said, "but I've got another trooper over there trying to set it up."

"OK. By the way, I'm from our (NYSP) SWAT team..." I was wearing tactical gear, so he gave me a look like *No shit.* "What I mean is, are any of your (SWAT) guys here yet?"

"Not that I know of, but I think they're en route," he responded.

"Please let them know I'm here, and I have more guys coming. We'll need to link up at some point. Thanks," I said.

By 7:15 AM, we had approximately 150 law enforcement officers, including SWAT and K9, on the ground.

To understand what I was dealing with here, I had to get airborne. I contacted the helicopter that had dropped me off. Although they were returning for fuel, the pilot advised me that a Huey was en route to my location with several of my guys on board, ETA approximately 15 minutes. *Perfect!* I thought. I returned back to LZ and awaited their arrival. As if on cue, they landed. Six or eight guys piled out, and I said to the team leader, "I'm taking two of your guys up with me for an aerial reconnaissance flight. Link up with the K9 guys, who just arrived, and see what you can do about establishing a track where he went into the woods."

With that, I talked to the pilots about the need for us to overfly the golf course and figure out what the hell was going on. The pilot was a former MRT guy, as I recall, and only too happy to oblige. He did not need to be told twice, and off we went. Once above the trees, as we gained altitude, it became clear this was no ordinary golf course. There were three sides surrounded by dense woods and corn fields, and the one open side contained the club house. Not average topography either; the surrounding terrain was heavily wooded, steep, and mountainous. Not being a golfer, I wondered, *who builds a freakin' golf course in the mountains?* While it would not be terribly difficult to set a perimeter around with enough officers (several hundred I estimated), it would be tough to clear it! Woods, mountains, streams, thick stuff with a bunch of fairways thrown in. The Huey was now running low on fuel, and my guys were starting to arrive by vehicle, so they landed and dropped me off. "You two (MRT operators) stay with the aircraft as sharpshooters," I said as I disconnected from the headset. This would later prove to be an integral decision.

Linking up with my team leaders, I provided a quick overview of what I saw by air. "We've got to lock this place down. Locate some maps, and see if you can find PA SWAT," I directed.

By the time I was back on the ground, increasingly more NY State Troopers had arrived, pouring over the border. They were not going to let this guy escape if *THEY* had anything to say about it. The good news was, they knew just what to do; they had been playing this game long enough. The NCOs were in charge, and they were expanding and strengthening the perimeter with the arrival of each additional patrol. It was a sight to behold – a thing of beauty, really. The arrival of a Commissioned Officer could only screw things up, in my opinion.

That was the good news. The not-so-good news was that in my absence, at approximately 9:10 AM, a K9 team supported by two troopers had moved into the woods on a track and had spooked Phillips from his hiding spot. Phillips fled, but turned and displayed a handgun, pointing at the officers. One trooper fired in response, but missed his mark. The K9 handler then released the dog, but the canine could not make it up the very steep, muddy bank on the far side of a stream. They lost Phillips, but now we had a "recent" sighting. We knew definitively that he was within our search area.

As the morning progressed, we continued to harden the perimeter and attempted to maintain continuous overflight of the area. We had to keep him boxed in until we had sufficient numbers to begin a coordinated "push." Finally, we ran into our counterparts Pennsylvania (PASP) SWAT. Agreeing that the perimeter was coming along and that anything we did had to be coordinated, we proceeded to the newly established joint CP where all agencies were coalescing for a meeting. Knowing that time was of the essence, since only the tactical teams had uniformly been issued night vision, we had to make our penetrations and sweeps of the surrounding terrain count. We knew, that if we didn't get him today, or hem him right in, he would look to make his move at night and slip away yet again. Consequently, we walked out of the meeting with a couple of phases to the tactical plan and set out to implement them.

Upon returning to the field, I briefed Superintendent Bennett, who had been checking on the troopers personally. I informed him and key staff that we were prepared to: 1) lock down the perimeter, 2) insert the MRT and PA SWAT deep into the woods in an extended L-shape ambush formation as a blocking element, where they could make use of their numerical advantage and thermal and night-vision equipment 3) collapse a portion of the perimeter in a concerted, on-line push towards the tactical backstop established by SWAT, and 4) keep the helicopters airborne with sharpshooters. The superintendent indicated his approval and the wheels were in motion. It was late afternoon before the "deer drive" commenced, and the feeling was one of intensity. We would either succeed, or the "ghost" would elude us again.

As darkness fell, everyone was switched on, regardless of how little sleep they'd had. Suddenly, a patrol car on the perimeter, a Warren County Sheriff Deputy, radioed in that an, "unidentified subject dressed in camouflage was hiding against a fence row." Someone appeared to be low crawling near his location. He had challenged the subject, but got no response…not assumed to be friendly.

I got on the air to Aviation, "Did you copy last transmission!"

"Affirmative," came the reply.

"Get overhead, and take the appropriate action," I directed the pilots and MRT onboard.

"Roger that," came the reply.

What seemed like forever, but was really a matter of seconds, the aircraft was overhead and had a bead on him. Finally, there he was, Phillips, the man who had shot three State Troopers, killing one, and had vowed to go down fighting, surrendered to a Deputy on the ground and a helicopter in the sky.

"Suspect in custody!" came the next radio transmission. "I repeat suspect in custody!"

Phillips, who'd been on the run for over five months, himself would later tell our investigators, "There were no holes in the perimeter. Police officers were shoulder to shoulder." Phillips who had recently been placed on the FBI's 10 Most Wanted List, was in custody at 7:56 PM.

Later, Superintendent Bennett addressed his troopers and the media: "He could run, but he couldn't hide. The pressure was so great on him. The game was up and he knew it." [Phillips would later admit to the shooting and is serving two life sentences.]

There were no words, just immense relief because the "nightmare" was finally over. Relief, and concurrent, deep sadness, because one of our guys didn't make it to see that day.

Upon return to the staging area in Fredonia, the superintendent addressed the troopers en masse, both commending the actions of everyone involved and acknowledging the extreme sacrifices made by a select few.

Afterward, Colonel Schepperly, the man who had initially reactivated me to assist the MRT, asked if I would consider returning to the team on a full-time basis. I must have had a puzzled look on my face, knowing that there was no slot for a lieutenant on the team, and he quickly added, "You made a difference out here. This team needs a lieutenant; an officer-in-charge, to assist the captain (Emergency Services), to work with guys in the field. I have floated the idea by the superintendent...let me see what I can do."

"Thank you, Sir," I said. It would be a privilege to work with these men again!

Two days later, we attended the funeral for Trooper Joseph Longobardo. It had been planned before Phillips' apprehension, but now that he was in custody, it was bitter sweet. Fitting. I think Joe would have wanted it that way. Trooper Don Baker had also sustained very serious physical injuries, and it is no exaggeration to say it was "touch and go" for a while. Ultimately, after several months, Don recovered, and although his injuries would prevent him from kicking down doors again, he progressed through the ranks and as of 2016, leads the very same tactical team as the OIC (lieutenant), of the Special Operation Response Team (SORT).

Over the next several weeks, a great deal of criticism surfaced about how the Division of State Police had handled the incident. You can't have three troopers shot and one killed without coming under fire. Following the manhunt in 2006, our union, the NYST PBA, wrote a scathing letter to George Pataki, then-Governor of New York. The letter was highly critical of what they considered to be flawed senior leadership and focused scrutiny on the actions of the incident commander, at the time, in Troop "A". The letter, included charges of *"inexcusable and unconscionable ineptitude."* Claiming the State Police dismissed the FBI, engaged in "internal turf wars," failed to adequately share information and intelligence, conducted unsafe road checks and observation post tactics, and did not provide troopers with adequate weapons and equipment.

Lastly, speaking only for myself, to address a separate area of concern – the ambush of Troopers Baker and Longobardo – this was an overall colossal failure of: intelligence dissemination, tactical protocols, and common sense. Had the intelligence been fully analyzed, vetted, and disseminated, it should have been noted the target was believed to be armed, at large, and in the area. This was definitely *not* a two-man surveillance mission. The request should have warranted notification to Division HQ and resulted in a tactical team-level response to conduct a multi-point surveillance operation. At a minimum, the size of the LP/OP should have afforded 360-degree security, the number of teams employed should have been increased, a QRF placed on standby for the duration, and a MEDEVAC dedicated to the operation. Hindsight is 20/20 but, *under no circumstances, should two men have been assigned alone.*

This was not the incident commander's fault, but a failure of the system.

Division of State Police embarked on an intense effort to conduct a thorough After Action Review (AAR) of the Phillips manhunt, resulting in hundreds of interviews and assessments. The net result was a report replete with significant lessons learned. Whether you approved of the PBA's evaluation or not, it was not lost upon me during the post-incident review, that the *on-scene commander* was the man on the "hot seat." Logically, it made sense. *The Incident Commander is the individual with the greatest responsibility for the effectiveness of the day-to-day search effort <u>and</u> the safety and welfare of the people assigned.*

Naturally, I had made my own first-person observations during the ordeal, regarding: the level and quality of leadership, inter-agency cooperation, strategic vision, tactical applications, and lack of protocols and safety issues related to the event. The AAR quantified that, to a degree, and more.

Now, nearly 10 years later, I vowed those shortcomings would <u>not</u> be repeated on my watch.

CHAPTER 9

CASE DEVELOPMENT

Although we did not have our targets in custody, significant work was being done. As I'd said earlier, "No stone was being left unturned."

As of **Saturday night, June 13, Day 8,** we had 800 plus officers on the ground and had investigated over 700 leads, but still had no "confirmed sightings." That said, in addition to the Village of Dannemora, searchers continued to scour the Towns of Saranac and Plattsburgh and the Hamlet of Caddyville. *Plus*, roving patrols, ATV's, and aerial assets had been deployed far and wide for a week, in an effort to find evidence of movement along the many powerlines and recreational trails in the region.

Sunday, June 14, Day 9, additional coordination occurred between SP and the Superintendent of the SCSD. This was final exam season, and schools that had been closed Thursday and Friday of the previous week, were now scheduled to reopen on Monday. Per our discussion, this would be accompanied by a significant increase in troopers in the district, enabling classes to resume and exams to be completed. Buses would go through check points and, as a precaution, be boarded and checked by law enforcement manning the road blocks. Additionally, road patrols would be increased near pick up and drop off points.

Monday, June 15, Day 10, with more than 800 personnel, over 1,000 leads, and 13 square miles (8,300 acres) searched to date, it was remarkable just how supportive the community had been. This fact was well-reported by the local media and summarized by the *Press-Republican*: In addition to vigilance, resulting in tips and leads called in, residents of the community were delivering coffee, Gatorade, snacks, lawn chairs, and even Easy Ups to searchers who were standing for hours on end at road checks; elementary school children were bagging lunches, complete with motivational notes on the side of paper bags; local businesses, colleges, hospitals, restaurants, convenience stores, grocery stores, community groups all were supplying food, goods, and services to assist responders from around the country, who had come to their community to help. Local EMS was always available for call out and tended to minor injuries and ailments when possible. Even a national entity, like Verizon, contributed by upgrading cell towers, boosting coverage and expediting service to improve command and control.[7]

Truly, too many benefactors to list, without inadvertently leaving someone off. Perhaps one of the most obvious symbols of support for responders, was the appearance, seemingly overnight, of the ubiquitous blue ribbon. Residents displayed so many blue ribbons on trees, mailboxes, telephone poles, and other public places, that I was told stores had run out of them.

That same day, Governor Cuomo called for the New York State Inspector General (IG) to conduct an investigation to run parallel to the State Police criminal investigation, into what factors led to the escape at Clinton. As a result, New York State Inspector General Catherine Leahy Scott stated publicly, "Apprehension of the two fugitives from CCF is the highest priority, and nothing will stand in the way of this primary mission." I certainly appreciated the IG's position. All I asked of my boss, Superintendent D'Amico, was that the parallel investigation in no way detract from our mission to apprehend the fugitives. He assured me that it wouldn't, and it did not. [Chapter 20, is dedicated to lessons learned from our NYSP AAR and the IG's findings regarding CCF.]

Additionally, June 15 turned out to be a significant day in the news cycle, when more information was provided to the media about Mitchell's complicity in the escape. Clinton County District Attorney Andrew Wylie, who had been working the case with us from the start, attempted to clarify public misconceptions by making the following comments: 1) "Basically, when it was go time, Mitchell got cold feet." 2) "There was no evidence that Matt and Sweat had a Plan B, once Mitchell backed out." 3) "No vehicles have been reported stolen in the area." 4) "The inmates had access to tools stored by prison contractors in gang boxes, which Sweat managed to open, returning them each night," and 5) "The inmates may have 'rehearsed' their escape for up to five weeks, based upon the admission that Joyce Mitchell had provided contraband on May 1st."

Ultimately, the investigation determined that the introduction of the first hacksaw blades occurred much earlier. Additionally, the manner in which these items were transported through the system to the inmates was still being investigated at the time. Now we know, according to Sweat's statement, he had been working on the escape for months and had been out of his cell up to 85 nights, behind the walls and down in the catacombs of the prison. In that case, it appears Mitchell may have first introduced hacksaw blades into the facility to Matt in the tailor shop as early as February.

Then, a surprise, when the media began citing "sources" as telling them that Mitchell, in her statement, admitted there had been talk with the inmates of killing her husband following the escape. While the DA and lead investigators were confidentially aware of this development, no one would officially confirm it.

Then, another "bomb" dropped when it was disclosed, again by "sources," that Mitchell allegedly had "sexual contact" with an inmate, performing oral sex on Matt.

Where was all this coming from, and who were these "sources? These were intimate details of interviews, and like other specific investigative findings, they were supposed to remain close-hold – confidential. We had not even completed all our necessary interviews and desirable reinterviews, yet information was leaking out.

Meanwhile, anonymous correction officers, both retired and active, were telling the media that: "policies" at the prison contributed to the escape. Retired C.O.s claimed overnight catwalk checks behind cells had been canceled; officers were prohibited from using flashlights to illuminate cells at night during checks, because inmates complained lights were being shined in their eyes; inmates did not want to "show skin," complaining their heads were cold, so they were allowed to cover their heads with pillows, blankets, and hoodies; inmates were allowed to paint their cells, and were routinely provided with the prison paint to do it, facilitating the ability to cover up a breach, even painting razor blades into the wall, to conceal them; gang boxes were located in catwalks and other project areas, affording access.[8] While generally accurate, this was considered another "shot" at the prison administration.

By **Tuesday, June 16, Day 11,** we were on our final "push" to wrap up the Dannemora search box. Again, the objective was to thoroughly search every inch of the 16-square-mile area, some 10,228 acres, to establish with certainty that the inmates were not hiding under our noses. And, it had not been easy. Troopers had been rotated in from all 11 designated troops in the SP. With over 800 personnel on the ground, we had been busy addressing some 1,200 leads, over 100 per day. Additionally, the terrain and elements, primarily the incessant rain, had hampered our physical search efforts, particularly affecting scent for canines, and thick foliage negatively impacted our use of airborne thermal imagers. However, as we increased our expansion into other communities in the region, the challenges presented by the environment around Dannemora paled in comparison to what awaited us.

Also, on this date, I was made aware that the DA had responded to an inquiry from the media, informing them that he had been told the multi-agency search and investigation was costing "more than $1 million per day." While it wasn't within my purview or concern, I would have to contend with that question myself, later, when the broader media became keyed in.

As of **Wednesday, June 17, after 12 days** of intense search efforts, in the immediate area surrounding Dannemora all homes and camps had been checked and rechecked, additionally, all rural and woodland areas methodically combed by searchers on the ground and canines. The superintendent and field commander, who had visited multiple times during the course of the investigation, supported our strategy and agreed with the necessity of relocating our Command Post to Caddyville. Resultantly, by that time, we already had a significant force of rovers and tactical sorties focusing 25 miles west and north from the prison. Our future planners were always thinking "outside the box," trying to *"What if...?"* the situation. We had done all we could, and then some, in the 16 square miles around the prison. Consequently, the Dannemora search box was officially considered closed.

Acknowledging this shift in focus, a press conference was held that afternoon in Plattsburgh, the county seat. In my prepared statement, I summarized the developments as follows: The decision to widen the local search is based on evidence. We've closed the Dannemora perimeter box after thoroughly sweeping the area. Our intention is to *continue* to look at the viable high-speed avenues of egress from the prison, in all cardinal directions. About 200 search personnel (mostly CERT) have been sent back to their facilities, leaving a force of 600 local, state, and federal personnel on the ground. No tactical, canine, or aviation units have been reduced.

Furthermore, my BCI Captain, Bob La Fountain, stated: "We have no information the inmates have been able to leave this area. Law enforcement officials, including 110 SP Investigators, have already received 1,300 leads and are checking every one. This will continue until these two are apprehended."

Additionally, we (SP) released progression photos, depicting an artist's rendering of what Matt and Sweat could look like after 12 days on the run.

DA Wylie then took the podium and confirmed Joyce Mitchell had told police Matt and Sweat planned to kill her husband. The plan was for her to drive her four-wheel-drive jeep to Dannemora to pick up the inmates at midnight, but instead checked herself into the hospital that night. She *never* told authorities that the inmates coerced her. Additionally, the DA advised, Lyle Mitchell would <u>not</u> be charged; based upon the results of his three-hour statement.

Before addressing the anticipated questions, I added a statement, regarding my growing concern pertaining to investigative leaks, which I considered a threat to the integrity of the investigation. "The volume of reported confidential information provided to the media by unnamed sources or those allegedly close to the investigation does not aid in this investigation. In fact, it imperils the investigation. Those responsible put our law enforcement officers and responders at risk, hamper our ability to get ahead of the fugitives, and prolong the threat to the general public. In my 25 years of law enforcement experience, I've never witnessed better interagency cooperation." Adding, "While no incident is perfect, especially with the volume of information, size, scope, and scale of the investigation, we are well-coordinated. We are doggedly pursuing every lead. We're not ruling anything out. We're not taking anything for granted."

Thus, on **Thursday, June 18, Day 13,** the day when the lockdown at CCF was lifted by DOCCS upon completion of necessary repairs and implementation of increased security restrictions, we had slightly over 600 searchers on the ground. We were checking thousands of seasonal homes and hunting camps in the region and stepping up our roving patrols. Then, out of the blue, it was widely circulated that Lyle Mitchell's attorney told the "TODAY" show, that his client was "blown away" by revelations that Joyce Mitchell talked to the inmates about having him killed after they broke out.

On **Friday, June 19, Day 14,** after two weeks without results, I publicly renewed our commitment to the citizens of the North County and the nation at a press conference, announcing: The USMS had added Matt and Sweat to its 15 Most Wanted fugitives list; reserved for the worst of the worst, increasing the total award to $150,000. I reminded the public that although the number of personnel has been reduced from 800 to 600, <u>no</u> reduction of aviation, K9, and tactical units has occurred. Furthermore, while we have transitioned from the grid search, we're continuing to fan out, going door to door, and have cleared more than 200 structures (seasonal hunting camps and cabins) outside the Village of Dannemora. Additionally, officers on ATVs have traversed more than 600 miles of trails, what we consider to be high-speed avenues of egress. Again, I urged the public to continue to check their trail cameras. I finished by saying, "I can tell you we're configured for a rapid response, and we're also geared for the long haul." **"We're not going anywhere."**

Later that day, in a statement released by DOCCS at 9:00 PM, it was announced that a Correction Officer, Gene Palmer, had been placed on leave. Subsequent to that announcement, Palmer was interviewed by SP and OSI Investigators for 14 hours on Saturday, June 20, but was not immediately arrested, as we believed there was more to learn.

Earlier in that second week, a sighting had been reported in Stueben County, in Troop "E", 315 miles away in Western New York. Upon receiving a report of two unknown male subjects walking in close proximity to a rail yard, an investigation was conducted by fellow members of the State Police headquartered near Rochester, NY. Investigators located video surveillance footage of two subjects, seeming to fit the general description of the escapees, but due to the distance and quality of the film, positive identification was not possible. Increased law enforcement resources were then dedicated to this region from the local troop, due to the viability of the lead; however, no solid leads were further developed. Still, that sighting, set the stage. We had to be open to the possibility of movement outside our region, and we were, so we were ready for the next development...

Early **Saturday, June 20, Day 15** of the search effort, a resident of Friendship, NY, 335 away in Alleghany County, reported that her dog alerted to two white males walking on the railroad tracks behind her home, along Route 20 and I-86. A resident, who'd been dialed into the news reports about the possibility that the fugitives may be travelling by rail in the Southern Tier, felt that the subjects resembled Matt and Sweat and immediately called 911. A large multi-agency response was initiated by NYSP Troop "A", Headquartered near Buffalo, to the area south of the city. A Command Post was established and a task force of 300 federal, state, and local agencies from that region assembled, to run the lead to ground.

Significantly, the superintendent and field commander made a decision at the time, _not_ to transfer any personnel from Dannemora. This would prove _crucial_!

Despite _not_ having two suspects in custody, the last 15 days had been productive. We had: built an enormous coalition of resources; maintained public safety; located and obtained a signed confession from one co-conspirator and arrested another for misconduct; completely integrated our command structure in accordance with ICS; ensured our tactical teams were all managed by a single branch director; shared appropriate intelligence; developed a future planning cell to guide operations; relocated and expanded our Command Post to Caddyville, in an unoccupied elementary school; and even received laudatory comments, in most circles, for our focus on inter-agency cooperation. Having achieved all the above, _most importantly_, we'd maintained an accident-free safety record.

As Incident Commander, I had attempted to build and maintain a collaborative, coherent, evidence-based strategy. Importantly, I'd conveyed my commander's intent which was based on sound, integrated, dynamic-tactics, that were easily executable by ALL members of the team.

I also knew, that as a *leader*, only hard-fought experience, based upon tragedies and triumphs, could prepare one for this level of responsibility. Considering the enormity of the task at hand, and not knowing what lay ahead, I reflected on an earlier period in my career, when, upon having assisted with the capture of one killer, on a golf course in Pennsylvania, in 2006, I was reconnected with the tactical team as their officer-in-charge.

As a result, on **December 27, 2006,** I was transferred to a newly created lieutenant's position in the Office of Emergency Services. Colonel Schepperly had kept his word. *I was headed back to the team, but the days ahead, would not be easy.*

CHAPTER 10

MARGARETVILLE MANHUNT

We began 2007 still licking our wounds after the stunning loss of Trooper Joe Longobardo, committed to making changes that would take us to the next level.

Returning to the Office of Emergency Services, now known as Special Operations, I had the distinct privilege of working under Captain Bob Nuzzo. Bob was a true professional, and we would become good friends over the years, working through some very tough times to come. As the captain, Bob was responsible for overseeing the MRT, SCUBA, BDU, K9, HAZMAT, etc. – all the acronym teams. With an already-full plate, and credit in the bank with Bob, for how I'd handled myself during the Phillips Investigation, he gave me a lot of latitude with the team. Bob knew I was tactically sound, committed to improvement, and loyal. And, I would never let him down.

Much speculation had occurred since the end of the Phillips Detail about the team finally going full time. As the author of the first full-time proposal, which I'd submitted to the superintendent after 9/11, I knew I had the template and believed I possessed the institutional knowledge and credibility to push it forward. After all, I reasoned, *If not now...when?* As the new OIC, I was chomping at the bit. We worked hard to make our case. But, even after what Division had just gone through, the executives were not ready to pull the trigger. Convincing them we needed a full-time team, became my Holy Grail. A position, thankfully, receiving full support from Captain Nuzzo!

While the 2001 proposal still existed, we needed to clean it up and modernize it. The team was larger, had new equipment, and had evolved since then. That progress had to be reflected in the "new" proposal. I figured we had one opportunity to get it right; one chance to make a compelling argument. While the captain and I worked the hallways to garner support, we were often cautioned about not overreaching. Although we knew we were "converting" some of the execs, we still faced an uphill battle. We were reminded there were hurdles and legitimate concerns, most of them cost related, to gaining approval. We worked tirelessly, the first several months of that new year, to identify the issues and resolve them. We worked just as hard to win over our critics.

We were making progress, albeit not fast enough for a number of operators on the team, who had by this time come to believe they were *entitled* to the change. What's worse, they were beginning to let their disenchantment with Division and the process show. Frankly, those carping to the Union or their fellow troopers, were beginning to seriously undermine our cause.

Then, at approximately 2:45 PM, on April 25, 2007, Trooper Matthew Gombosi was working routine patrol out of SP Margaretville, in Troop "C". The trooper pulled into a convenience store on Main Street, after observing a vehicle with a missing front license plate, a minor infraction. Trooper Gombosi approached the subject and requested his license and registration. The driver made a comment about being lost and could not produce his documents, ultimately providing a false name and date of birth. Now suspicious, the trooper noted a buck knife on the subject and a rifle in the vehicle, both of which he secured. Upon receiving a reply from his Communications point that the vehicle was registered to a specific person not with the vehicle, and unknown to the subject upon questioning, Trooper Gombosi elected to place the subject in custody. Ordering him to turn around for handcuffing, the subject turned and fired a .22 caliber handgun from point-blank range, striking Gombosi in the abdomen. Fortunately, the round struck the trooper's body armor, saving his life. Stunned and injured, the trooper sought cover and called for assistance. The congested scene and innocent bystanders in the parking lot prohibited the trooper from returning fire. Subsequently, the subject reentered the vehicle, a maroon Dodge Caravan, and sped off. Investigation would later reveal the shooter/driver was identified as Travis D. Trim. Trim, a 23-year-old with a minor criminal record from Upstate New York, was driving a stolen vehicle at the time of the shooting, and was wanted by authorities for probation violation.

Resultantly, an APB was issued for the subject and vehicle, and hundreds of troopers descended upon the small community in the Catskill Mountains searching for the attempted murderer. Nearly three hours later, the vehicle was recovered, unoccupied and secreted among trees, in a rural area on Searles Road, a relatively short distance from the original scene of the shooting.

Included in the massive response, was the South Team of the MRT, led by Sergeant John Gomez. John, a highly experienced leader responded with his team of seasoned operators, to the Command Post, which had been established at the Margaretville Barracks, and went to work coordinating the tactical piece of the search. At Division Headquarters, we knew from experience to plan for the long haul and Gomez's team would require coordinated relief at both the supervisor and operator level. Accordingly, I responded to the Command Post early the next morning. By that time, we had two teams on the ground and a third, out of the four teams, en route. As I drove in, the perimeter was static. Apparently, there was nothing "hot" going on at this early hour. I passed through a number of road checks established by uniformed troopers and saw our MRT members positioned in small, mobile clusters of vehicles known as Quick Response Teams (QRTs). QRT – a hybrid tactical element consisting of a specified mix of MRT, Riflemen (snipers), and K9 handlers – a concept I had developed and deployed during the Phillips search to act as a force multiplier. As I pulled into Margaretville, the radio was quiet, and everything appeared as it should be at this point in an operation.

Entering the station, I passed the front desk and walked by the Communications area. John had set up his version of a TOC in the adjoining room, which consisted of maps, a white board, and photos. "Morning, John," I said.

"Morning, Chuck," he replied, "C'mon in. Let me show you where the guys are." By that he meant where deployed on the map.

I took off my coat, and we were only minutes into the briefing, when all hell broke loose in the radio room next door. I recall, hearing, "MRT to Command Post! MRT to Command, shots fired. I repeat shots fired! We have two members down and need MEDEVAC!"

Sergeant Gomez immediately stepped through the threshold of the doorway and said to the COMSPEC "Who is that?!" John obtained the call sign and knew who it was right away.

"What's happening, John?!" I asked.

He said, "Joe Schmidt and six guys (MRT) responded to an EID (electronic intrusion device) at a farmhouse up the road, about half a mile away from where the stolen vehicle had been recovered last night. They made entry to check it, and were engaged!"

"OK. You're already plugged in here, so I'm heading up there to assist. Get whatever you've got headed that way, and notify Headquarters for the deployment of the other team and the Bearcat," I directed.

"You got it," he said, multi-tasking and simultaneously verifying that a MEDEVAC helo was en route.

I grabbed the address of the farmhouse on Cemetery Road from Communications, plugged it into my GPS and raced up the road.

As I drove, I could see and hear the helicopter streak past me, en route to the scene. I blew past a couple of road checks and set my sights on a farmhouse near a "Y" intersection at the end of the road. I pulled in behind the MRT van, a box truck issued to each team containing tactical equipment, just as the helicopter was lifting off. *That was fast!* I thought, as I jumped out of my truck, popped open the back and began to don my Tac-vest (Level 4 tactical body armor).

Reaching for my radio, I called out to, "ANY MRT member at the scene," advised I was on location, and requested a "SITREP."

Trooper Joe Schmidt came on the air and asked, "Where are you LT?!"

I said, "Down by the cube van, Joe."

He simply replied, "En route."

Trooper Schmidt ran down the slope to my location from the farmhouse. As he drew closer, I observed he was covered with blood, which was actually dripping from the handguard of his M4 assault rifle. "You, all right, Joe?!" I asked.

"I'm good," he said reactively. "But, the two guys I just sent out of here are in bad shape!"

"What about security," I asked.

Joe said, "LT, I've got everybody out of the house, and people posted on the four corners of the perimeter. I think the shooter's still inside!" Trooper Schmidt, was an outstanding operator. His team had been ambushed. He had extracted all members, secured the perimeter, and loaded the two casualties on MEDEVACs, all before my arrival. He was a Trooper's Trooper, and the rest of story he was about to relay to me would prove it.

"Who was hit?" I asked.

"Brink and Matson," he said. "Brink's in bad shape…"

"What happened here?" I asked.

The back story is as follows. Working as a Quick Reaction Force, comprised solely of MRT operators, a seven-man element of the South Team, under the supervision of Assistant Team Leader (ATL) Pete Verdesi, had responded to a report of an EID. The burglary alarm had occurred at a seasonal farmhouse used as a hunting camp by an offsite owner from NJ. These alarms, occur thousands of times around the country each and every day and are routinely responded to by one of more law enforcement officers. Ninety-nine percent of them being false alarms, triggered by the home or business owner, a cat, high-winds, or malfunction. Officers typically respond to them, attempt to contact the home owner, or wait for a "key holder" to respond, and then clear them. End of story…or is it? Officers respond to so many during their careers, they become common place; therefore, they run the risk of becoming complacent. But, that was not the case here!

In this instance, given the events of the previous day, with a subject wanted for attempted murder on the run, a SWAT team with K9 support responded to the location. After inspecting the exterior of the residence, the team determined there was no sign of forced entry, but it couldn't end there. A red flannel shirt, similar to the one the subject who had shot the trooper the day before had been wearing, and several weapons had been found in a barn on the property. SP Margaretville contacted the alarm company, and although a key holder was not available, the team was advised that the owner lived in New Jersey, and the seasonal residence should not be occupied. The house had to be cleared. At the direction of a Troop "C" Commissioned Officer, the team effected entry on the ground floor, announcing their entry with, "State Police!" Posting security on the stairs leading to both the second level and the basement, they cleared the first floor. Continuing to cover the basement access and their "6," their backs, the team methodically proceeded up the staircase to the second floor and broke left and right to secure the rooms. Being that this was an older farmhouse, the rooms and hallways were particularly tight, without much excess space for five fully outfitted tactical operators toting assault rifles. Additionally, there appeared to be several doors off the hallway, which adjoined bedrooms, and a shared bathroom.

As the men were clearing the target, Trooper Rich Mattson took point and proceeded down the short hallway towards a partially closed bathroom door, with his weapon raised at the ready. Suddenly, the silence was broken by the loud reverberations of gunfire within a confined area. Their assailant, suspect Travis Trim, had apparently entered the farmhouse to avoid the external area patrols and executed a textbook near ambush. Firing his .30-.30 lever-action rifle through the door, he struck Trooper Matson in the upper left arm, shattering the bone and damaging his radial artery, effectively taking him out of the fight. Mattson called out, "I'm hit!" Unable to return fire due to his injury (because he sure as hell wanted to shoot back), he pulled out of the hallway, seeking cover in an adjacent room, in need of immediate medical attention.

Nearly simultaneous with the shooting, Troopers Dave Brinkerhoff, an eight and a half-year veteran of the State Police, and Pete Verdesi broke right and entered a bedroom off the same hall. Verdesi cut left off the doorway, hugging the near-side wall and cleared the corner, his forward progress being obstructed by a bed. Brinkerhoff continued straight across the threshold, along the wall. Upon reaching the corner, Brinkerhoff pivoted 90 degrees to his left as a shot rang out, dropping him to one knee. Brinkerhoff had been shot from a doorway on the back wall, which afforded access to an adjoining bedroom and the very same bathroom where Mattson had been engaged seconds earlier.

Brinkerhoff, struck in the chest, was saved by the body armor chest plate integrated into his tactical vest. Although the kinetic energy of the round knocked him down, Brinkerhoff reportedly regained his footing and returned fire, ultimately back tracking to the doorframe they had just entered seeking cover. Verdesi, his partner, returned fire as well from his corner of the room, although he had little to no angle on the perpetrator.

Schmidt attended to Matson, applying a life-saving tourniquet, and escorted him down the stairs and out of the house to the inbound helicopter. To cover this withdrawal, others continued to briefly lay down suppressive fire in the ambush.

Suddenly, amid the chaos, Trooper Brinkerhoff went down. One second, "Brink" had taken a knee in the doorway, the next he was down. MRT members recognized that it was time to extract from the target. Carrying Brink, who was unresponsive, they exfilled down the stairway and out of the house for another MEDEVAC. Schmidt ensured both wounded members were placed on board the helos and returned to the fight. Locating his friend, ATL Verdesi, together they ensured everyone was accounted for and redistributed personnel on the perimeter to prevent the shooter's escape.

All that had happened in the moments before my arrival.

More units responded, and we hardened the perimeter. In short order, we had another full team on hand, and the perimeter was locked down; however, we could not be 100 percent certain Trim was still in the residence. I advised the troop commander, upon his arrival, recommending that we had to ascertain if the shooter was still contained and that we didn't have time to waste. We could not permit this dangerous assailant to slip back into the community. That would be a *shit sandwich.* If he wasn't contained, we needed to know, and he agreed.

So, a plan was devised to introduce chemical munitions, CS gas, into the structure. We brought in key leaders, went over the detailed plan together in the van, and distributed the gas. We did not plan to enter at that time; our aim was to get Trim to surrender, or at least, confirm his presence by a reaction to the chemical agent. This was fairly straightforward. At approximately 11:00 AM, we introduced the gas. The house was adequately saturated, but no sign of Travis Trim. His failure to respond proved nothing definitively. Wisely, out of an abundance of caution, the troop commander had ordered troopers to check on the welfare of surrounding residents and maintain their vigilance in this relatively rural area.

Now the big bosses were arriving from Albany. I recall my captain and I briefing the field commander on the scene regarding our next proposed course of action: a deliberate entry. We could not allow this to go on for days. Sitting out here would be a dangerous fool's errand, if he were on the loose. So, I gathered our team leaders, and we devised a comprehensive plan to conduct a multi-breach point, three-team entry, into the structure. Again, immediately prior to entry, we would introduce copious amounts of chemical agents, something our guys were trained for. The key to this operation would be to reduce the possibility of cross fire, so limits of advance were set up internally.

As we prepared for the entry, assignments were given, chemical munitions were distributed, and weapons and communications were checked. Ambulances were put on standby and a local fire department had been called out and pre-positioned in case of fire. Frankly, we believed there was little chance of our CS rounds and canisters causing a fire, as we intended to use the type of munitions designed specifically for *indoor* use. However, make a mistake by utilizing a device meant for *outdoor* use, such as crowd control, and there would be a problem, as those munitions are pyrotechnically enhanced to aid deployment of the agent. So, although we made a point of reiterating the appropriate selection, use, and distribution of chemical munitions for this assignment, a fire truck from the Arkville Volunteer Fire Department was still brought up and positioned just out of small arms range, as a safety measure. In the past, we've experienced deranged, barricaded subjects set their own homes on fire and learned having fire services on site is always preferable. We had covered our bases, or so I thought, and told the bosses there was little risk of fire.

A final briefing was given, and it was time to get into position. At approximately 5:55 PM, we began attempting to "call out" Travis Trim. At approximately 6:00 PM, with all teams in position and no response, we commenced introducing chemical agents, in advance of our intended entry. Rounds were being deployed through windows by selected officers on the perimeter via 37mm and .12 gauge launchers. Additionally, I joined teams on the ground making the approach and deploying hand-held canisters into basement and hard-to-reach windows. As CS gas began dispensing, our team on the "two" side, or left side as you look at the house, observed flames around the window frame. In addition to the fire trucks, each team had a member in the stack (formation) carrying a fire extinguisher, per SOP, and we directed him to extinguish the blaze. Unfortunately, it didn't knock it down. A piece of upholstery and drapes must have been burning, because suddenly tall flames and plumes of smoke began pouring out of the window.

I got on the radio, "Get the fire truck up here!" I shouted. They were already moving, so a spotter on the perimeter must have noticed our attempt to extinguish the growing blaze. The fire truck arrived within seconds, and hoses were deployed expeditiously, but the fire was spreading. This old farmhouse is a *fucking tinderbox* I thought, and although water was being deployed, the flames were now into the second floor and spreading quickly across the front of the building, from left to right. The ambush and last known location of our target was in the top floor bedroom on the far right, and the fire was heading that way.

Suddenly, rounds started flying. Out of the corner of my left eye, I saw a firefighter drop to the ground and start rolling down the hill. Initially, I assumed he had been hit, but then he jumped back up and ran off behind a truck to seek cover. As luck would have it, this old hunting camp was chocked full of rifles, shotguns, and ammunition, much of which was beginning to "cook off," sending rounds everywhere. The firefighters were dropping their gear and retreating to safety behind cover, and who could blame them? They weren't getting paid for **this**! We were the only ones *stupid* enough to stand in front of this inferno.

Well this day can't get much worse, I thought, as I bent down and picked up an unmanned fire hose. Turning it on, I was now lamely putting water on the house. Then, out of nowhere, my friend and colleague Trooper Jay Curry, emerged from the dark with a ballistic shield, and positioned himself right in front of me, providing protection. I wasn't the only one playing "fireman," two or three other MRT pairs were trying to do the same thing.

Almost as quickly as it started, after burning for what seemed like forever, it burned itself out. The fire had consumed about 95% of the structure, including ravaging our target room. But, we're cops, not firefighters, and still had a bad guy to locate. So, we kept our perimeter weapons trained on the smoking mess and called for a ladder to access the second-floor bedroom from the ground. Carefully, our guys climbed onto the roof and through what was left of the window. Inside, they located what appeared to be a corpse, seated/slumped in the doorframe of what used to be the bedroom. Unfortunately, Travis Trim's life had ended here. Although we could take a deep breath, having apparently located our subject, I still would have to answer for how this fire started.

So, I went around the perimeter, searching in the dark for shell casings, knowing that the type of gas would be stamped right on the projectile's case. Three fourths of the way around the building, everything seemed in order. So far, all shell casings matched a munition deemed appropriate for *internal* use. Then, I reached my final stop, the pine tree-turned-firing-position, on the one-two corner, near the front left corner of the residence. There, on the ground, was a shell casing affiliated with a chemical munition recommended for *outdoor* use, most appropriately crowd control. Bingo. *That would do it!* I thought. I bent over to pick it up, just to make sure my eyes weren't playing tricks on me, when I spotted another. *Whoever had occupied this position,* I reasoned, *had been issued the wrong shit!* I thought,...*and I've got to advise somebody!* I dropped what I had in my hand, and got on the radio to my captain. "Sir," I said, over a secure frequency, "Looks like we may have caused this. Can you come to my location?"

"On my way...," he replied.

Within two minutes, Bob Nuzzo was standing in front of me under the tree, and I pointed at the shells on the ground.

"Are you sure?" he asked.

"Yes." I replied, pointing to the culprit shell casings.

"Fuck," he said, to no one in particular. "Before I came up here, I was told the superintendent was going on live TV to discuss today's events.

Undoubtedly, he will be asked about the cause of the fire, and we told him there was no real cause for concern."

"True," I said. "Apparently, we issued someone the wrong shit." Both of us knew instantaneously, we had to stop the superintendent before he went on camera.

Bob called ahead and got one of the execs on the line. The response was basically, "Get down here to the CP ASAP!" Totally understood. We pulled into the barracks I had left nearly 12 hours earlier that day, and approached the front steps. The door opened quickly, and Colonel John Melville stepped out. Although he rapidly closed the door behind him, we could hear the voices of the occupants inside, and they weren't happy. Again, completely understandable.

Colonel Melville knew why we were there. In fact, by the end of the discussion, it was obvious he had stepped in to save us. The colonel asked, "Just how did this happen? I thought we were OK with the gas."

I explained the error. Basically, despite my directives to ensure we were issuing the correct chemical munitions, something went wrong, and we had issued chemical munitions intended for outdoor use only. Put the wrong stuff into a house, and there's a good chance of starting a fire. "This is on us, Colonel," I said.

Later review would reveal that part of the blame could be attributed to the fact that each team separated and stored its chemical munitions in different containers, within their respective vehicles. There was no standardization, something that would be addressed in the AAR and resolved by SOP. We accepted responsibility for the foul up. That said, the Incident Commander at the time, the Troop "C" Commander, still characterized the overall mission, stating publicly: "The only thing I can tell you is that our operation yesterday was well-planned, well-thought out, and well executed."

Before the deployment to conduct entry, we'd found out that teammate Rich Mattson had undergone a lengthy surgery and was fighting for his life at Albany Medical Center and, tragically, Trooper David Brinkerhoff had died at Margaretville Memorial Hospital. A second fatality on the team, in less than a year, but this wouldn't be the worst of the news.

Within days, a colonel walked into the office Captain Nuzzo and I shared and asked, "Does our .223 rifle ammunition have a "T" imprinted on the bottom of the round?"

"Yes, Sir," I said. "It stands for "tactical bonded," knowing the crime scene guys were processing what was left of the house in Troop "C".

He stepped into the office fully and closed the door. He said, "What I'm about to tell you two, does not leave this room. Understood?"

"Yes, Sir," we both replied, straightening up.

"Trooper Brinkerhoff was killed by one of our rounds," he said. The words came out of his mouth as if in slow motion. "The Medical Examiner (ME) has determined that the entry wound came from behind, and the round that penetrated his helmet is a .223, marked by a "T". He continued, "The superintendent himself will be the one delivering the news, first to your team, and then to the media. Keep it between yourselves for now."

This was a crushing blow. One that no one could have seen coming.

Acting Superintendent Preston Felton gathered the team in the Academy library and broke the tragic news, as well as anyone could. We experienced an array of emotions, shock, disbelief, anger, denial – the gambit. It all came crashing down upon unsuspecting team members.

Months of investigation and forensic analysis would reveal that Trooper Brinkerhoff was, in fact, shot upon entering the room by the assailant, but the vest saved his life from that first round. Brink then returned fire and took cover in the doorway. It was Dave Brinkerhoff himself, who had fired the round in self-defense that was responsible for killing Travis Trim. Thus, explaining why Trim's body was found in the doorway, where he knelt while cocking his lever-action rifle to chamber another round. Unbeknownst to the team at that time, Trim was dead, but additional rounds were fired, as Mattson was being evacuated. It was at this point that tragedy struck, and an MRT member firing from behind Brinkerhoff, at the shooter's last known position, inadvertently hit Dave in the back of the head, killing him instantly.

However, we would not learn that level of detail for months, and it opened a bitter wound on the team. One that would take months, if not years, to heal.

Days later, we were attending another funeral, for our beloved Brother, and fellow MRT operator, Trooper Dave Brinkerhoff. Months earlier we had buried his classmate Trooper Joe Longobardo, feeling some solace that at least we had captured Phillips. This time, the loss was punctuated by the reality that it occurred as a result of "friendly fire." Although it was completely accidental, even rationalized by some as a chaotic moment during the "fog of war," it tore us apart. Trooper Rich Mattson, former professional soccer player and fellow MRT member survived, but did not regain sufficient use of his arm to permit his return to the State Police and was retired as a technical sergeant.

I can only imagine the *unrealized* potential that existed between these three men. My heart goes out to their loved ones and fellow troopers.

Acting Superintendent Preston Felton, our new boss, publicly addressed our team and our loss from this tragic incident saying: "This was a very volatile situation. While it's clear something went wrong, nothing can detract from the bravery and dedication of the men who entered that house. They are a highly trained and dedicated group who understood the dangers of what they were doing, and they accepted the risks."

At the conclusion of the funeral service, Superintendent Felton gathered the MRT together at the SP Coxsackie Barracks, Brink's former station in the Catskills, and told the men that he supported their move to full time. It is what the guys needed to hear, although there was no celebrating. However, the superintendent wisely issued a caveat: this would be done in an orderly fashion, supervised by the field commander, and only after the requisite SOPs and program modifications were in place. I agreed wholeheartedly. This is a marathon, not a sprint. *Let's do it right!*

The process, including two successive basic schools to replenish and increase our numbers and a name change for the team, would take the better part of a year and a half to accomplish.

Chapter 11

TRANSITION

That summer two important steps were taken: First, creation of the team's first comprehensive SOP, and second, and more critical, a complete revision of the way in which candidates were selected for the team.

Although the MRT had been in existence since 1984, it had always been <u>part time</u>, except for the year, immediately following 9/11, when the team was deployed to Ground Zero. That meant only one full-time member, a sergeant, known as the Team Coordinator, tended to every need – administrative, training, equipment, etc. One man, a veritable jack of all trades. Without any dedicated assistance (all other members were assigned to road patrol), the team coordinator lacked both the time and depth of knowledge necessary to independently construct a comprehensive SOP.

In July of 2007, as a necessary precursor to proceeding to full time, that task fell to me, as the OIC. I was pleased to do it, as it indicated progress, but required assistance. So, I set about identifying the committee of SMEs, a cross section of 14 select MRT members representing each team around the state, who would assist me over the next four weeks. This was a massive undertaking. I had identified at least 25 separate, detailed chapters for development, covering such subjects as: raids, woodland searches, barricaded subjects, fast roping, helicopter operations, rope rescue, chemical munitions, firearms, armored vehicle operations, less-lethal munitions, dignitary protection…you get the picture. At first, I received unexpected resistance from Headquarters. "Why do you need so many people? Can't two or three of you just lock yourselves in an office and put it together? Why do you need a month to accomplish this?"

Frankly, I was stunned. This team had existed for 23 years without an SOP, and now, they did not want to invest the time and personnel to get it right. In light of recent tragic events, I pushed back…hard.

"Look," I said respectfully, in sum and substance, "Our list of capabilities is enormous. Although there is some operational crossover, each capability requires very specific protocols, and in some instances, detailed procedures to govern and guide our execution. Remember the mix-up on chemical munitions? In order for us to prevent that, and things like it, from happening again, we've got to get this right. As far as the number of people, I need our best SMEs on this. We've got people who have received advanced training, instructor-level status, in a variety of areas: firearms, chemical munitions, aviation operations, high-angle rope rescue and the like, and they <u>must</u> be involved in production. I've assigned a cross section from the various units to keep the teams balanced in the field, for everyday, real-world responses and to achieve across the board buy-in. If we attempt to put together a document with two guys in a vacuum at HQ, operators will rightly challenge its credibility. You've asked me to do this, and we're not going full time without it; so, let's do it right!" With the staunch support of Captain Nuzzo, I got my wish.

"OK, you've got exactly 30 days to wrap it up. No more!" came the admonishment from above.

We worked tirelessly, including several nights and weekends on our own time, to get it done. Exactly 30 days to the day, we presented the completed manual to the Field Commander of the NYSP in a brief presentation held in the Academy library. "Good work, men. I appreciate what went into this," he said from the heart.

When he left the room, I then inquired behind closed doors, "What's next...?"

Well, I was told, it must go through the various sections in Division HQ for sign-off, then to the superintendent for approval. I knew the superintendent had to approve it, but the "various sections...?" What the hell does somebody in HR or Planning and Research know about operating a Bearcat? *This will take forever!*

Unfortunately, I was wasn't wrong. With the variety of questions and flat out delays in circulating the binder around the building, it would be two and a half years, and <u>two</u> superintendents *later*, before it would be approved. In the interim, we'd graduated two new classes, and even transitioned to full-time operations, *absent* the SOP. This was UNSAT! One day, I received another request for rewrite, from some genius questioning our reference to the Bearcat armored vehicle. We had included on the specs page that the Bearcat had "12, 4.5 inch gun ports"; this information had been taken from the manufacturer. The reviewer wielding the red pen had corrected it to "12.5 inch gun ports." I lost my damn mind and walked directly into my new boss, Chris Fiore's office. Chris knew the building as well as anyone and was as sick of the BS regarding this SOP, as me.

I said, "Major, apparently instead of <u>twelve</u>, 4.5 inch gun ports, we now have 12.5 inch gun ports, the size of freaking *basketballs* on the Bearcat! It took us 30 days to write the SOP, and we've been operating full time now for *a year* without it." Imagine the agency's liability! He agreed, wholeheartedly, and managed to somehow finally bypass the nonsense and obtain the new superintendent's signature. UFB!

Frankly, the time had come in our pivotal history, that the caliber of MRT candidates and the training regimen had peaked. Tragedies over the summer of 2006 and spring of 2007 were dissected, and the lessons learned clearly dictated a change was necessary. And, I believed that*: To truly honor our fallen comrades and attempt to prevent similar occurrences, the desired changes could not be subtle; they must be far-reaching and transformational.* So, the next, even more-vital aspect of transitioning to full time, was to address the unit's <u>selection</u> process.

If we'd learned nothing else from the tragic loss of Troopers Joe Longobardo in Fredonia and Dave Brinkerhoff in Margaretville, it was this – tactical team members would be subjected to the worst of the worst conditions. By definition, they would have to enter the most volatile of environments, often times long after the possibility for a peaceful resolution had passed, and without fail or defect, be expected to take care of business. This would include dynamic entries and shootouts, requiring the ability to maintain a clear, logical, analytical thought process, while being fired upon; and maintaining fire discipline and operating with surgical precision, under the most extreme and chaotic conditions. Failure in either of these areas could mean the difference between life and death.

Historically, although we drew from a pool of highly motivated, physically fit, troopers, clearly, <u>not everyone</u> was cut out for this type of work. So, while maintaining our previous two-day tryouts (consisting of a PT test, obstacle course, firearms qualification, and interview), as what is now known as *Pre*-Selection, we recognized we needed a completely <u>new</u> method of selecting candidates for our revised Basic Operators Course.

In talking with my good friend, the team's NCOIC at the time, Sergeant Ron Pastino, both of us knew that to make a difference, we would need a complete departure from what had become the established "norm." Recognizing also, that anything we came up with would be an almost-insurmountable tough sell to Division, we wisely opted to approach the FBI Hostage Rescue Team (HRT) for advice. Besides, *why reinvent the wheel?*

HRT, the nation's premier Tier One domestic law enforcement tactical team had been in existence since 1984, and through extensive collaboration with the U.S. military and other top-flight tactical teams around the world, had finely honed their skills and were rated among the best of the best. Not the least of which was their outstanding Selection Process, something for which they were well-known and respected within the special operations community. Having worked with them briefly at the Phillips Investigation, I knew their worth. Equally, I knew that they had come to assist us, in our hour of need, because Ron Pastino himself had personally and quietly cultivated a relationship with HRT. So, Ron had the *in* and reached out to his contact in Quantico to inquire if this was an area in which they'd be willing to assist. Typically, this is not something the FBI gets involved with, but desperate times call for desperate measures. Because the HRT had been with us at the Phillips manhunt right before Troopers Baker and Longobardo had been shot, <u>and</u> knew we had sustained another hit recently with the loss of Trooper Brinkerhoff, they agreed to help us.

None of this would've been possible if not for Ron Pastino.

I first met Ron in 1996. I was a trooper at the time on routine patrol out of SP Newburgh, Zone Two, Troop "F". There I was, sitting just off the road on RT 9W running stationary radar when, out of the corner of my eye, I noticed some "mope" approaching my troop car on foot. I'm sure any cop can relate, because they've all been there before. Although I could see his hands, and he looked harmless enough, without enough time to exit my vehicle, I still rested my hand on my gun as I rolled down the window to ask, "Can I help you?"

I was greeted by, "Excuse me, Trooper. I just got my acceptance letter to the Academy and report next week. Can you tell me anything about what to expect?"

Before opening up, I asked him a couple of probing questions – *you know, trust but verify, right?* I came to learn that Ron had been an active duty Army MP and, most recently, a local town police officer. Based on his military experience and past assignment as a MP Special Response Team member, the conversation ultimately turned to his interest in our MRT. With our chance encounter, Ron sort of struck gold. Having been an active Army soldier myself for six years, joining the State Police, and recent graduation from the MRT school, there was an immediate connection. However, I cautioned him, "Dude, you've got a long way to go. Let's make it through the Academy first!"

Over the years, I kept tabs on Ron; commencing with my role as a DT instructor, while training him and other members of his 1996 Academy class. Ron not only graduated from the Academy, but earned the award for highest physical fitness. A good start for a wannabe SWAT guy!

Upon graduation, Ron was initially assigned to a neighboring station. As an FTO, I'd heard "good things" about his progress from those working with him. But, it was when Ron transferred down to Newburgh, that I really got a chance to know him. Trust me, you learn everything you need to know about someone when you're responding to calls together night after night. I was duly impressed. A few short years later, the MRT was about to hold tryouts. By this time, I had been promoted to sergeant and was the South Team Leader, so you might think that Ron had a leg up...not exactly. First, although Ron was turning out to be a great cop, he would face very tough competition coming from other outstanding members trying out. Second, my philosophy is, *it doesn't matter who you know, you have to earn your own way,* and the proof would be during tryouts. So, I wished Ron, "Good luck," and told him, "Don't hold anything back."

Ron, as it turned out, crushed it. He was a natural and earned one of the coveted slots on the team. A hard worker and quick study, Ron became a "go to" guy in relatively short order. He had a remarkable ability to get things done and didn't shy away from a challenge. Perhaps most importantly, Ron possessed the one quality, above all, that would make him a natural selection for future leadership responsibility on the team, and that is *selfless service*. Always looking for ways to elevate the team and take care of the men, Ron was intently focused on bringing this team to the next level. He and I had countless discussions on the subject. Constantly assessing where we were as a team and where we needed to be. Safety and operational effectiveness were driving concerns, for we envisioned a day when the team may be called on to do more than we were perhaps capable of. The world was changing, and so must we.

To his credit, Ron would not rest until he did everything in his power to ensure we would be ready, and for his efforts, he was promoted to technical sergeant and administrative sergeant in late 2001, later taking over as team coordinator in 2004.

Ron's most enduring legacy to the team, in my view, was his drive and ability to make contact with other tactical teams around the state and federal agencies, including direct outreach to Tier One entities within the military. He established personal and professional affiliations, which would benefit the team, especially in the critical areas of selection, equipment, and tactics, techniques, and procedures.

Subsequently, several of us were invited to visit the FBI Academy, where I had spent nearly three months in 2005 attending their National Academy with 250 other law enforcement professionals from around the world. During the visit, we spent a great deal of time studying the HRT's two-week Selection Process. Modeled after some of the military's top Special Operations Forces, it results in identifying the "right" candidates for further tactical training. It is a proven concept, but one that would likely face hurdles within the State Police, because of its radical departure from the past. The task of selling the new program would fall largely to me. Fortunately, after much convincing, the powers that be supported our plan and adopted the program.

So, in the fall of 2007, we conducted the first NYSP Selection Program, modeled exactly after the HRT's proven process. The program was an immense success, and without going into detail, delivered exactly what we were looking for. Like the FBI, we experienced a 70% attrition rate and in early 2008, commenced a revamped Basic Operators Course, with those candidates who had successfully finished Selection.

During the six months of the school, I performed double duty as *both* the OIC of the school and remained responsible for supervising the four operational teams in the field. So, it was critical that I chose just the right man to run the day-to-day training program. That individual was Sergeant Shad Crowe. A hard-charging, detailed-oriented NCO, who lead by example in everything he did. Shad, ever cognizant of the importance of his role as the first NCOIC of our revitalized training program, brought those studs through to graduation. They are now known as Generation One, or Gen. 1. This was proof of concept! Since then, Shad shepherded a second school through for me in 2010 (Gen. 2), a tremendous act of service to the Division and the team. Certainly, something for which I would be forever personally grateful. Since then, two more classes, Gens. 3 and 4 have joined the team, forever cementing the shift in paradigm.

During the interim, after receiving the first graduating class, the MRT finally, *officially* transitioned to full time, onto what is now called the Special Operations Response Team (SORT). Due to an across the board change in our work rules, a name change was deemed necessary by Human Resources, in order to make a clean break. I chose and put forward the name SORT, which was approved by the chain of command, because it was straightforward, described what we were about, and preserved at least some part of our original title (Response Team), in deference to those who had come before us. So, in February 2009, after much effort, tumult, triumph, and great sacrifice, Division <u>finally</u> had a full-time tactical team.

By the summer of 2010, I had my 20 years on with the State Police, figured I had done what I could for the job and my teammates, and was considering what else might be out there. At the time, the United States was winding things down in Iraq, but stepping things up in Afghanistan, looking for law enforcement advisors. I was looking for a change, a new challenge, and applied. With my resume, I received immediate attention and began processing for a well-known contractor. With the background check nearing completion, I had been requested to provide uniform sizes and was being earmarked for deployment to Afghanistan in October 2010, some 45 days hence.

That changed in late August 2010, when I received a call from the Office of the Superintendent; he wanted to see me on the third floor. I reported in and was greeted by Acting Superintendent John Melville, a life-long trooper, who enjoyed the deep respect of everyone in the agency. "Have a seat, Chuck," he said. Continuing, "I'm in position to make a few promotions, and I'd like to promote you to Captain." That was great news, as I'm sure he could tell by the look on my face. "It gets better…," he said, "The best part is, I plan to keep you in Emergency Management. You'll continue to remain involved with SORT, in addition to providing direct oversight of: K9, BDU, SCUBA, CCSERT; all things you're very familiar with."

"That's outstanding, Sir!" I said.

"Chuck, your leadership has been instrumental to the team. I think it's a good fit," he replied.

"Thank you, Sir! I said. "It would be an honor and a privilege. I won't let you down."

Later that afternoon, I contacted the corporation that had been processing my application for overseas assignment and, citing promotion, withdrew my name. I was looking *for a "new"* challenge, and now I had it, as a captain, within the Office of Emergency Management, in charge of Division's specialized units.

CHAPTER 12

PERSEVERANCE LEADS TO A BREAKTHROUGH

By the morning of **Saturday, June 20,** we had been at it for 15 days, two weeks – that had seemed like an eternity. We had closed the 16-square-mile search box around Dannemora days ago, having swept through a portion of the Town of Willsboro, during a two-day push in response to a "sighting," coming up empty. Additionally, we were in the midst of responding to tips in Alleghany County, some 350 miles southwest of the prison. Having investigated over 2,200 leads by this point, we were incrementally expanding, regionally, and throughout the North Country, sending patrols in cruisers, by boat, by helicopter, on foot, and by ATV, in ever-expanding vectors into the woods and along the network of trails, seasonal roads, power lines, train tracks, and waterways, which intersect throughout the area.

These were trying times. We had been on a continuously heightened state of alert for two weeks. Having saturated the area with more than 800 law enforcement and correction officers, who'd intently prosecuted the target area; still we had little to show for our efforts. The public had been incredibly supportive, but nerves were on edge, and who could blame them.

As troopers from around the state, and federal agents from around the country, were cycling through the detail, some for their second deployment, morale was waning. You could see it in their faces. My concerns were two-fold: 1) We would become complacent and someone would overlook some small detail, or fail to carry out a necessary investigative step, and the inmates would complete their escape, and/or 2) We would become complacent, and someone would get killed. Either way, *complacency* was the "enemy." Additionally, I reasoned, as time went on, Matt and Sweat would become increasingly desperate and therefore more dangerous, not less so. If a member of the public or law enforcement let their guard down, they could become an easy target.

I was convinced there was nothing these two men wouldn't do to affect their escape. Maintaining morale was a challenge. I told our law enforcement team repeatedly, "Today is the day!" to remind them that at <u>any</u> given moment, inside the trunk of a car they were about to check, hiding in a seasonal camp or outbuilding, or lurking behind a tree in the woods, these guys could pop up and take your life. *"You must remain focused and vigilant,"* I urged. It was not only vital for the investigation, it could also save their lives.

The first time I used that phrase, about seven days in, was in front of a mostly "new" group of 200 or so State Troopers and Forest Rangers, who were assembled for a briefing occurring in a Dannemora gymnasium. They had just received their post assignments and safety instructions for their tour of duty, something Troop "B" officers and NCOs had been providing twice daily since the beginning of the search. I was standing off to the side and could tell from the looks on some of the troopers faces, and glances they casually exchanged among each other, that the constant media hype that: *"These two are long gone…probably in Mexico by now…,"* was having a negative effect. Doubt had crept into their minds, and that could lead to complacency, and *"complacency kills!"* So, when the Safety Officer asked, "Do you have anything you'd like to add, Major?"

I stepped forward and said, **"Today is the day!"**

I could read in the eyes of those in the front row, that they had no idea what I was talking about. I repeated myself, "Today is the day! That <u>must</u> be your *mindset* when you walk out this door and take your posts. If your head is not in the game, you <u>will</u> make mistakes! Block out that crap you're hearing in the media. They, and those talking heads they hire, don't know a freakin' thing about what we're doing here. This investigation is based on facts: 1) We don't have any evidence they have made connection with anyone on the outside who has assisted them out of the area. 2) We have no evidence of any stolen vehicles. 3) We don't see any money transfers, or hits on the phone taps, that indicate they're talking to anyone. 4) There is no evidence they've hopped on a train, stolen a boat, or crossed any border. Therefore, if we have *no evidence* that they have left the area, we *must* act as though they are still *here*, and conduct the search accordingly. If you can't wrap your minds around that, then see one of my sergeants, because we'll have to send you home for your own safety."

I was not being dramatic. Remaining focused was critical to the operation. As I spoke, I could see heads nodding in agreement. This group understood. But I knew this was fleeting, and we, the leaders, would have to remain resolute and push that message. Our survival and success would depend upon it. And, so it happened, the phrase "Today's the day!" became sort of a mantra. Due to the buy-in and additional emphasis provided by my staff, I was pleased to see that from time to time, throughout the remainder of the detail, troopers would pass me in the hallway or in the field and greet me with, "Today's the day, Sir!" Internally, I prayed for the day it would become reality, but we still had a long way to go.

However, **June 20, 2015,** the courageous actions of a local man, would lead to our biggest break in the case so far. As our investigation revealed, and would later be reported *directly* to me by the man himself, John Stockwell took it upon himself that Saturday morning, to check his seasonal hunting cabin near the Hamlet of Mountain View, NY, a mere 14 miles southeast of the Village of Malone. Arming himself with a .38 caliber handgun, he saddled up his ATV, and with his dog, a six-year-old Lab named "Dolly," headed out. During our numerous press conferences and releases, we had been soliciting the assistance of the public, "Call us with any tips or concerns. If you happen to check on your hunting camps or trail cameras, let us know if anything seems out of the ordinary." Stockwell, an off-duty correction officer, was going to take a look for himself.

Access to the remote cabin, called "Twisted Horn Hunting Club," on Black Cat Mountain, in the Town of Bellmont, NY, (population 1,444) was difficult. Leased by several area residents, including correction officers, the cabin contained few amenities: a sink, gas stove, wood stove, and electricity supplied by generator. This is representative of most seasonal camps in the area. Access required Stockwell to embark on a journey down a dirt road, Wolf Pond Road, with an ATV in the bed of his GMC pickup, followed by a quad ride of roughly two miles farther down a remote, rocky trail, of alternating mud and ruts, encompassed by thick brush and overhead canopy. This trail, however, was nothing special, just one of hundreds like it traversing the area, leading to secluded cabins in the region. At three or four miles per hour, the ATV ride would take 20-30 minutes on a good day.

As Stockwell entered a small clearing and approached the cabin at around 10:00 AM, he noticed his dog had stopped dead in her tracks. Facing the front of the structure, her ears had reportedly perked up, and the hair on her back bristled. Stockwell, knew immediately something was wrong, dismounted his ATV, and stepping closer toward a tree for cover, drew his handgun. Focusing on the large window on the front door, Stockwell could see clear through the small, two-room cabin, all the way to the window and door along the back wall, which led to a deck. Simultaneously, he observed what he thought was the figure of a man step back from the window. Moving further to the right, to improve his angle and cover, he saw through the same window what appeared to be a man with a hood up over his head, moving near the rear of the cabin. Fearing the worst, that there was at least one intruder, and quite possibly two, Stockwell, gun drawn, "challenged" the intruders, ordering them to come out with their hands up, to which he received no response.

Stockwell was well-trained and smart enough to know, that if he attempted to just swing the ATV around and drive out of there, he might well be shot in the back, merely to prevent his departure and facilitate taking his vehicle, so he held his ground. Challenging them again, he suddenly heard a commotion outside the cabin, and then heard what he believed to be two men "crashing" down off the back deck, running down the slope towards a stream behind the cabin. Finally, the stalemate was broken. This was the opportunity Stockwell needed to escape. He had a cell phone, but no service and was, quite possibly, out-numbered by two fugitives. *Had they armed themselves?* he mused. It was a hunting camp, so that was certainly possible. Stockwell, wisely, did not stick around to find out. Hopping back on his ATV and calling to his dog, who'd likely just saved his life, he headed out, determined to notify the State Troopers!

To obtain a cell signal, Stockwell knew he had to go all the way out to the main road, and then some, just to find coverage. Along the way, he met other civilians on the road, who said they had just observed a troop car pass them minutes earlier. Stockwell briefly relayed the encounter and asked the others to try to catch up with the troopers. He would continue toward an establishment down the road, where he was certain he could get cell service or use of a landline phone. They agreed, and before long, as a result of Stockwell's 911 call and his cohorts catching up to the roving troop car, he was able to meet State Police Sergeant Bob Dixon and two of his troopers at the trailhead. Together, they radioed-in the location and the nature of the sighting, requested back up, and headed deep into the woods to investigate, knowing that time was of the essence.

Arriving at the cabin, the troopers tactically cleared the interior and searched the immediate surrounding area. In the cabin, Stockwell noted that a map had been taken from the wall, a coffee pot was out of place, a jar of peanut butter had been left out on the kitchen table, and a water jug had been opened. It appeared the fugitives had been there, at least overnight, used the generator, a radio (to monitor law enforcement), cooked food, and availed themselves of alcohol.

Additionally, it appeared, and would later be confirmed, a .20-gauge shotgun was missing from the cabin. Proceeding out the rear door, onto the back deck, and down the slope some 30-40 yards into the woods, the troopers also observed that, whoever had been in the cabin had sure left in a hurry. They had dropped numerous articles of "personal" property while scrambling down the bank and along the stream, in their haste to escape. Cautious not to get too deep into the woods, as they did not want to contaminate a possible "track" for the canines that were en route, or disturb any evidence, the troopers wisely held their ground. This was a major development! For the first time in two weeks, it appeared we had a valid sighting. More work would need to be done to confirm that, but this lead would ultimately prove to be of vital significance. As for Mr. Stockwell, his role, vigilance, and courage, in this 30-second encounter, is to be saluted. Humbly, he gives the credit to his best friend, his dog, Dolly, telling me, *"If Dolly wasn't with me that day, I could have walked right into camp where they were."*

In relatively short order, the cavalry arrived: additional troopers to secure the perimeter; K9 handlers with their German Shepherds and

Bloodhounds; a tactical team to recon deep into the woods; Aviation to conduct an airborne search; and the Troop "B" Forensic Identification Unit. FIU, our superb crime scene technicians and specialists, so integral to everything we'd done since Day 1, and would continue to do going forward, responded to the scene to process, document, and photograph the site with numerous items of evidence, which had been left behind in the inmates' hasty departure, such as: latent fingerprints, water bottles, a plastic spoon, cigarette butts, a jar of peanut butter, in the cabins interior. Items dropped near the brook, as they rushed to vacate the area included: black boots, socks, a camouflage rain suit, trail knife and sheath, Ziploc bag containing a bar of soap wrapped in cloth, hair brush, roll of duct tape, Ziploc bag containing socks and Corcraft boxers (produced at DOCCS by inmates), and Moccasin-style slippers. The inmates also dropped a cloth toiletries bag which contained: a hair trimmer, toothbrush, Bic lighter, toothpaste, nail clippers, deodorant, light wand, and a bag with a quantity of pills. A virtual treasure trove for our analysts.

Throughout the remainder of the day, and into the night, Black Cat Mountain, Mountain View, and the Owls Head area in general, were bustling with activity. A temporary Tactical Operations Center, was set up at the nearby Owls Head Fire Department, as nearly 600 officers attempted to set up some semblance of a "perimeter;" including: roving patrols, check points, road blocks, light towers, and an aerial Quick Reaction Force, an enormous, nearly impossible task, in this wilderness. At the Twisted Horn Hunting Club itself, activity continued late into the night. The target area was thoroughly searched and the evidence, once photographed, and collected in accordance with scientific protocols, was packaged, secured, and transported to the New York State Police Forensic Investigation Center (FIC) in Albany.

The very next day, **Sunday, June 21, Day 16,** at approximately 11:30 AM, we had what we had been waiting for, confirmed DNA matches from the cabin, proving that both inmates had been there. In a remarkable turnaround of less than 9 hours, the FIC (lab) had found DNA matches of both inmates, obtained from items that had been dropped from their packs as they exited the cabin. This was proof positive that Matt and

Sweat had been at the Twisted Horn Hunting Club as recently as the day before; not Mexico or Canada, as the press had come to infer. And, while we didn't know for sure, we had no reason to believe they weren't still travelling together; although, our tactics allowed for the possibility of their separation.

With this development, the State Police could now call off the recently initiated search occurring in Western New York's Troop "A", which had been searching in Alleghany County, 350 miles away, for the better part of 24 hours. Once again, we could focus exclusively, on the North Country, something *we* never took for granted. Our "full- court press" had yielded our first big break. Accordingly, within the next 24 hours, my numbers of personnel on the ground would increase from 600 to more than 1,000, including a surge of additional tactical teams, ATVs, and aircraft.

After intense searching and activity, on **Tuesday, June 23, Day 18,** we held another press conference at our Command Post, Headquartered at Caddyville Elementary School, during which I read a statement summarizing the events and developments of the last few days, stating: "As a result of a burglary to a seasonal camp in Mountain View, on Saturday, June 20, evidence has been discovered in a remote cabin near Owls Head (25 miles west of the prison), 'conclusively' determining that both Matt and Sweat had been there." Considering the recent activity, 350 miles away in Western New York, I wanted to set the record straight and said, "The region around Dannemora (meaning Northern New York) remains the primary focus of our investigation. We ask the public to remain on alert and take any necessary precautions. Report anything out of the ordinary. This is especially true of seasonal camp owners, now that the summer season is here." I continued, "We have recovered specific evidence from the cabin and forwarded it to the appropriate laboratory and reached a conclusive determination, but are not prepared to release that evidence at this time, so we do not jeopardize the continuity of the investigation."

Adding, "We currently have more than 1,000 law enforcement personnel now involved in the search in a remote section of Franklin County, but there are a number of factors that make this a complex search:

weather, the terrain, the environment and frankly the vast scope of the North Country of the Adirondacks." I further acknowledged the difficult work ahead for our searchers (due to pouring rain, thick vegetation, swamps, bogs, mountainous, nearly impenetrable landscape in some areas) and renewed my call to the public to check their camps and trail cameras, requesting: "Let us know if you have captured footage of any suspicious activity."

Most of the questions I received afterward focused on DNA and weapons. *"Sources"* had already advised the press that we had recovered: DNA, from a variety of items recovered at the scene and that a shotgun may be missing. As a matter of investigative protocol, I could neither confirm, deny, or offer clarity on those subjects. Although this was the first confirmation we had that the inmates now possessed a .20-gauge shotgun, we had always operated under the assumption they were armed, so this did not affect our tactics or strategy one bit.

I was then asked how I justify the growing cost of the search. I said, "I don't concern myself with the cost of the search; I concern myself with finding the inmates." Thinking to myself, *If this is your most burning question, pal, considering the danger to the community and first responders, and this latest development, then this is a good place to wrap it up!*

I closed by reminding residents, who, many if not most, had armed themselves at home, to keep their doors locked and lights on, and by thanking them for their continued patience and cooperation.

The enormous influx of additional resources was an example of our resolve, and the State Police, would later release the following notice: "All available assets are being deployed around the clock. Law enforcement is maintaining a strong and visible presence in the region, and that will continue until we bring this matter to a close."

Clearly, we were excited, as we had recovered DNA, a concrete lead pinning them to the area, which provided us a much-needed shot in the arm! In fact, the media got it right when the *Press-Republican* quoted "sources" as saying: *"The energy* (among law enforcement) *is just fantastic"* and *"It looks like Mrs. (Joyce) Mitchell was Plan A. There was no Plan B. They don't have a plan now, other than to evade us."* [9]

Fortunately, residents did not view our enhanced police presence as overly intrusive, but appropriate for the circumstances. In fact, Terry Bellinger, owner of Belly's Mountain View Inn, in the heart of the search zone, perhaps put it best, when upon observing the massive police response in the area, remarked to the *Adirondack Daily Enterprise*, *"Normally, we don't get this much excitement in Mountain View in three lifetimes."* [10]

We later learned through interviews with Inmate Sweat, that he and Matt had been holed up at Twisted Horn for several days, staying out of some particularly nasty weather. Weather that our search crews had to endure day and night. According to Sweat, the only one of the two we could interview, Matt had become comfortable at the cabin. There was food, water, alcohol, a stove – all the comforts of home. They had located a .20-gauge shotgun between two mattresses in the bunkroom, but much to their disappointment, <u>no</u> ammunition. This would later bode well for Mr. Stockwell during his approach to the cabin.

Sweat claims that Matt was "drunk" most of the time and in no hurry to depart the cabin, to reenter the mosquito-infested woods. Sweat, however, reasoned that with the improvement in weather and approach of the weekend, it was entirely possible that one or more camp owners may come out to check on their property. It turns out he was prescient. When Saturday morning came along, it was a beautiful day and the weekend. An argument reportedly ensued between the two men, with Matt proclaiming if anyone came down the trail, he'd take them hostage, or just kill them and take their vehicle.

That morning, the 20th, Sweat was packed up ready to go, when they heard an ATV and a dog entering the clearing. Armed with a shotgun, but no ammunition, and noting the approaching individual (Stockwell) was armed, Sweat headed out the back door. Matt, was apparently scrambling to get his personal effects into his open backpack, while he too headed down the slope, dropping a number of items along the way. Items we would retrieve and scientifically exploit. However, turning that new intelligence into actionable, operational success would require unyielding operational synergy and a dose of luck.

Knowing we had the "A-team" in place, and with more resources arriving daily, I believed we were *tightening the noose*. All I had to do was continue to instill confidence, provide a bit of vision, and let the "big dogs" run!

While it had taken decades to develop my personalized brand of leadership, I recognized that I had recently completed a command assignment that had tested and honed that skill set in unexpected ways. *I was a better leader for it, and I would tap into every bit of that experience going forward...*

CHAPTER 13

AVIATION

By June 2011, as the captain in the Office of Emergency Management, I was in my element, and was viewed as a subject matter expert by Division; I fully expected to finish out my career there.

Each of the units under my purview was run by a sharp NCO, who defined the term "consummate professional." I thoroughly enjoyed working with these experts, and the teams they represented. However, they were *so* good, I did not feel particularly challenged. Yet, as I fought going on auto-pilot, I thought to myself, *Who's got it better than me?*

Then, our new Superintendent, Joseph D'Amico, would make me an offer I couldn't refuse and catapult my career in an entirely unexpected direction.

Walking into HQ one morning, I was aware of the buzz surrounding the current major-in-charge of Division Aviation, an accomplished pilot, a colleague from my days in Troop "F". The rumor mill was churning, as it had been released over the preceding weekend, that the press had published an article claiming a Division helicopter assigned to an air show on Long Island had been used to give off-duty troopers rides, around the venue. Although, this may have been a longstanding, discrete practice at the air show, and was not intended to detract from the mission, it had. Clearly, it was not a "mission-essential" use of aircraft, and the "optics" for the agency were terrible. To make matters worse, the major – detail commander – himself, had been on site. Before long, word circulated that the major had filed his retirement paperwork.

This unexpected development came as a shock to the Aviation Unit. The XO at Aviation, a lieutenant, suddenly had his hands full and making his life infinitely more difficult, was the ensuing Internal Affairs investigation. As a result of the recent transgression, the Internal Affairs Bureau, or

IAB as they were commonly known, was directed to conduct a thorough audit of unit operations. The thought being, if there was one non-standard practice occurring, perhaps there could be more.

During the audit, a keen IAB Investigator, who had been conducting an inventory of Division-issued equipment at the unit, in this case GPSes, came up short. In essence, open-source reporting and court records alleged that: months earlier, during the recently retired major's tenure, six aviation-capable Garmin GPS units had been purchased and delivered. These units were destined for aircraft located at SP Aviation facilities across the state, but would have to get checked in through the system first to be issued a property number. The six boxes were left on the unit's staff sergeant's desk for entry into the system. The NCO noticed that of the six boxes, only five were sealed; the sixth box was open and contained a "used" older model GPS. Something was not right with the order, and the NCO contacted Garmin and the vendor, wondering if a reconditioned GPS had somehow made it into the order in error. "No," came the response from the vendor, "All models shipped were new." Sensing a problem, the NCO brought the GPS unit in question to the major, who allegedly said words to the effect, "Leave it with me, I'll look into it. Get the others out to the field." And that was that.

Eventually, the months-long investigation revealed that the "used" GPS had found its way into service at Newburgh Aviation, one of the outlying satellite offices, and the issue was not pursued. Furthermore, according to Garmin's serialized subscription records, the "new" unit, which had been missing from the start, allegedly had been registered for use by the former major and utilized privately, outside the unit. Later, that same GPS, was allegedly sold by the former major, to an innocent third party member of the State Police, who was not even a member of the Aviation Unit, but was completing private pilot's training in an off-duty capacity. In any event, the unsuspecting trooper, had unwittingly ended up in possession of the missing Division property.

But, all that would not be known for months, it was still early June, the major had just retired, and the missing GPS recently discovered. This was brought to the attention of the executive officer, a lieutenant, who did his level best to answer these questions and wrap his mind around what he was hearing. Ultimately, running the unit while contending with an intensifying IAB investigation proved overwhelming for the XO, and it became obvious to Division execs, he was in need of assistance.

On June 18, 2011, I was on the road, returning from a security exercise at one of the State's nuclear power plants, when I received a call from then-Field Commander, Colonel John Melville. "Where are you?" asked the colonel.

"Heading north, on the Thruway, back to HQ," I replied.

"Can you be here by 4:30 PM? Superintendent D'Amico wants to see you in his office ASAP," he said.

"Colonel, that's pushing it. Depending on traffic, I'll be cutting it close. What's this about?" I asked respectfully.

"He's going to offer you the commander's spot at Aviation. He's got to leave at 4:30 PM, so get here as soon as you can," he said.

"Yes, Sir," I replied.

As suspected, Friday traffic on the NYS Thruway around Albany precluded me from getting there on time, but I would be briefed by his number two, First Deputy Superintendent Kevin Gagan. I had not previously met either man, as both of them had joined the agency within the last six months. "Captain Guess, c'mon in and have a seat," he said. "I understand you're a pilot."

"Yes, Sir. A former Army Aviator," I said.

"Good," he said. Followed by, "That will help," as if to himself. "Are you aware of our ongoing issues at Aviation?" he asked.

"Vaguely," I answered. I'd never been much for the rumor mill, frankly always being too busy to listen to the griping and speculation, and I was only aware of what was happening on the periphery.

"Well, he said, "…they've got problems; the major's out, and I don't have time to go into the rest right now. The superintendent and I will have you back first thing next week to brief you. As of now, you're the 'Acting'

Detail Commander, Captain. It's Friday afternoon. Advise the unit you're in charge, exchange phone numbers, and make sure they let you know when they're up flying over the weekend. <u>No one flies without your knowledge</u>; understood? Call me if anything out of the ordinary comes up. Any questions?"

"I've got quite a few, Sir," I said, "…but nothing that can't wait till I see you on Monday."

"Good. Congratulations!" he said, extending his hand. "I'll send out the teletype message making it official. Good luck!"

I walked out of there, and I'll admit, my head was spinning. First thing I did, was contact the Aviation Unit Headquarters and get the phone number for the senior NCO. It was getting late on a Friday evening, and I had no time to waste. I didn't want the teletype "orders" to come out before I'd even had a chance to notify someone in the unit. *How would that look?* I obtained the number and spoke to the unit's staff sergeant; this was the top of the food chain at the time, as the lieutenant was currently unavailable. Quite accustomed to taking requests for service from officers around the state, in fact he had taken several from me during my time with SORT, the sergeant answered routinely, "Hello, Captain, what can I do for you?"

I said, "Good evening, Sergeant. Sorry, I've got to deliver this message over the phone, but I've just left Division HQ, and have been designated the new Acting Detail Commander of Aviation." You could have heard a pin drop. "So, please take down my cell number, and of course, I'll need yours. Ready to copy?"

"Yes, Sir," he replied. We exchanged numbers.

"How are we set up for the weekend?" I asked.

"Nothing on the calendar, but you never know what calls for assistance will come in," he said.

"Understood," I said. "What is the mechanism for advising me when we have something going airborne?" I inquired.

"We send out a Flight Notification, by e-mail," he said, "I'll contact dispatch and have them add you to the list," he offered.

"Thank you. I appreciate that," I said. "I have a meeting with the superintendent next week and will have more to share with you after that. Other than that, I'm looking forward to working with you. Have a good weekend."

"You too, Sir," he said, and hung up.

It had been 21 years since I had officially flown a helicopter, not counting my trip to Flight 800 in 1996. Of course, I had been around them throughout my career with the State Police, rappelling, fast roping, as needed in search and rescue, helicasting as a SCUBA diver in training, etc., and I was familiar with several of the pilots. Two I knew fairly well, as I had been their field training officer at Newburgh, when they first came on the job. Now they were seasoned aviators. But, this would be quite different. The unit had become accustomed to elevating their leaders from within. Only one other time, did they have an outsider come in, and that, I'm told, was not universally well-received. This would likely ruffle a few feathers as well, but orders are orders.

I went home that evening wondering what I was getting myself into, but knowing I would give them 110%. Out of operational necessity, the unit of 21 aircraft (13 helicopters and 8 fixed-wing) and nearly sixty personnel (pilots, mechanics, flight dispatchers, and support staff) was decentralized, with a substantial hangar and HQ at Albany International Airport and smaller satellite offices at airports in Batavia, Syracuse, Newburgh, and Saranac Lake. Given the ongoing internal affairs investigation and current issues at HQ, I braced for the fact that it may take some time to get around the state to meet everyone, but knew I could not afford to delay introducing myself. Therefore, over the weekend, I generated the following memorandum, the recognized communications medium within the State Police, addressed to all members of the unit:

NEW YORK STATE POLICE

MEMORANDUM

Troop "H" Station Headquarters

Date June 21, 2011

To: **Aviation Unit Members**

From: **Captain Charles E. Guess – Detail Commander**

Subject: **UNIT UPDATE**

I wish to take a minute of your valuable time to introduce myself and briefly discuss our way forward.

First, effective immediately, I will be joining the unit as Detail Commander. As a former Army Aviator, I have an understanding and deep respect for the work you do. That appreciation is directed to ALL unit members; sworn and non-sworn. Clearly, the success of SP Aviation is a team effort, dependent upon the commitment and professionalism of each and every one of you. It is my strong belief that the diversity of this unit and your unique backgrounds are its strength. Because the decentralized structure of this unit prevents our assembly, I wanted to immediately get ahead of potential rumors as an information vacuum is never beneficial. Naturally, I look forward to expeditiously visiting every station and meeting each of you.

In the way of introductions, I spent 6 years on active duty in the U.S. Army as a commissioned officer attaining the rank of captain. I began as an Infantry officer but was quickly assigned to Initial Entry Rotary Wing training (flight school) serving the balance of my time in primary flight and staff assignments in an Air Cavalry Squadron and an Attack Helicopter Battalion. Additionally, I have over 20 years of service with the State Police and have served in a variety of assignments. My longest and a very satisfying role was the nearly 10 years spent as a Road Trooper in Troop "F". There, I learned the value of Division's core mission...Law Enforcement. I have served as a supervisor in the Field in Troops B, F and ESD – Capital. I've also had the good fortune of training and assignments during my career as a member of the following specialties: MRT/SORT, SCUBA, Firearms Instructor, Defensive Tactics Instructor and FTO. Until today, I served as the Captain – Emergency Management at Headquarters, assisting with the oversight of Division's special mission units. Throughout my career, these assignments often brought me into close contact with the many professionals in Aviation.

Now, to the point, I recognize this proud unit is in the midst of an internal investigation and a difficult transition. Although I have none of the details now, in due time, I expect to receive a briefing on the findings and we will address those issues together. My intention is to work with all of you as we navigate through this trying experience while continuing to perform the daily tasks, missions and assignments with the safety and professionalism for which you have come to be known. Over time, I am confident this unit will emerge stronger and more unified than ever. To accomplish this, I will need your assistance, patience, continued dedication to duty and loyalty. In return, I will reciprocate those values and pledge to be an engaged advocate for progressiveness and your welfare as we re-establish forward momentum. This will be a collective effort.

You should also know that while I am a firm believer in the chain of command, I also have an "open door" policy and am interested in what each of you has to say going forward. I do ask however, that when considering use of this policy, any issues that can be addressed within the chain of command first be brought to the attention of the appropriate supervisor to afford that member an opportunity to remedy the situation.

Understand that with the responsibility of leadership (at all levels) come difficult and occasionally unpopular decisions. I am cognizant that each decision I make will have an impact on members of this command and will endeavor to solicit the appropriate input while determining the best course of action. You may rest assured; ALL decisions will be made with the best interest of the unit and Division in mind.

My immediate objectives are as follows:

- Re-establish a sense of order, normalcy and chain of command.
- Ensure unit activities are driven by and support Division's core mission.
- Open lines of communication and clearly articulate expectations.
- Restore trust and confidence within the ranks.
- Review SOPs, best practices and potential areas of improvement, and
- Ensure the unit's outstanding Safety record remains central to what we do.

I would like to acknowledge the tremendous achievements this unit has made over the years and thank the leaders who have come before me for it is their vision coupled with your efforts that brought you this far.

Once again, I consider it an honor and privilege to have an opportunity to work with you.

With that, I reported to work on day one, eagerly anticipating what the future would hold. The unit was, by far, the largest of its kind within New York State, resembling a small air force and responsible for support, upon request, to: law enforcement agencies, MEDEVAC, Search and Rescue, SP SORT and SCUBA divers, Department of Environmental Conservation support missions pertaining to biology and wildlife preservation, aerial firefighting of wild fires, and executive transport of the Governor and NYSP Superintendent. A full plate, so there would be no time to waste.

Over the next eight weeks, I conducted a detailed, 360-degree review of the unit's policies, procedures, and personnel. I scheduled visits to all the outlying stations and interviewed each member of the unit, to gain an appreciation and understanding of their issues and concerns. Additionally, I had been briefed, daily, by our Internal Affairs Bureau regarding the status of the audit and ongoing investigation. Naturally, I met regularly with the superintendent, the first deputy superintendent, and field commander, to receive guidance and to request additional personnel and internal appointments and promotions for key members, as I began to restructure the organization.

As a result of my discussions with supervisors, pilots, mechanics, civilian support staff, Internal Affairs, and executives at Headquarters, I identified ten areas of vulnerability in need of immediate and sustained attention:

1) Leadership/Unity of Command
2) Intra-unit Communications
3) Clarity of the Unit's Core Mission
4) Outdated Policies and Procedures
5) Professional Development and Training Concerns
6) Unresolved Safety Concerns

7) Inventory Control, Accountability, and Administrative Records
8) External Customer Support Challenges
9) Fiscal Support Challenges
10) Supervisory, Pilot, and Maintenance Schedule coverage

To address the matters listed above, I knew would take a concerted effort, and I looked forward to engaging each member on the path forward. During the interviews, I found that it was the collective view of unit members that previous administrations had not *fully* utilized the unique skills of *all* personnel. Something I assured them we would focus on going forward. Subsequently, I unveiled a new organizational structure, identifying additional, internally designated roles and responsibilities. The objective being to streamline unit operations and afford each member greater opportunity to contribute to the program.

I further assured unit members, that as an "outsider" coming in, I would level the playing field, and recognized there was a wealth of talent, dedication, and commitment at *all* levels. Despite perceived shortcomings and the distraction of an internal affairs investigation, the unit continued to function at a high-operational level – a credit to the professionalism of its employees. A point I repeatedly stressed to the superintendent and IAB.

My point would be proven, and the unit's operational efficacy vindicated, at the end of August 2011, upon its performance during one of New York's largest natural disasters: Hurricane Irene and Tropical Storm Leigh. Beginning on Sunday August 27, and over several succeeding days, extreme weather continually hammered the state. First, in the form of a Category 3 hurricane, which was followed up by a knockout punch from a prolific tropical storm. Collectively, the resulting flooding was responsible for ten deaths statewide and $296 million dollars of devastation to cities, towns, and villages along vast swaths of territory across the Southern Tier, Central New York, Capitol Region, and Northern Adirondacks. Entire communities were cut off and devastated. Food, water, and health care were severely compromised, temporarily non-existent in some areas. Amid all of this, and the massive response rolled out by Governor Cuomo, was the contribution to the rescue and recovery effort by the NYSP Aviation Unit. During the disaster, the unit flew virtually around the clock, logging hundreds of accident-free flight hours, transporting life-saving supplies to victims and conducting aerial reconnaissance with the emergency managers, providing decision makers with "eyes in the sky." Most importantly, the unit conducted 44 live-hoist rescues of stranded citizens, 42 in New York, and 2 in Vermont, undoubtedly saving lives as these victims were plucked out of harm's way.

Not since Hurricane Katrina, in 2005, had so many individuals been hoisted to safety by helicopter during a natural disaster. Accordingly, unit aviators and crew, were recognized by Bell Helicopter Textron with an award for service.

While not surprised at their performance, I was extraordinarily proud of the achievement. With the internal investigation continuing in the background, it was a well-deserved shot in the arm for the unit. They had stepped up when New Yorkers needed them most!

Over the coming months and years, there was much to do. Along the way, some five months after taking command, I began refresher training in the UH-1 Huey helicopter. Up to that point, I had been flat out addressing one organizational need after another. I figured my primary responsibility was to manage the unit, obtain scarce resources for training, sustainment (maintenance), recruiting additional pilots, and developing future initiatives, including an aircraft fleet modernization program. In fact, over my three and a half years with the unit, I spent 99% of my time doing just that, "flying the desk," as it's called, vs. the "friendly skies." But, by November of 2011, I was looking forward to spending some time in the cockpit again. Responsible for my requalification effort would be one of the unit's most-seasoned flight instructors, Technical Sergeant Phil Crane, another classmate of mine from the 168th Session. Phil was a highly experienced aviator. He was qualified in everything the unit flew, even possessing some ratings we didn't have need for currently, such as seaplane pilot. A friend and colleague of many years; I knew I would be in "good hands."

First order of business, Phil put me through "ground school." I had flown and qualified in the Huey during my time in the Army, but that was

20 plus years ago, so relearning the systems, capabilities, and Emergency Procedures was essential. It's amazing what the mind is capable of retaining; things I hadn't thought about for two decades, had apparently taken root in the recesses of my brain, and were relatively easily recalled. Next, we proceeded to the flight line, for aircraft refamiliarization. This was the part I was most looking forward to, the actual flying. I had been told that, flying the helicopter, once you had it, as I did back in the 1980's, was much like "riding a bike"; it would come right back to you. I was sure hoping that was true, especially since much of the initial training would take place right there at Albany Airport, on the ramp, sod, and taxiways, right outside my HQ, in full view of any member of the unit who wanted to observe through our huge glass windows or hangar doors. I didn't want to put on a "show," if you know what I mean, but it was time to go to work.

Thankfully, with Phil's coaching and my muscle memory, it *was* a lot like riding a bike, the skills seemed to come back quickly. And although my control touch was a bit rusty, I was pleased with my progress. We progressed from hovering, to maneuvers such as: air taxiing, accelerations and decelerations, straight-and-level flight, normal and steep approaches, slope landings, auto-rotations, you name it. Obviously, there was much more to come, but not a bad showing for the first flight.

After about 90 minutes or so, it was time to return to base, which meant, perhaps the most difficult task of the day, landing the helicopter on the dolly, a wheeled platform, just slightly larger than the aircraft's skid footprint. This enabled the mechanics to hook up a tug post-flight, to drag the helo back into the hangar daily. Although I had seen it done a thousand times outside the window of my office which faced the flight line, I had never performed the task myself, not even in the Army, where we would land on the ramp or flight line. To top it all off, visibility from the Huey's cockpit, while adequate for forward flight, was limited out the windscreen and chin bubble when looking down. While sufficient during most maneuvers, the chin bubble affords visual access forward and slightly down; the side windows, for 90 degrees side to side; and the overhead, plexiglass-tinted "greenhouse" suitable for looking straight up; none of them actually covered the belly of the aircraft, or the 95 percent of the skids that had to be planted on the dolly.

Obviously, it could be done, as I'd lifted off the dolly at the beginning of my flight, but putting it back where you found it the first time, would be a whole different matter! And frankly, I knew that this was the only part of my flight any member of the peanut gallery would pay attention to, the landing; so, *Don't screw it up!* I thought.

So, we came in for the approach, Phil coached me into position. "OK, a little farther," he said, while I was holding a hover over the platform, "Now, a little back. Hold what you got…Wait, a little to the left now. Good! Stop! Too far! Shit! You lost it; back up. Let's start over." One aborted landing; the folks inside were getting their money's worth.

Round two, I approached the dolly again. Trying not to overcorrect it, but just kind of "will it" onto the platform. Because, like a Jedi, there comes a point where you must establish a sight picture and just land the damn thing by using the "Force." Finally, after more coaching, I obtained the proper sight picture and nailed it. "Good job! See that wasn't so bad," Phil said.

Well, I was down, but I was sweating my balls off! *WTF!* I'd been in more stressful situations than this before! It was November and relatively cool outside, and even though the sun was shining through the plexiglass providing a little "greenhouse" effect, this was ridiculous. We shut the aircraft down, by the book, and when the blades were spinning down removed our flight helmets. Now it would be obvious to Phil how much I was perspiring, so as a preemptive strike I said, "Man, everything felt pretty good today, but, I've got to tell you, I sweat my ass off on that landing."

Phil looked over at me and said, "Oh, hey, Sir, did I tell you the Huey has heated seats, you didn't have your heating pad on by mistake, did you?" he said grinning.

Jesus Christ! I thought, …*that's it!* I remember reading that in the manual during Ground School, but the Huey's I'd flown in the Army didn't have them, so I must have filed it away. Either some "candy ass" before me had left the seat heater on and hadn't noticed, or Phil had turned it on for me, just to make things more interesting. I'll never know!

By the Summer of 2013, after two years in command we had essentially reversed and resolved the myriad of administrative, training, and operational issues in the unit. This was largely due to the exceedingly hard work of my staff, led by Lieutenants Mark Haskell and Bill Carraher (Administrative Officers), Technical Lieutenant Phil Napolitano (Chief Pilot), Staff Sergeant Ben Albizu (Maintenance Supervisor), Staff Sergeant Michael Greenwood, Technical Sergeant John Healy (Fixed-Wing Coordinator), Bill Wadsworth (Training Officer), Nancy Pennick and Lynn Bruno (two, *superb* FAA Flight Dispatchers), et al.

That progress, hard fought and won, would <u>not</u> be without its challenges...

We had an aging fleet of aircraft, which at times, despite the best efforts our professional pilots and maintainers, limited our performance and detracted from our operational readiness, capabilities, and maintenance sustainability. Resultantly, we experienced occasional bumps in the road while striving to service and meet the demands of external customers. But, despite the difficulties, we received stalwart support from the superintendent and field commander and persevered. Like all units, we evolved.

As personnel transferred or retired, opportunities opened for others to jump in and move the ball down the field. Looking back, one such individual was John Healy. Upon taking Command in 2011, then-Trooper John Healy, was the first individual I recruited to the unit. Although, I did not know John personally, I knew of his qualifications: a retired USAF colonel, who was a combat-tested B-52 Bomber and C-5 Galaxy pilot. In fact, he had been on the detail previously, starting the Executive King Air Program, until he was called upon to serve his country during overseas conflict, and did so for an extended five and a half-year tour of duty. Upon conclusion of his military service, and return to the NYSP, Healy was not immediately returned to the detail. In fact, at the time I met him, Healy was serving as an Interstate Highway Patrol trooper. Whatever shortsighted rationale had precluded his return, it was clear to me that I could use a man like John Healy on my team, and it proved to be among the most *astute* personnel decisions I ever made.

Healy, returned first as the newly appointed fixed-wing coordinator and executive pilot in command. Subsequently, when the position opened in the fall of 2013, John was promoted to Technical Lieutenant and Chief Pilot. Teaming up with Administrative Officer extraordinaire, Lieutenant Bill Carraher, together they continued to hammer out outstanding results.

As well-suited for the OPS job as Healy was, there wasn't anything Carraher couldn't do. And for three years, working side by side with me, he proved it every day. Right after taking command, I had an opportunity to hire a new staff sergeant, who would, on paper, assist with the administration of the entire unit. I impaneled a committee to select the best-qualified candidate, and upwards of 14 people from around the State Police, including several from within the unit, applied. Taking the candidates in one by one, Sergeant Bill Carraher from Troop "G", whom I had never met, reported to the Board and handed over his resume. In addition to acing the standardized interview format, and being a highly regarded NCO in the State Police, Carraher's resume revealed he was an Air National Guard major, C-130 pilot in command, and flight/tactics evaluator, in the very Air Force unit responsible for the South Pole mission. This guy was a home run! In short order, I would later have an opportunity to promote him to technical lieutenant. Again, among the *best* personnel decisions I ever made.

Combined, nobody could touch these two men for their competency, fairness, and loyalty. The unit was better for their service, and I was fortunate to ultimately consider them close friends.

Time went on, and we continued to forge ahead, correcting and shrugging off the substantive administrative defects that once plagued the unit, and while not perfect, becoming infinitely more standardized and capable of handling the operational challenges than when I found it.

In October 2014, I was stunned when I received a phone call from the International Association of Chiefs of Police advising me that I had been selected from candidates around the world as the 2014 recipient of the *"Excellence in Police Aviation Award."*

Invited to the Annual Conference in Orlando, FL, I accepted the award for leadership on behalf of my unit and the Division of State Police, knowing that if not for the members of my team and the support and confidence of the superintendent, there would be no such success, or recognition.

In November of 2014, there remained one personal objective in the State Police that I had not attained, command of a troop in the field. As a major since 2012, I had attained the necessary rank. Now it was a matter of formulating a request for transfer that made sense, in keeping with potential vacancies and the "best interest" of Division. I requested a meeting with Field Commander Patricia Groeber and presented my case. In my view, I had taken on the challenge of command of the Aviation Unit when Division needed me to step in and stop the hemorrhaging. In fact, I had given it my all, believing in my heart that I had left it better than I found it. My request of the colonel was, if there is any future movement within the organization, I would like to be considered. She indicated there may soon be an opening working in her office as an inspector, a promotion, and I was honored that she would want me to work in Field Command, but she could tell by my face and response that a promotion was not what I was looking for. What I was hoping for, was the rare and great privilege of commanding one of our operational troops in the field. Colonel Groeber herself had commanded Troop "G", and she knew exactly the experience I was looking for. "Chuck, I get it," she said. "You've done a great job for us in Aviation. I will speak to the superintendent and relay your wishes. But I can't make you any promises."

I completely understood and was grateful for the consideration.

CHAPTER 14

TROOP "B" - DREAM" ASSIGNMENT

In early December 2014, while at my desk at Aviation, I received a call from Superintendent Joseph D'Amico. "Chuck," he said, "Joe D'Amico."

"Good afternoon, Superintendent," I replied. I had taken many calls from the Boss, right on this very phone, about unit-related business over my three and a half years of command. I had no reason to believe this was any different.

"Listen, I've been talking with Patricia, and she tells me you're looking for a change," he said.

"Yes, Sir," I responded.

"I'm going to send you up to Troop "B", he said.

"Sir, you've just made my day!" I replied, "I would love to go to Troop "B"!

"No, look," he continued, "…you've done a great job at Aviation, everything I've asked you to do. You've earned it. I always felt comfortable having you at the helm of Aviation, and I know you'll do great things in "B."

"I'm honored, Sir, I said. "I won't let you down!"

After all my staff and I had been through together at Aviation, it was more than a little difficult breaking the news to them. I'd had a "good run," thanks to them, but no one is irreplaceable. I was leaving the unit in the highly capable hands of Carraher and Healy, and it was time for me to move on.

On December 18, I arrived in Ray Brook, NY, right down the road from Lake Placid, site of the 1932 and 1980 Winter Olympics, ready to go to work. I was replacing a long-serving troop commander in the North Country, Major Rick Smith, who had been at the helm for the last eight and a half years. While the troop was running efficiently, and there was no need to turn the proverbial "battleship" around, I did set about making adjustments that suited my style of leadership.

But, it was a week before Christmas, and there would be time for all of that. I settled into my new office and sent out a holiday message to members of the Troop, wishing them peace and prosperity for the year ahead, reminding them to be ever vigilant in the dangerous world in which we live.

It was at this time, I was asked to contribute to the Winter 2014-2015 issue of the PBA Trooper magazine, which was being dedicated *"In Memory of New York State Trooper Ross M. Riley, 1969-2013."* Ross, was a SORT/MRT teammate of mine and a dear friend, perhaps the closest, to me and my family. I wrote in memorial:

"As I look back on my career with pride, I remain humbled by a devastating loss. Near the end of 2013, November 20 to be exact, tragedy struck, as my close friend and longtime confidant, Trooper Ross M. Riley, was killed in a tragic training accident.

Ross embodied the core values of the New York State Police. His, respect for the rule of law, compassion for members of the community, quest for continuous education, and indomitable spirit made him a Trooper's Trooper.

Ross was a quiet professional, and unless you knew him well, you may not have realized that he was also a United States Marine, paramedic, rifleman, world-class instructor, and SORT operator at the very top of his game. Fortunately for Division, it was his chosen role as a trooper that allowed him to put into practice everything he'd learned.

As important as his work was, that's not what defined him. Ross was truly defined by his commitment to his family. That was his greatest quality. Husband to Heidi, a sergeant in Troop "A", and father of three beautiful daughters. If you really wanted to know what made him tick, what he was most proud of, it was his girls. They could not have asked for a better man.

I had the honor and privilege of knowing Ross for his entire career and watched him come up the ranks from recruit trooper to seasoned veteran. He was a mentor to many troopers and a role model, whose impact on this job and SORT was enormous."

One of my favorite recollections of Ross is of one of the many times we climbed Mt. Marcy, in the Adirondack High Peaks, in February. We were taking a group of new SORT members up for cold weather survival training, and Ross, who was one of the co-instructors and a bit of a gear guru, happened to be trying out a <u>new</u> pair of boots with his snowshoes. "<u>Rookie mistake, Bro!</u>" I can still hear him saying. The boots were causing him some serious difficulty and he began to fall behind as the hot spots worsened. Now, I knew his dropping back wasn't a fitness issue, the guy was a stud. So I stopped and waited for him to come around the next pine tree. After teasing him, by asking if he needed MY help carrying HIS pack, and receiving a smart remark in return, he informed me that the boots just weren't cutting it, but HE HAD A PLAN! He and Trooper Brian Brass were going to hike out, get cell service, call Heidi at home in Olean, have her get his old boots, meet him on the road in Bath, some 250 miles away (in the middle of the night), and he'd be back by morning to complete the climb. Mind you, that's a round trip of 500 miles. I shook my head, but there was no talking him out of it. Giving him the old five-point contingency plan, that we would have to move out to the summit with the students in the morning if he wasn't back in time, we split up, with Ross and Brian headed back down the mountain. Next morning, we got suited up for the hike to the top and waited till the agreed upon time…no Ross. We had no choice but to move or freeze. After tagging the summit, in virtually zero visibility, we began the trek back to basecamp. Just as we descended into the tree line, who should be heading up the mountain, but Ross and Brian! Huge grins on their faces and a story to boot. Ross said, indeed they'd hiked out, met Heidi and the girls on the road, exchanged the boots, drove back non-stop, resumed the climb, and here they were 24 hours later…fueled almost exclusively by Red Bull, Gummy Bears, and Snickers on their way to the summit! That was Ross! Didn't know the meaning of the word quit! If there was a way to make something as simple as climbing the state's highest mountain in the middle of winter even more epic, he'd find it!

"What a legacy. Ross lived a life full of *love, achievement,* and *adventure,* never failing to bring out the best in us. The motto of the New York State Police Special Operations Response Team is *Salus Populi,* which means: 'For the Safety of Others.' Trooper Ross Riley lived his life in accordance with that motto."

I started 2015 off with a series of meetings to get the lay of the land of the largest troop within the NYSP and to get to know my staff. I started out with a Commissioned Officers meeting, with my 10 subordinate officers, on who I would rely to help me run the troop by commanding three subordinate zones, the BCI, and one serving as the troop's administrative or executive officer, my right-hand man.

Truthfully, my real right-hand man, administratively speaking, was not a man after all, but a wonderful woman named Barbra Buckley, Troop Commander's Secretary. A sweetheart of a person, Barb had been among the very first to welcome me to Troop "B" in 2004, when I was first assigned as an administrative lieutenant, working for the troop commander in an adjoining office. The major at the time, Pete Person, was a hard corps Recon Marine and Vietnam Vet. He had a reputation as being demanding, but working for him, I preferred to think of it as: *The man's a hell of a cop and knows what he wants. If you're doing your job, there's nothing to worry about.* Knowing what the Boss was looking for, Barb kept me in line, and I never ran afoul of the major. Now that I had returned to troop as the commander, Barb was my go-to for just about everything. She had a "heart of gold" and could be trusted implicitly – two, among her many, outstanding qualities.

Right from the start, I had each subordinate commander and section head formally brief me on their respective areas of responsibility. Then, I visited each zone and station, meeting with as many troopers and Civilian Employees as I could along the way, without disrupting the flow of operations. Additionally, while out with the Zone Commanders, Captains Brent Gillam, Mike Girard, and John Tibbitts, and touring the area with the BCI Captain, Bob LaFountain, I stopped in to introduce myself to the various police chiefs, sheriffs, federal partners, DAs, prison officials, and supervisors whenever possible throughout my five-county, 8,335-square-mile region. These actions, learning the strengths and weaknesses of my staff and cementing pre-exisiting relationships with my regional partners, would prove *essential* to establishing our forthcoming coalition during the manhunt.

After settling in and digesting all the info I had been briefed on by the various commanders and staff section heads, I began to implement, with the assistance of my XO, Captain Walt Teppo, several initiatives I hoped would strengthen an already-solid troop, chief among them:

First, it was my observation, and opinion early on, that the troop was strategically more BCI centric than necessary. As preeminent in serious cases as the Bureau is, it was my intention to rebalance and reinvest greater responsibility and authority to the hands of the three zone commanders. In this way, I reasoned, the zone captains and BCI captain would have to work hand in glove, communicating routinely for optimal efficiency. Any "draws" would be settled by me; however, that almost never occurred, once the players knew I was serious about making it work. The beneficiaries, I hoped, would be uniformed troopers and plain-clothes investigators, who are the backbone of the organization.

Second, I had long held the belief that within the State Police, we were not making best use, certainly not using the full potential, of our first sergeants. Generally speaking, in many troops, the person selected as the first sergeant, or senior NCO, often possessed the most experience, was a tenured zone sergeant adept at supervising troopers, subordinate NCOs, and sometimes civilians, and had responded over the years to a fair share of emergencies. For those reasons and more, that individual was often ultimately selected for the top NCO billet. However, they were then typically locked away in an office at Troop Headquarters, dealing with leave requests, administrative staff, construction programs, lost property, and the like. Certainly, all of those areas are of vital import to the effective, administrative, functionality of a Troop, but none of them took *full advantage* of the NCO's, finely honed _leadership_ potential. This was about to change in Troop "B". One of my first orders of business was to engage the first sergeant in just such a shift of focus.

Before rolling this one out, I consulted with my XO, Captain Walt Teppo. Walt was another classmate of mine from the 168th Session. In fact, fortunately for me, I had two more 168ers on my command staff: my good friend Captain Brent Gillam, Zone One and Captain Mike Girard, my superb Zone Two Commander, who innately knew how to take care of business. Teppo could barely contain himself, squirming in the chair as I was describing what I thought the problem was, and how I intended to address it.

"Jesus Christ! What, Walt. What?!" I demanded of him, as he sat there grinning from ear to ear.

"This is so cool," he said in his deadpan manner, "I was just talking to the first sergeant about this the other day! He's going to shit himself and will never believe I didn't put you up to it!"

I had known Walt my whole career; in fact, six years after we graduated, we met up again at Defensive Tactics School at the Academy and spent the next three weeks knocking the hell out of each other. Walt was a good man. Also, he was some sort of brilliant Naval Reserve intel analyst, one of very few people who would talk to me that candidly – perfect for an XO and confidant. "Well then, what does the first sergeant think?" I asked.

"He agrees with the basic premise, but wonders about the implementation; would the officers go along with it?" Walt responded.

"Well, he can leave that part to me," I said. "I'll grease the skids for him. All I'll need him to do is execute. Go get him."

Five minutes later, First Sergeant Steve Lacey entered with Captain Teppo. Steve had a smile on his face as I asked him to sit down. "The captain get to you, Sir?" he asked.

"Not exactly, Steve," I said running through our previous discussion, now breaking it down for him as to the details of what I hoped to achieve. "I recognize your concerns, Steve. You handle the NCOs..."

"They won't be a problem," he interjected.

"And I'll handle the officers," I added.

Once this concept was fully introduced Troop-wide, Steve ran with the ball. Newly empowered, Steve would prove to be a game changer during the manhunt.

Third, as 2014 ended and 2015 commenced, it was time for all troops, details, and sections to submit their recommendations for yearly awards to the superintendent. Naturally, this involved a significant process and committees were formed at Division Headquarters to review the nominees. One of the first directives I received as the new TC, was to submit the awards package by a certain date, in the not-too-distant future. Turning to my XO, I said, "Walt, have the captains get in their recommendations ASAP," thinking it was a routine request.

"Yeah, about that," Teppo replied,…that's going to be a problem."

"Why's that?" I asked.

"Because we don't do a very good job recognizing our people around here," he said with sincerity. "We beat the hell out of them if they do something wrong, or don't arrest enough drunks; but rewarding them, that's a different story."

"Well that's fucked up…" I said.

"I agree," he replied.

"All right, get the word out to them. Let's see what we get?" I directed.

"Is this a test?" he asked.

"It sure is," I said.

Days passed, and like most groups in any organization, they let the clock tick away, waiting to submit their response until the deadline. *The wait better be worth it,* I thought. Walt was absolutely correct. Two out of three zones submitted a one-liner indicating they had nobody to recommend." I was pissed, "Walt, how the hell can that be? Troopers work a whole year on the road, risking their lives _every_ day, and nobody is worthy of recognition?!"

"I don't want to say, I told you so…," the smart ass began, but he sensed I was not in a joking mood.

Meanwhile, he, the XO, had been writing his ass off, taking care of his troopers assigned to our Headquarters. To their credit, so had the BCI Captain Bob LaFountain and the Zone Three Commander, Captain John Tibbitts. Clearly, I was blessed with a terrific staff and Tibbitts was among the best. A tenured zone commander, he had cultivated an outstanding relationship with the Forest Rangers in his zone, the Adirondack High Peaks, which would pay off in spades during the search. John would later go on to succeed me as Troop Commander, upon my retirement.

Because of their efforts, we had superlative nominees, now it was just a matter of submitting them, and getting them through the review process at Division HQ. That year, Troop "B" snared the NCO of the Year and George M. Searle Award for Training for 2014, Superintendent's Commendations for two Zone Three members, and the Unit Citation for the BCI's FIU, crime scene technicians. I couldn't have been prouder of our people, as they, and their families walked across the stage at the Academy in the Spring of 2015 to receive their well-deserved awards. Captains Teppo, LaFountain, and Tibbitts had saved the day, boosted morale, and ensured our troopers received the recognition they deserved.

Fourth, and finally, utilization of SORT and K9. Having been a member of SORT/MRT for over 12 years and having supervised all special operations as their captain, I had institutional knowledge regarding what I considered to be a lack of appropriate and consistent utilization of these specialized units. Troop "B" had a team, the SORT North Team, assigned to their geographic area of responsibility since 2009, something I had previously pushed for as the SORT lieutenant/OIC, but since I left Special Operations as a captain in 2010, the North Team had very little activity to show for their time in the region. Upon taking command at the end of 2014, I thoroughly reviewed statewide SORT activity reports, making a statistical comparison between the number of details (calls for service) between the various troops and teams, as it related to most common missions, such as: narcotics raids, barricaded gunmen, hostage situations, search and rescue (SAR), etc. Upon review, it was immediately apparent that, with the exception of SAR, the North Team was being *significantly* underutilized, in each of the high-risk categories.

This was not just significant because the Team in the northern region of the state was not realizing their full numerical potential, compared to other regional teams, it was significant and worthy of attention because each and every time traditional uniformed troopers and plain-clothes investigators were assigned by their supervisors to handle these most-critical events (armed/barricaded gunmen, hostage scenarios, high-risk entries, and narcotics raids) without specialized assistance, they were facing underscored and excessive risk. *Clearly, a full-time tactical team, possessing Tier*

One tactical training, weapons, body armor, equipment, night observation devices, and armored vehicles would be better suited to the task. I had long been of the opinion, that as supervisors, we had a <u>moral obligation</u> to do everything within our power to protect our people and make them as **safe** as possible. The jobs they did, on a daily basis, were already dangerous enough. We had a responsibility to stack the deck in *their* favor, and utilization of the appropriate assets, in this instance SORT, was a grounder. Accordingly, I immediately instituted a written policy mandating use of tactical assets, under very specific, incrementally increasing criteria. I never wanted to be in the position of explaining to a parent, widow/widower, or family of a fallen trooper, why their loved one was <u>not</u> coming home, when we had people specially trained and equipped to handle such incidents.

In my opinion, we were off to a great start. I love the Adirondacks, and there are no better people than the troopers and civilians in Troop "B". My wife and I had long contemplated moving here upon retirement, my nine-month commute was getting old, and this would enable us to get a head start. We were determined to make this our new home. Going *"all in"* and *"living the dream"* as I like to say!

As June 2015 began, everything was going according to plan...

CHAPTER 15

TIGHTENING THE NOOSE

It had been two days since the sighting at the Twisted Horn Hunting Club, and a massive search effort was underway.

The evidence collected on the afternoon of Saturday June 20 had been transported to the New York State Police Forensic Investigation Center (FIC) and arrived at 3:00 AM, early on the morning of **June 21, Day 16.** The FIC had recalled staff and immediately began analysis of the evidence. By 11:30 AM, in a remarkable span of less than nine hours, the first lab results were obtained, which verified that *both* Inmate Matt's and Inmate Sweat's DNA was present on evidence secured from the camp. Evidence such as latent prints and DNA collected from: water bottles, a plastic spoon, cigarette butts, jar of peanut butter, <u>and</u> items dropped outside near the stream, as they rushed to vacate the area, including: shoes, rain suit, trail knife, and Ziploc bags containing toiletries and clothing.

This was the first confirmation that the inmates were still in the area and had been unable to complete their escape. Immediate notifications of the DNA confirmation were made to the various other federal, state, and local law enforcement agencies and additional resources were dispatched. Spirits soared! "ALL HANDS" were on deck, and the game of cat and mouse intensified exponentially.

As difficult as our work in the Dannemora search box had proven to be, it would seem like a walk in the park compared to the remote nature of <u>this</u> landscape, dotted with mountains, waterways, streams, bogs, and black bear. It has been said many times, that good leaders make their own luck, and I wasn't leaving anything to chance.

With approximately 25 miles between our formal Command Post in Caddyville and this expanded area of operations, we established a Forward Operating Base (FOB) at the Titus Mountain Family Ski Center; the location's use had been graciously offered by the owners. Titus Mountain, at 2,025 feet and 900 acres, was a superb landmark and facility. Use of the

Upper Lodge afforded us a phenomenal structure on the upper mountain, from which to command and control ground operations, land helicopters, deliver food (with the assistance of their staff and the community) conduct briefings to hundreds of officers, provide a staging area for tactical teams, a multi-purpose facility. Establishing an FOB on the mountain improved our communications. Titus Mountain allowed the SP and DEC to use its repeater, and the USMS and Verizon also erected temporary cell towers and communications equipment on Titus, facilitating improved coverage. Overall, this location allowed us to have a significant footprint right on top of the action.

The "noose" was tightening, but we didn't have them in cuffs. Anything could happen! Late **Monday, June 22, Day 17**, at approximately 10:30 PM, we received a reported sighting. One of our CERT members on the perimeter reported that possibly two male subjects were sighted near a wood pile, across the street from a trail entrance, off County Route 41 (CR 41); and we brought the "heat!" Lieutenant Pat Ryan, the Operations Officer at the CP, immediately deployed tactical teams, helicopters, canines, and additional roving patrols to scour the rural area. The problem was, the pouring rain and low cloud ceiling in the mountainous environment constrained the effectiveness of our helicopters and limited the opportunity for our canines to develop a credible track. Like ghosts, they were in the wind, again. Ryan, a superb officer, who I would later recommend for promotion to captain and assignment as my future XO when Teppo took over a zone, had done everything right during the response. It just wasn't our night.

On Tuesday, June 23, Day 18, with over 1,000 personnel on the ground and more than 2,000 leads investigated, we announced, in a press release, our move from the temporary TOC at Owls Head Fire Station, to the new FOB at Titus Mountain. Out of necessity, the Caddyville Command Post would remain our HQ for the duration of the search. Also, in addition to the intense activity in rural areas, the Vermont State Police Tactical Team, in conjunction with the Village of Malone Police Department, checked several apartments on Main Street, after hearing that an associate of one of the fugitives lived there; however, the claim was unfounded.

A day later, on **Wednesday, June 24, Day 19,** a reported burglary had been called in by another seasonal camp owner at a camp, deep in the woods off CR 41, on Fayette Road, in Malone. Like the previous sighting two days earlier, this location was about 11 miles north and west of the Twisted Horn camp, and it appeared by virtue of location, that if related, the inmates may have covered some ground over the last two days. It was not a "burglary in-progress," as there was no one to chase, but the screen had been cut and entry gained. Although the perpetrator(s) was (were) long gone, importantly, there was evidence to be collected and analyzed: Corcraft brand underwear, a T-shirt, and a DNA swab of an outhouse door handle, <u>later</u> confirmed the presence of <u>Matt's</u> DNA. Again, evidence one, or both, were still in the area.

Indeed, so much activity evolved around the ubiquitous camps, one caretaker commented to a reporter, *"It's been wild around here...kind of exciting. My neighbor up here, he's almost 80 years old. He's all excited watching this. He's got his shotgun by his chair, and he's watching the show."*[11]

At a press conference, in Caddyville later that day, after a brief introductory statement reaffirming our commitment in the area, a question was posed to me regarding the location of the inmates, whether they may have left the area near Owls Head and Mountain View, to which I replied, "That's entirely possible. We now have a 75-square-mile area, as the primary search area. They could have made it out before law enforcement encircled them. The fact of the matter is, we are not limiting our investigation to Owls Head. We continue to look nationwide. We have all the assets at our disposal – U.S. Marshals, FBI, and others – to take this thing nationwide and around the world if necessary."

I also indicated, we had begun searching the Village of Malone, out of an abundance of caution and to ensure the safety of the residents. I reminded them, that morning, we had sent out automated calls through Franklin County Emergency Services – advising residents to expect a strong police presence, as part of the expanding search.

When pressed for more on whether we had recovered a gun and if the inmates were armed, I said, "There have been reports, widely made, that a shotgun is missing, but I do not have confirmatory evidence that a particular shotgun is missing. Just about every cabin or outbuilding in the North Country has one or more shotguns or weapons. These men are extremely dangerous; they are cunning. Why wouldn't they try to arm themselves immediately upon escape? We have, since Day 1, operated under the belief that these men are armed." Furthermore, I added, "Law enforcement officials are trying to search and secure every cabin they find. But, from interviewing cabin owners and users in the area, police have learned the camps are often occupied by multiple people throughout the year. This abundance of weapons and ammunition in seasonal hunting camps, makes an accurate inventory very difficult."

I then turned the podium over to Forest Ranger Captain John Streiff, for a perspective on the terrain. John said, "Searchers are methodically moving through an area where it's not only difficult to navigate, but the [sight] distance in front of them is sometimes only a few feet or less. The area is also known to have logging roads, ATV trails and paths, and hundreds of seasonal camps, all potentially aiding the fugitives and complicating the search.

I closed by stating we had investigated over 2,200 leads to date, and that the "Bottom line is, we don't want them to have a restful, peaceful night. Whether this ends here today, in Owls Head, or an indeterminate period of time going forward, we will resolve this case and capture these individuals. *What you're seeing here is the face of relentless pursuit."*

On Thursday, **June 25, Day 20,** news turned to reports of the arrest of Correction Officer Gene Palmer, the previous day. The charges: 1) Promoting Prison Contraband (Felony), for knowingly introducing needle-nosed pliers and a flathead screwdriver allegedly for use on artwork, between November 2014 and June 6, 2015, 2) Official Misconduct (Misdemeanor), regarding his overall conduct, such as: taking Sweat out onto the catwalk behind their cells to change wiring on electrical boxes enhancing inmates ability to cook on hot plates, and accepting paintings from Matt, and 3) Tampering with Evidence (Felony), for destroying, or trying to destroy, paintings, created and given to him by Richard Matt.

Palmer, who worked eight years in A-Block, transported frozen hamburger supplied by Joyce Mitchell to the inmates in plainly wrapped packages, on one or more occasions, *but* claimed he did <u>not</u> know about the tools (hacksaw blades) secreted in the meat by Mitchell. Palmer also *denies* knowing about the escape plan, and there is <u>no</u> evidence to the contrary. Additionally, Palmer *passed* a polygraph to that effect after a 14-hour interview.

Also on June 25, the Editorial Board of the *Press-Republican* published the following – VIEWPOINT [12], which addressed the fact that after 19 days, the inmates were still unaccounted for, writing: ***"We believe the law-enforcement agencies have made the right, by-the-book decisions in coping with a wholly unexpected and historic situation."*** Further, outlining their case, in sum and substance, they wrote:

- the prisoners, were last physically seen at a 10:30 PM standing count, discovered missing at 5:30 AM, had at least a *5-hour head start* [determined to be a six-hour head start];
- CCF notified SP at 5:45 AM, two inmates were unaccounted for, SP immediately activated its pre-existing escape plan, notifying: DEC, CCF, FBI, USMS, USCBP, ICE, VSP, PPD, Lake Champlain Ferries and more;
- *Press-Republican* advised soon after 8:00 AM, and had a story posted within minutes, including TV and radio; SP issued news release with photos and descriptions of inmates;
- the local landscape consists of large dense forests, creeks, crevasses, thick brush, downed trees, all starting within a stone's throw of the Dannemora prison;
- the inmates had help (later revealed by investigation);
- every one of 2,200 leads have been checked out, along with numerous false alarm sightings;
- searchers responded to a parallel sighting in Allegany County;
- officers responded to a burglary of a seasonal camp, and obtained DNA confirmation the next day.

The Editorial Board concluded by saying: ***"We are confident that the unrelenting effort and dogged determination of the massed searchers will snare the fugitives. They (law enforcement) have earned our patience."*** [13]

I felt secure that our strategy of saturating the area and denying them the ability to punch through our search layers was effective. *We must be wearing them down,* I thought. That, plus the vigilance of citizens of the North Country, was tipping the scales. Tactically, I knew we were ready. The fixed-posts, roving patrols, troopers, and investigators responding to calls, tactical teams permeating the area, and omnipresent aircraft overhead were poised to strike. I was gaining confidence that it would just be a matter of time. All the while, praying no one would get injured.

First thing **Friday morning, June 26,** as the manhunt was entering its 21st day, the *Press-Republican* reported we had issued another, "Warning Call – Just before 7 AM Friday, automated phone calls alerted residents in Malone, and to the north, the Town of Constable, to expect an increased police presence. It was the start of a day that saw 1,100 local, state and federal officers, guns drawn, combing forests, fields and homes near two cabins where Matt and Sweat's presence had been confirmed by DNA." One local resident got it right when he commented, "They (police) told me they're trying to control them from moving any further north." 14

With over 1,100 officers and more than 2,200 leads by this point, I was at our FOB, when a call came in that CERT Members conducting one of a dozen grid searches going on between CR 41, Malone, and the Canadian border to the north that day, had found something on Webster Street Road, approximately two and a quarter miles from the most recent burglary location. This time, however, searchers had found what appeared to be a "hide site." A bed-down area, about 25 yards into the woods, off the east shoulder of Webster Street Road, north of the intersection with CR 41. The CERT supervisors in the field, sounded excited about what they found, and I proceeded out to see for myself.

Upon my arrival, I was escorted by a CERT NCO and the correction officer who had made the discovery. Twenty-five yards into the woods, and overlooking the road, was an obvious spot where someone had "laid up." Estimated to be approximately 24-48 hours old, the grass was matted down. M&M wrappers and salt and pepper shakers littered the ground. We knew by this point, and would be reinforced later in interviews with Sweat, that the inmates utilized an abundance of pepper, attempting to throw off the dogs, "Cool Hand Luke-style." Search teams expanded and combed the woods, while the crime scene techs were called in for collection. [In time, these items were found to be consistent with Sweat's DNA; although they were *not* tested for Matt's DNA, due to Matt being deceased by the time they made it to the lab; and the whereabouts of Sweat was now the priority.] Taking in the sights, and being cautious not to disturb the scene, I concurred with DOCCS CERT, that this was an outstanding find.

Knowing, that momentarily I had another national press conference scheduled at the SP Malone Barracks, I headed back out to the road towards my car. Wanting to thank these officers for their efforts before departing, I walked up to a group of CERT supervisors huddled in the middle of the dirt road. No sooner did I start to speak, did an arm penetrate the circle holding out an *ice-cold* Diet Mountain Dew. "Here ya go, Major! We heard you had a thing for Diet Mountain Dew!"

I said, "You got that right!" From the beginning of the incident, 20 days earlier, I had had very little food and even less sleep. At times, it was as if I was holding it together on Diet Dew and 5-Hour Energy. I immediately accepted the gesture. After all, it was already a hot day, and I had the press to deal with. But, the best part about it was that I got a chance to celebrate this "find," with some great people. Looking just beyond the inner-perimeter of our group, I noticed a big smile on the face of CERT Lieutenant Darryl Menard. Darryl, was the OIC of Clinton Correctional Facility's CERT in Dannemora. He and his team had taken capturing these two fugitives *personally*. Darryl, knowing my penchant for this specific soft drink, had apparently spread the word, and I was fortunate to have him on my team.

Driving north to the press conference, I will admit, I was a little tired of doing them. While I understood the purpose of a free and transparent press <u>and</u> the importance of getting the message out, frankly, I felt we had more pressing concerns right now. Fortunately for me, I had a superb Unified Command staff, and had delegated the necessary authority to act in my absence. I knew my staff was fully capable, but still, *another* PC? I had been in front of the cameras so many times; I had stopped counting. The good news was, I also had a tremendous staff of public information officers, under the direction of Director Beau Duffy and his deputy, Kristin Lowman, from Division HQ. Together with my own Troop "B" PIO, Trooper Jennifer Fleishman, who had been with me from the start, and Trooper Jack Keller, on loan from Troop "D", I was always well-prepared. I know, and am thankful for, the amount of BS they dealt with, so I didn't have to. Anyway, I arrived at SP Malone, with just minutes to spare. The front lot was full of cameras, commentators, and journalists, and I almost couldn't make it to the back lot to park.

I walked into the building from the rear entrance and was handed a set of prepared remarks, that I would deliver, before opening it up for questioning. Having been through the mill before, I knew this was where it always got interesting. The reporters were never satisfied with the prepared statement and pressed hard for facts and something newsworthy. And, who could blame them, it was their job. It was tough, at times, withholding case specifics, like DNA, confessions, pending arrests, and the like, but that was MY job. Release *nothing* prematurely that would compromise the safety of my people, our tactics, techniques, and procedures (TTPs), or the integrity of the investigation.

Just about everything's fair game during these encounters, including: "Major, how much is this search costing the taxpayers?" a reporter asked.

Granted, it's a legitimate question. I simply replied once again, "I do not concern myself with the cost of the search, **I concern myself with capturing two escaped murderers**."

Still, sometimes you get a truly off-the-wall question, and this would prove to be one of those times. After fielding numerous questions, mostly about DNA, weapons, and evidence from burglaries, I got: "Major Guess, as you stand before us today, citing the 1,000 police officers you have in this intense search effort, how is it that the State Police is going ahead with a promotional exam (for sergeant) tomorrow (Saturday)? Doesn't that detract from your mission here?" As the words were coming out of his mouth, I could feel my jaw tensing. A look my wife was familiar with, and as she watched the press conference at home on TV thought, *Here it comes!*

[The NYSP holds promotional exams every two years. Troopers had been intently studying around the state for this infrequent opportunity for the previous 6-12 months. Accordingly, I had worked with the Division's Office of Human Resources, to ensure my numbers were NOT impacted and that this search, MY PRIORITY, would continue unabated.] But that was more than I wanted to relate to this jackass, who, I felt, was trying to catch me with my pants down around my ankles. So, I simply replied, *"Fortunately, the New York State Police is capable of doing more than one thing at a time, and doing it very well."* With that, I declared the PC was over, turned immediately away from the podium, and walked back into the barracks.

I had more important things to do and couldn't wait to get back to the CP, or in the field, where the real work was being done. Thus, I jumped back in my car and headed out of the lot, having to pause momentarily at the front entrance, while waiting to merge into traffic. Just then, out of the corner of my eye, I noticed a reporter making his way over to me. I thought, *Here we go. I can't even get out of the parking lot. Well, at least it's not the same guy.* Ever respectful of my position, we'd made eye contact, so I rolled down my window. "Major," the journalist began, "You're doing a great job out there. Be safe!"

I was blown away. "Thank you, Sir. Much appreciated," I said to Rick Leventhal, a Fox News reporter. What a class act!

Exiting the lot, I was headed south out of the Village of Malone, intending to head back to the FOB on Titus Mountain, to get an overview of how the search was progressing. On the way back, I was monitoring a radio transmission involving troopers responding to another alleged "burglary" of a seasonal camp off Route 30, approximately 10 miles south of my location. Nothing out of the ordinary yet, just patrols, including BCI Investigators, en route.

The complainant and owner of the camp, Robert Willett Jr., an off-duty correction officer and area resident, had discovered the intrusion while checking on his cabin, the "Humbug Mountain Hunting Club," a good-size, brown structure, complete with bunk beds, a red felt pool table, and an outbuilding, situated back in the woods off the east side of the highway in the Town of Malone. At around noon that day, Willett noted a bottle of Seagram's grape gin had been moved and spilled on the countertop in the camp. Cognizant of the recent burglary activity in the area and the sighting at the Twisted Horn camp, approximately 12 miles southeast, just six days earlier, he contacted his friend, Leland Paul Marlow, another DOCCS employee, and registered nurse at Upstate Correctional Facility, to inquire if he'd been through the cabin and possibly moved the gin bottle. "No," Marlow responded, then agreed to join Willett in a search of the camp, which after arming themselves, both men accomplished.

Upon second look, not only was the bottle out of place, but Willett also found empty bottles of rum and thought one might even be missing. Observant, he'd also detected that his Bushnell Binoculars were gone. Upon this discovery, Willett and Marlow each made calls to the NYSP; Willett dialed a SP hotline, and Marlow reached State Police Investigator Jason Pelkey by cell phone, an acquaintance of his who happened to be working at the FOB at Titus Mountain, less than 10 miles away. Both men were instructed to standby for the arrival of investigators.

While waiting for the officers, both men heard a gunshot, and called 911 to report it. Troopers and SP Investigators arrived on the scene, armed with patrol rifles. While conducting an interview with the complainant another shot rang out, just as vehicles passed by, resulting in one, a truck towing a fifth-wheel trailer, pulling off the side of the road. The driver pulling the trailer, thinking he had blown a tire, checked his vehicle, while two investigators approached to check on his welfare. Seeing no flat tires or damage to the trailer, the driver departed the area, just as a third gunshot was heard. The troopers then raced back toward the cabin.

Subsequently, at approximately 1:11 PM, before I could arrive back at the FOB, I monitored a radio transmission of, "Shots fired, in the vicinity of State Route 30 in the Town of Malone." This location, I knew, was extraordinarily close to the reported camp burglary currently under investigation. In fact, the area was right on top of the highway, where interviews were being conducted. Due to my proximity, and the urgency of the situation, I headed directly to the scene.

Minutes later, as additional officers raced to that location, a fourth gunshot was heard emanating from the wood line, just south of the cabin, along RT 30. To assist members on scene, tactical assets were deployed both by helicopter (FBI HRT, and BORTAC) and by vehicle (Technical Sergeant Pena and his riflemen, and SORT), as anxious troopers attempted to determine the location of the shooter and protect the civilian residents. At the same time, the Troop "B" FIU, was dispatched to process the site of the burglary. [Ultimately, evidence was subsequently secured and later analyzed by the FIC, confirming the presence of <u>Matt's</u> DNA.]

At that time, a State Police roving Patrol Rifle Team member advised his supervisor, Sergeant Mike Pena, he had heard a gunshot after his arrival, approximately 100 yards south of original call. As the Patrol Rifle Team deployed south along RT 30, they observed and entered an over-grown, grassy pathway, leading into the wood line, and proceeding about 30 yards off road. Upon arrival, the element noted a small, camping-type trailer, approximately 12 feet long, in a thickly wooded setting. Leading his team, Sergeant Pena first cleared the immediate surrounding area and searched the camper, detecting the smell of gunpowder still in the air. Troopers also noted a set of footprints, travelling away from the camper door and into a ravine. Aware that the United States Border Patrol Special Operations Group Tactical Unit National Team (BORTAC) was in the area, Sergeant Pena met with the Team Leader, Christopher Voss, a Supervisory Agent with U.S. Customs and Border Protection, and advised him of his findings. BORTAC, based out of El Paso, TX, was assigned as an aerial Quick Reaction Force (QRF) that day, and had responded by helicopter when the "shots fired" call went out. Accordingly, the team, one of four responding to the area (including FBI HRT, VSP Tactical Unit, and NYSP SORT), entered the woods south of the camper.

Shortly after my arrival, a fifth shot rang out. I closed the road and obtained a SITREP from Sergeant Pena and Captain Teppo, who had responded when the first "shots fired" call was made. Sergeant Pena advised that he had just cleared a "camper" where he had located a bottle of spiced rum, smoldering incense, and detected the odor of gunpow-der...maybe 15 minutes old. Furthermore, he stated, that a trail led out of the camper and down an embankment. He'd located a knife and a pair of shoes near the steps of the camper. The camper door was wide open, as if someone had darted out in a hurry. Presently, Captain Teppo advised me that tactical teams were moving into the area and searching the property around the cabin, but thus far, canines did not have a track. With that, Sergeant Pena relayed his conversation with the BORTAC Team Leader, and that they (BORTAC) had dropped over the bank searching south, with troopers covering the high ground along Route 30.

Suddenly, at 1:30 PM, another report of "shots fired" came in. This one, reported at Meacham Lake Campground, eight miles south, where a driver was reporting his trailer being struck by gunfire while travelling on State Route 30. "What the fuck?" the three of us said in unison, not knowing that the driver had previously stopped to check for a suspected "blow out." We reasoned, "If they'd (inmates) hijacked a vehicle, they could have gotten that far." We had to know what we're dealing with.

Captain Teppo and Sergeant Pena said, "We're on it!" and headed out.

In the meantime, this entire event was a huge development, and I knew I had to advise Division HQ, ideally, before they heard about it on the news. I picked up my BlackBerry, no signal. *Figures.* This area, in fact the entire region, is notorious for poor cell coverage. But, I didn't have time for this. Hopping back in my car, I raced up the road, in search of a few bars indicating coverage. I got Field Commander Colonel Patricia Groeber on the phone, first ring, and relayed what we had. She was intrigued, to say the least, and indicated she would advise the superintendent. "Keep me updated," she said.

"Of course," I replied, "But, be advised, cell coverage sucks. I had to drive three quarters of a mile up the road to get this signal. Now, I'm heading back to the action." That's how it went for the rest of the afternoon – command and control from the scene, punctuated by incrementally advising the colonel by driving up and down the road. *Whatever it takes...*

When the captain and sergeant arrived at Meacham Lake Campground, they interviewed the rattled driver and noted a shotgun slug hole on the left side of the trailer, approximately six-feet high, passing through and through. When the driver, who had only minutes before been travelling southbound down RT 30 and thought he had a blowout, arrived at the park's check-in kiosk, he'd observed the fifth-wheel RV trailer he was towing had sustained damage from an apparent gunshot, and reported it. This interview, left no doubt in the troopers' minds, that the gunshot had come from the same area they had just left. Subsequently, Sergeant Pena contacted the Forward Operating Base, via radio, and reported *confirmation* that a shotgun had been utilized in the location of the initial report <u>and</u> ensured the information was relayed to members searching the area.

[Although we will never precisely know Matt's intention, one may reasonably infer from the investigation, that Matt had been shooting at vehicles from a firing point along the sloped eastern bank of RT 30. Four 20-gauge shotgun shell casings were recovered near a downed log, approximately 40 yards south of the camper, just 10 yards up the slope from RT 30, while a fifth shell casing was found half the distance to Matt's final location, in the wood line. The location of his firing position, and hole in the trailer, portrayed an attempt to commandeer a vehicle for escape. The fifth-wheel trailer that was struck, was being towed by a pick-up truck. Hypothetically, if a highly intoxicated shooter wielding a sawed-off shotgun had taken a shot at the driver of a moving vehicle and had failed to adequately compensate for movement of the vehicle, it is entirely plausible that a slug hole could end up in the vehicle, at a position behind the driver's head, at roughly the same height.]

Upon returning to my location, Sergeant Pena stopped an additional tactical team about to enter the woods and advised them of the presence of the BORTAC Team already in the area, to deconflict the potential for a Blue-on-Blue, friendly fire incident. He was then joined by several uniformed State Police members from across the state, and took a position on the wood line along RT 30, just north of the BORTAC location. As troopers held the perimeter, Troop "E" Sergeant Scott Reinard stated that one of his men heard movement in the woods along RT 30, south of the camper. Sergeant Pena and Sergeant Reinard exited the wood line at approximately 3:20 PM, and observed a trooper draw his sidearm and point it east, into the woods, about 40 yards south of trailer stating, "I heard someone cough!" Pena, who'd been talking to the tactical teams all day, then transmitted this information to BORTAC, who stated they were still in the vicinity, patrolling in the woods along the ridgeline, approximately 30-40 yards in from roadway. Sergeant Pena, relayed that information to me, then reported hearing movement and another cough, just prior to a helicopter flying over. At that point, I directed all helicopters to exit the area, to isolate and enhance the search.

At approximately 3:45 PM, Sergeant Pena again heard movement and advised BORTAC, who responded, "Let us know when close..."

With the troopers holding the perimeter, Sergeant Pena radioed, "That's good. You're in the immediate area."

Following that transmission, Sergeant Pena heard verbal commands, "Let me see your hands!" and "Drop the gun!" before hearing multiple gunshots.

In the heavily wooded area, just off the roadway and bordered by a large swamp, here's what had just transpired: BORTAC had responded, and while patrolling the area, the team's point-man located a subject lying in a prone position yards in front of the group. Despite not having a clear view, he commanded the subject to put his hands up. It was at that time, Team Leader Voss, who had been in communication with the troopers, moved forward in the formation and began commanding the subject to put his hands up – no response. Subsequently, Voss could see the subject lift his face up and noted the subject was pointing a firearm directly at him, creating a life-threatening situation. Now, Voss commanded him to drop the gun. The subject failed to comply, and Voss fired his M4 rifle in rapid succession, striking the subject in the head twice, terminating the threat to himself and his team.

BORTAC quickly established 360-degree security, both covering the subject and safeguarding against the threat of another shooter, as they sought to determine positive identification. Checking immediately for scars, marks, and tattoos, they observed the tattoo "Mexico Forever," on the subject, confirming it was indeed Richard Matt. Voss made a radio call stating, "Shots fired, one suspect down hard!" Later adding that no friendlies had been injured. BORTAC then requested Sergeant Pena and troopers on the perimeter to penetrate 30 yards into the wood line, to their position, to form a tight perimeter, securing Matt's body, while they (BORTAC) continued the search for David Sweat...

While numerous individuals distinguished themselves that day, Technical Sergeant Mike Pena had performed in an outstanding manner. Over the duration of the manhunt, Pena had worked to establish an extraordinarily high level of trust and rapport with outside agency tactical teams, and had become an invaluable liaison between these assets in the field and Incident Command. So much so, that while Supervisory Agent Voss may not have even heard the "cough" troopers referred to on the perimeter, Pena's observations and recommendations were nevertheless considered valid and logical to the BORTAC National Team Leader, aiding in the search. Thus, the capture of escaped murderer Richard Matt was largely the result of the trust in the troopers' observations and Pena's communication of that information to our law enforcement partners. [For his exemplary actions, Sergeant Pena would later be awarded the Superintendent's Commendation.]

The weapon in Matt's possession was later determined to be the same .20-gauge shotgun that was stolen from the Twisted Horn Camp. Matt, an escaped murderer, had been firing the gun, ostensibly in an attempt to commandeer a passing vehicle, and had oriented the gun in the direction of the tactical team, refusing commands to drop it, forcing the BORTAC Team Leader to utilize deadly physical force to end the threat and take him into custody. [Voss' actions would later be found to be fully justified by an investigation conducted by the Franklin County District Attorney, as reported November 12, 2015.]

On June 27, 2015, an autopsy was conducted on Matt's body by Forensic Pathologist Dr. Michael Sikirica, who determined the cause of death was severe skull fractures and traumatic brain injuries, due to gunshot wounds to the head; with a residual BAC of .18%.

Matt's apprehension was a significant development, but it was not time to celebrate. *This thing was far from over, and it could still go south.*

CHAPTER 16

NO PRESSURE...

National and international media exploded. Matt's capture, and death, as a result of a spectacular encounter with authorities, captured everyone's attention and stoked the already-intense flames. It seemed the eyes of the world were very much upon us. Among law enforcement participating in the search, there was a visceral sense of expectation. Alertness engulfed our operation! For me personally, while there was relief we'd captured Matt and none of the "good guys" had been injured, I knew history would not judge us kindly, unless Sweat was also apprehended.

Thus, every member of the search detail was now fortified and "leaning forward," as is said in the military, in the proverbial "foxhole."

As BORTAC darted off deeper into the woods, we were consolidating the perimeter in a significant way. While the Border Patrol to the north remained on high-alert, and our roving patrols continued north of Malone in the area between the village and the Canadian border, every other available asset engaged in the search was pulled off other assignments (i.e. localized grid searches and redundant rovers) and committed to reinforcing this site. This meant that hundreds, upon hundreds, of police officers (including plain-clothes investigators), Forest Rangers, deputies, federal agents, and correction officers would now flood into the zone. Even the night shift was recalled early; but, the infusion of additional resources would have to be done in a highly coordinated manner. Now was not the time for everyone to focus on the "shiny object" just off RT 30, where Matt's last stand occurred, and *miss* David Sweat altogether. Who knew if he was holed up in a hide site, within small arms range of where Matt was taken down, waiting to ambush us, how fast and where he was travelling on foot, or if he made a break for it when Matt opened fire. *Had he even still been with Matt when law enforcement closed in that day?* That was a question we needed an answer to and fast!

So, a perimeter of enormous proportions was locked down, and it took everyone we had to do it. Essentially, a box consisting of approximately 20 miles of perimeter roads was secured. There was a patrol car or dismounted officer every 50 yards, less if the curvature of the road, or sight distance, was an issue. Darkness was fast approaching, and dozens of light poles were expeditiously trailered in and deployed. Remember, this is the wilderness. State Route 30, a primary north-south state route, then forming the western border of the box, is sporadically populated with only the occasional home visible and accessible from the roadway. The other three sides of the box were extremely low-traffic county and town roads, with the eastern border being Studley Hill Road, consisting of an old, dirt logging road. Locked within this new focal point was 22 square miles of densely wooded, swampy, mountainous state and private land.

As the Incident Commander, I issued further instructions to Captain Teppo, who had been assisting me on the ground all afternoon, regarding the necessary level of containment. I checked with OPS regarding the current location of the tactical teams presently committed in the woods and where we wanted them over night. Then, after updating HQ, I headed out myself to check the perimeter, driving the entire circumference. It looked good, but nothing was impenetrable. I knew once we locked it down, ultimately, the area would have to be partitioned up and searched. All of it. Just like Dannemora. As a former Army Ranger and SWAT operator, I knew precisely how difficult and time consuming that task would be.

Committing nearly all my resources was a gamble, but one I had to take. As the night shift arrived for duty, the day shift would remain on post, and I didn't hear a word of complaint. They were "all in!" Maintaining this level of commitment, could not be sustained indefinitely, and would be influenced by two things: 1) How many additional resources (reserves) I could obtain, and 2) DNA evidence, or the lack there of...*Had Sweat been with Matt at Humbug Mountain Camp and the camper? Or hadn't he?* Our crime scene techs were processing the scene as I contemplated the question, and I knew our FIC (lab) in Albany was about to pull another "all-nighter" to find the answer. It was that vital!

Later that evening as I remained on scene, a press conference was held at the SP barracks in Malone, attended by Governor Cuomo and Superintendent D'Amico, amid throngs of reporters and the public. The Governor took the podium and confirmed, what the media had been reporting, a fatal shooting had occurred off RT 30, in the Town of Malone. Richard Matt was dead, as a result of his refusal to surrender to law enforcement, and David Sweat was still at large. Governor Cuomo stated: "We have no reason to believe that Mr. Sweat was not with Mr. Matt at the time, but we don't have any confirming evidence that he was, either." Superintendent D'Amico added, Matt was confronted by BOR-TAC, was armed, but had not fired, and refused to comply with orders to raise his hands. [We later learned he was out of ammo, having fired all five-rounds.] The media asked numerous questions about the whereabouts of Sweat, but we were not about to get into a discussion of our theories or strategies.

After 21 days, Matt was dead. The media began to piece together his last movements connecting him to a recent seasonal camp burglary on Fayette Road (CR 41). They based this on unauthorized "sources" telling them that our evidence collection and testing showed feces and associated DNA found at the cabin had belonged to Matt, and the sources weren't wrong. Earlier Friday, at a press conference in Malone (before Matt's death), I had told the media that the "progression of evidence left by Matt and Sweat, including some candy wrappers found Friday, seemed to indicate they were headed in a north-northwest direction."

Our assessment now was, the inmates were last known to be together on Saturday, June 20, at the Twisted Horn camp on Black Cat Mountain, in Mountain View, just off Wolf Pond Road. The focus now was on 22-square-mile area, with heavy security along the Canadian border." That was it, the summation of where we stood.

Returning to the FOB at Titus Mountain, at around 8:30 PM, I called the superintendent directly. This was the first time I'd spoken to him all day, appropriately deferring to communications with the field commander throughout the mission. But, I figured I needed to provide him a SITREP directly; plus, I had a specific request. Upon briefing him with the latest, including our posture going forward during the over-night, he asked, "Chuck, what else do you need?"

"Sir, I need an additional 200 troopers standing on post by 7:00 AM."

"You got it," he said, "Call Field (Field Command) and make it happen." Perfect. No nonsense with Joe D'Amico. That's just how he rolled. We already had approximately 800 troopers here from around the state, so I knew this was a big lift. Committing another 200, would come close to breaking the backs of some of the other troops in the field, but the superintendent sensed, as I did, that this was it. Finally, we had momentum and had to maintain it.

I thanked him and hung up.

As the night wore on, there was much to do. Operationally, it had become relatively "quiet." The perimeter was in place; tactical elements were in the woods, occupying key terrain, and significant planning was underway for the next day's relief. We would be withdrawing and replacing individuals and units that had been rushed to the scene the day before, many of whom would have been up for 24 hours by that point. And it all had to be done seamlessly. We could not afford to create gaps in our coverage. Planning went on into the wee hours, and I collapsed into my troop car in the parking lot at about 2:30 AM, for a few hours of much-needed sleep.

Throughout the day **Saturday, June 27, Day 22,** we received the extra personnel, now greater than 1,600 total, relieved our units in place, and cleared a significant number of the surrounding homes, camps, cabins, and lake side cottages in the Lake Titus area. We also conducted proactive sweeps with CERT and tactical teams, checking off search sectors in the western portion of the grid. Now, with night approaching again, we were continuing to hold the perimeter and attempting to deny Sweat any chance of squirting out through areas previously checked. Going into to Saturday night, I had requested our SORT Team coordinator to come up with a comprehensive plan to insert fresh (recycled) teams into the woods, with the task of occupying multiple vantage points (choke points, high ground, water crossings, trail intersections, etc.) in preparation for the next day's concerted "final" push west to east through the box. This was another significant operation. One that was 100% required to clear the area and apprehend Sweat, if he was in there. *But was he...?*

Late Saturday night, I got the news. Receiving the call personally from one of the FIC (laboratory) supervisors in Albany, she said, "Major Guess, the results of the DNA from Humbug Mountain (the area we were working) are in…there are <u>no</u> matches for Sweat."

"So," I said, a little slow on the uptake due to lack of sleep, "You're telling me Sweat was never there?"

"Well," she said, as any scientist would, to be precise, "…we have no DNA evidence of him being there." The folks in the Lab, this supervisor included, were "Rock Stars," as far as I was concerned. They had processed hundreds of pieces of material and accurately dialed us in several times, and this time was no different. "Sorry," she said.

"No apologies necessary," I said. "Good work." Although, I was disappointed that Sweat was not definitively contained in the box, I had no time to dwell on it. It was pouring rain, and within hours, we were about to reload the woods with a *massive* influx of ground searchers and tactical teams; and I had to turn that off.

Calling the SORT team coordinator, I gave him the news. "Well, I'm glad the guys aren't going out in this shit!" he said, "But, now what?"

Exactly, I thought. They were last-known to be together on Saturday, June 20, at the Twisted Horn camp on Black Cat Mountain, in Mountain View, just off Wolf Pond Road. We now needed a *new* plan for Sunday morning, having only hours to redirect resources elsewhere.

And, so it was, on **Sunday, June 28, 2015,** I arrived at the FOB before first light to review our deployment plan for the day. Last night, we had been able to exfil the tactical teams from the woods and diminish the hard perimeter that had stood for the previous 24 hours. Relieving those officers would be instrumental in today's effort of ground searching another 10-12 grids and resuming our full-fledged reconnaissance of the region north of Malone to the Canadian border.

Although we had never given up that territory, even during the last 24-hour push south of the village, we had diminished those resources to allow for the full-court press some 10 miles south. Now, with no clear indication of where Sweat may be, everything was back on. There was even discussion among investigators in the CP that Matt, perhaps the more volatile of the two, may have grown frustrated running around the woods with Sweat and killed him. If so, we'd still have to find the body. This case had to be brought to closure, one way or another. The morning briefing was well-attended, but it was evident, with the disclosure that Sweat had not been with Matt, the wind had been let out of our sails. Understandable, but no time to lament. New assignments were issued, and the troops headed back out.

One of those receiving his instructions for the day, at the 6:00 AM briefing, was Sergeant Jay Cook, Troop "B" Traffic Incident Management (TIM) supervisor. Sergeant Cook, a 21-year veteran of the State Police, was a local guy, stationed out of SP Malone. In fact, this was his "back-yard," and he knew the area like the back of his hand. Additionally, Sergeant Cook was the "gun winner" in his Academy class years earlier, graduating in 1994, as the top-marksman of his class of 150 recruits and the former Senior Firearms Instructor for all of Troop "B". His new gig, TIM, gave him an opportunity to lead a unique unit within Troop that focused exclusively on Traffic and Highway Safety. During the manhunt, Sergeant Cook had been routinely fulfilling the role as one of our roving team supervisors, which meant he oversaw one of numerous squads of highly mobile troopers, responsible to patrol a designated sector and respond to sightings, calls for assistance, back up, or to perform countless building searches. Cook, with first-hand knowledge of the area, all the way up to the Canadian border, and a high degree of tactical acumen, couldn't have been better suited for this responsibility.

At approximately 3:00 PM, Sergeant Cook and his team were utiliz-ing his knowledge of the patrol area, searching the Town of Constable for David Sweat. With the knowledge that the evidentiary items recently gathered south of the village lacked Sweat's DNA, indicating Sweat had separated from Matt, we refocused our anticipation that Sweat was travel-ling toward the Canadian border. Sergeant Cook's area of responsibility was included in that possible route of travel. In fact, contrary to what some casual observers believe, since Saturday going into Sunday, we had saturated the border area north of Malone with 150-200 officers. Sergeant Cook told the *Press-Republican's* Joe LoTemplio, *"We all knew we were on to them. Absolutely. We were anticipating."* [15]

While patrolling *alone* on Coveytown Road, as the supervisor of a larger roving element, Cook observed an individual 500 yards ahead of him, crossing the road from south to north, near a stone wall, heading across a farmer's alfalfa field. Cook also noted that a *single* individual, dressed in camouflage and operating alone in this area, was suspicious, because our Border Patrol, Forest Ranger, and tactical teams operated in pairs or teams, not alone. Cook accelerated his troop car up the road in an attempt to intercept and question the subject. As Cook approached, the subject crossed the low stone wall and walked purposefully away from the decelerating troop car. Stopping, adjacent to the subject, now 25 yards away, Cook called out to him to, "Stop!" The subject, carrying a back pack, did not comply and continued, with the wave of a hand. Again, Sergeant Cook commanded him to, "Stop!"

This time, the subject looked up briefly, raising his hands, reflexively framing his face and said, "No, I'm good, Bro," as if nothing to see here.

At that moment, Sergeant Cook got a good look at the jaw line and profile of the subject, immediately recognizing him as David Sweat and renewed his commands for Sweat to, **"Stop!"** Telling the *Press-Republican*, "[Sweat was]…*making hand gestures, then, he like, framed his face with his hands like he was trying to bluff me, and I knew 100% it was him."* [16]

As soon as Cook exited his troop car, Sweat, by now with a 30-yard head start, took off running. Cook, sprang into action, cleared the roadside ditch, entered the field, drawing his firearm, and pursued Sweat on foot. During the pursuit, Cook continued to issue verbal commands, as Sweat continued to attempt to evade capture. Cook, a very physically fit trooper, began to gain on Sweat, as the inmate ran north, carrying the backpack. Sweat noticed the gap was closing and ditched his backpack, now outpacing the trooper, who was carrying 12 pounds of protective gear, including his body armor.

Finally, after pursuing Sweat for over 100 yards and knowing he would lose him in the woods ahead, now just 40 yards away, Cook had a decision to make. He knew, that at just two and a half miles south of the Canadian border, if Sweat made it into the trees, he would lose him, and the inmate would likely make it into Canada.

Accordingly, having no other option to gain custody of the fleeing, escaped murderer, Cook told the *Press-Republican*, "I yelled at him one last time: If you don't stop, I'm going to shoot." [17] Cook then stopped, planted his feet, quickly assumed a shooting stance, and discharged his Division-issued Glock Model 37 (.45 caliber) firearm, striking Sweat from a distance in excess of 50 yards.

Hit in the upper torso, Sweat stumbled, but continued to flee, ignoring commands to stop. Sergeant Cook again took aim and fired a second time, striking Sweat again in the upper torso, this time knocking him to the ground. Two phenomenal shots, taken after a 100-yard sprint, by an expert marksman, with a handgun at over 50 yards, resulted in Sweat being taken into custody.

Cook quickly closed the distance and radioed for Constable EMS and backup at 3:17 PM. Cook provided immediate attention to Sweat, which, along with medical care provided by responding troopers and the application of Quick-Clot, a coagulant applied to stem the bleeding, undoubtedly contributed to saving Sweat's life. Sweat was taken by ambulance to Alice Hyde Medical Center in Malone; he was later transported by air to Albany Medical Center, a Level 1 Trauma facility, in the New York State Capital Region, 206 miles away for treatment.

I was on the road, as all this went down, but could not hear Cook's initial call for assistance on the radio due to gaps in coverage. Almost immediately, however, I received a cell call from First Sergeant Steve Lacey, advising me that Sweat had just been shot, and taken into custody. My first question was, "Have any of our people been hurt?"

"No," came the reply.

Thank God! I thought. "Who shot him?" I asked.

"There's still some confusion on that ..." he said, "Might be a "T" Trooper...no wait, hold on, (I thought I could hear voices or a radio in the background) "...a "B" Trooper! Jay Cook!" he said triumphantly.

"And, the trooper's OK?" I reconfirmed...

"Yes, Sir!" replied the first sergeant.

Today was the day!

Had Sergeant Cook not located David Sweat on Coveytown Road, Sweat would have undoubtedly fled into Canada, greatly complicating the search effort, placing countless other lives at risk. Cook's actions were courageous and nothing short of heroic!

We would later learn, from interviewing Sweat, that he had separated from Matt a few days after their flight from the Twisted Horn Hunting Club. Matt had become a liability. He was drunk as often as supplies would permit, had become increasingly volatile, and was slowing Sweat down. Sweat had determined that he'd had enough. Finally, an opportunity presented itself when, according to Sweat, the pair was travelling along the shoulder of a dirt road, and upon hearing a patrol car coming, they ran deeper into the woods to avoid observation. In doing so, Matt, the less physically fit of the two, tripped and crashed to the forest floor, making sounds which would threaten to give their position away. Sweat, seized the chance, bolting away from Matt, leaving him behind. Matt, as investigators deduced from his final location, headed back northwest on his own, deeper into the array of our forces, finally boxing himself in. Sweat, on the other hand, by virtue of his stolen map and compass, more in tune with where he was *and* where he wanted to go, continued generally north, towards Canada.

While on the move, Sweat avoided built-up areas of population and stuck to the woods and fields along the way. [Despite what was being said in the media about power lines and rail beds, we now know through interviews, the inmates avoided them, believing, correctly, we would cover them with search teams.] Sweat noted a significant police presence in the northern sector, as we maintained roving patrols and grid searchers in the region, and he settled on spending his final two nights of freedom in a tree stand, watching law enforcement officers encroaching on his hide site. From his elevated position, he could see officers on ATVs, on foot, and in patrol cars saturating the area. Fearing that he might be discovered by staying put, Sweat, who routinely traveled at night to avoid detection, looked at his map, noting that Canada was just a stone's throw away, and decided to travel in the daylight that Sunday morning, to complete his trek to Canada and freedom.

For his part, Jay Cook has repeatedly heard the term "Hero" and shrugs it off, telling the *Press-Republican*: *"You never think it is going to happen to you, until it happens."* He went on to say, *"I don't know why I was the one to spot him, but I was so thankful that I was able to successfully capture him because I could have easily been the one who let him get away. And that would have devastated me."* [18]

Others, including me, would respectfully disagree. Cook *is* a "Hero," and his actions, for which he would later receive the Superintendent's Commendation, successfully concluded a manhunt of international significance and brought accolades from our law enforcement partners around the world.

As the Troop "B" Commander, who headed the search efforts, I've said many times: *"Cook was the perfect person for the job of apprehending Sweat."*

Unquestionably, Cook's quiet professionalism, dedication, and perseverance are truly *exemplary* and in the finest tradition of the New York State Police.

CHAPTER 17

"TODAY IS THE DAY!"

R acing towards SP Malone, where Jay Cook was about to be brought, I had heard the news I'd waited 23 days to hear. *It's over.* My first call was to the NYSP Field Commander, my good friend, Patricia Groeber. Like me, she verified that none of our people had been hurt *first*, before taking a breath. Patricia would then notify the superintendent.

I have been asked many times during interviews given since, "How did it feel, when you heard the news? How did you celebrate?" Truthfully, I did not celebrate. That normal human response, was eclipsed by an overwhelming feeling of immense relief. For the last 23 days, I felt as though I had the weight of the world on my shoulders. It was one thing, to have the responsibility as the Incident Commander to "catch" the fugitives; it was clearly another, even greater weight, to know in my heart that I was responsible for the safety and welfare of the community and every member of law enforcement participating in the search.

The odds had been so completely stacked against us: two, highly dangerous, killers broke out of New York State's most-secure, hardened facility, with a *six-hour* head start, vanishing into some of the most remote, inhospitable terrain in the country, eventually separating and compounding the difficulty. Juxtaposed to that, the sheer complexity of our response. At the high-water mark, we had over 1,600 law enforcement and correction officers on the ground, in vehicles, and in the air. It is nothing less than miraculous, that we did not experience a serious, or fatal, accident among officers on the ground, or those responding lights-and-siren to the hundreds of calls for service, or an aircraft accident (given the severe weather and proliferation of aircraft).

Perhaps most significantly, I am thankful that with tensions as high as they were, we did not have a "friendly fire" incident among our officers, or inadvertently committed by one of thousands of armed citizens in our area of operations, who, as a result of extreme fear, with nerves on edge, could have easily and mistakenly fired upon law enforcement searching the area. The ability of officers from nearly two dozen disparate agencies to come together successfully and safely for this common purpose, was a testament to their training, discipline, and leadership, as well as our consistent focus on safety.

Driving through Dannemora and eventually into Malone, it was obvious the citizens had gotten the word. Despite the pouring rain, streets in both villages were lined with relieved and grateful members of the community who were cheering and waving flags. Their relief and gratitude was apparent. I was overwhelmed by the sight, but I was even more grateful, that none of these good people had met with any harm. They had supported us and been with us every step of the way. *We wouldn't have been successful without them.*

Upon arriving at the Malone Barracks, I immediately sought out Sergeant Cook. He was sequestered in a room, drinking a bottle of water, and deescalating from his recent, intense encounter. "Jay, how are you? Are you, all right?" I said to him.

"Yes, Sir," he replied. I had already been assured he was "fine," and uninjured, but I was relieved to see him in person.

I said, "Listen, this is not an official debriefing, there'll be time for that later, but give me a quick rundown of what happened."

Jay, relayed the basic facts to me, as I listened in awe; *not* as his commander, but as a fellow trooper. He had performed brilliantly! In fact, the thought flooded into my mind, *Right man, right place, right time.* I couldn't have been prouder of him!

Knowing, I had to head back to the FOB, because the Governor and superintendent were inbound, I pulled him in for a quick hug and pat on the back, "Once again, nice job!" I said. "Here's my personal cell number, if you need anything, anything at all. We'll talk later."

En route to the FOB at Titus Mountain's Upper Lodge, I was redirected to the lower, Main Lodge, as some quick-thinking staffer correctly determined that the Main Lodge would be a more appropriate location for the executive briefing I was about to participate in and the follow-up press conference. My staff scrambled around a bit, to develop as many up-to-the-minute facts as possible (details of the shooting and apprehension, Cook's condition, Sweat's condition, etc.), prior to the Governor's arrival. I knew we had one chance to get it right, before he and the superintendent spoke to the media, and we had to ensure accuracy. In short order, even though it was a Sunday, every agency head that had people participating in the manhunt was present, or had representation. When Governor Cuomo arrived, everyone took a seat at the conference table, which had been fashioned by combining tables at the ski lodge. I'd had Captain Streiff, of the Forest Rangers, mount our latest operational map on the wall, and at the request of Superintendent D'Amico, I stood and briefed the Governor on the day's activity. I ran through the events, highlighting the superb conduct of Sergeant Cook. At the end of my comments, I added, "I said from the beginning, that I honestly did not care who brought these two to justice, but, Sir, I will admit, there's something special about a single, hometown "B" trooper, taking the last guy down just two and a half miles from the Canadian border!"

Proceeding to the next room for the press conference, the Governor took the podium and acknowledged that the weeks-long manhunt was now over. He said, "The nightmare is finally over…today ends with good news. These were dangerous men." The Governor continued by congratulating the first responders and Sergeant Cook, by name, calling Cook, a "Hero." "He was alone when this happened. He knew the area very well. It was a very courageous act."

He then turned it over to Superintendent D'Amico to fill in the details, acknowledging, among other points, Sweat was captured about 16 miles from where his partner, Matt, was shot and killed Friday. D'Amico continued, "We were pushing southward from the border; this was right in that search area." Also, acknowledging that, the inmates may have used black pepper, attempting to mask their trail. The superintendent was most gracious in his remarks, going out of his way to thank the various federal, state, and local agencies who had participated from around the country. In closing, the superintendent acknowledged me, personally, something I was not expecting him to do, stating, *"Major Guess, what a tremendous leader!"*

A round of spontaneous applause broke out among the agency leaders gathered behind the podium, and even among most of the journalists present. The Governor turned to shake my hand, and I will admit, I was truly humbled by the experience. I accepted that thanks on behalf of *every* member of the search coalition <u>and</u> the community, that had endured so much, maintained their confidence in us, and remained ever vigilant, offering the very leads that broke the case wide open. For without them, there would have been no success.

State Assemblywoman Janet Duprey, who did so much to support the correction and police officers during, and after the search, was on hand to join us, and said at Sunday's press conference that she felt *"Exhilaration,"* *"This is just wonderful. A lot of prayers have been answered today... The happiest place in the state right now is Clinton Correctional Facility."* [19] [Janet Duprey, a tremendous, engaged and compassionate, 40-year civil servant, would go on to sponsor an Assembly Resolution, honoring the successful search effort in the Adirondacks; particularly, acknowledging contributions made by DOCCS CERT, Sergeant Jay Cook, and me at the New York State Capitol.]

Additionally, State Senator Betty Little, another staunch supporter, "...extended her thanks to the many law enforcement personnel involved, led by State Police Troop "B" Commander Major Charles Guess. Little said in her statement: *"Their patience, persistence and professionalism, with the eyes of the nation on them, have been nothing short of extraordinary. I also want to commend the North Country residents not only for their patience in the face of uncertainty and danger, but their tremendous outpouring of support for law enforcement these past few weeks. This remarkable and riveting chapter in our Adirondack history will now be known as one of its finest."* [20]

Clearly, residents had endured nearly a month of searches, armed check points, lockdowns, lockouts, helicopters, school closings, cancellation of events, and fear. One local resident summed it up: *"I feel like I can sleep tonight. Life can go back to normal. It's over now."* [21] Another local resident, thanked authorities stating: *"They were bound and determined they were going to get these two guys and they did."* [22]

We wrapped up the press conference, and after shaking the hands of my terrific partners in the room, I headed out, careful to avoid the press outside, back to the Upper Lodge, our FOB. I was exhausted. Both physically and mentally. All I wanted to do was spend a few minutes with my troopers and key staff and to thank them! By the time, I rolled into the lot, most of the folks were gone. Troopers from every corner of the state, from Long Island to Buffalo, had participated in the effort and had been dismissed to return to their "home" troops, while I had been participating in the debriefing down below. The same would apply to the other federal, state, and local men and women, who had coalesced in the Adirondack Mountains for this one common purpose. My most heartfelt thanks and gratitude goes out to them. Despite what you sometimes hear about police at the national level, these professionals departed knowing they could hold their heads high. When their state and country needed them, they answered the call, and at great personal risk.

Late that Sunday night, I was heading back to my Troop Headquarters in Ray Brook, just drained, when I got a request from the NYSP Director of Public Information to go "live" the next morning on "New Day," with Chris Cuomo.

"OK. Time and place?" I asked. The response was 8:00 AM in front of our Command Post in Caddyville. *Figures... No sleeping in, Guess!* I thought. So, I dragged my tail out of the rack, and just as I had done so many days before, reloaded with Diet Mountain Dew and 5-hour Energy, for the one-hour ride north. Upon arrival, I was miked up and waiting for my turn, as Chris was finishing with other news. Then, he turned to me. Chris introduced me and asked a brief series of questions, which I answered, and it was over in minutes. Grateful to have that behind me, it wasn't long before someone sent me a message saying, in effect, "Just saw you on TV; man, you look tired!" I laughed it off, but that night I finally made it home and my wife showed me the "tape." *Holy shit!* I thought. *I DO look awful.* My eyes were red, and my face drawn, having lost about 18 pounds from the start. The stress had taken its toll. I remember thinking at the time, this probably knocked a year or two off my life...But, it was worth every minute. We couldn't have had a better outcome. Quicker, maybe, but not better. ***Both fugitives back in custody, and no one got hurt.***

The very next day, I was at home on a rare day off. My cell phone rang, with caller ID of "Unknown Number." Normally, I do not answer those, preferring to let them go to voicemail, and sort it out later. But, during the last three weeks, I had received a number of them, and knew odds were high that it was an important call.

"Major, Andrew Cuomo," I heard the Governor say.

"Good Morning, Sir," I replied.

Governor Cuomo is a very-direct man. And, I had taken numerous calls from him personally, day and night, throughout the manhunt, when he had a specific question or wanted to discuss strategy. I will say, he sets the bar high, but, it is precisely this way that he gets things done. Additionally, he told me from the start, that I would get whatever I needed from him and the superintendent, to prosecute this mission, and they <u>never</u> let me down. The Governor continued, in sum and substance:

"Major, for a number of years, certainly since the fiasco out west at the Bucky Phillips investigation, the State Police has lost ground…lost credibility as an agency. From the start, your superintendent (D'Amico) said, 'We've got the right guy in charge. If anybody can catch them, it's Chuck!' He was vindicated and right. Through your actions and leadership, the State Police is back on top. You are now, perhaps, at a high-point in modern State Police history. It's a great day!"

These were kind words indeed, and I humbly accepted them on behalf of the <u>entire</u> coalition of forces, that brought the incident to a successful close.

THE AFTERMATH

CHAPTER 18

ESCAPE: HOW IT HAPPENED...

This account is a synopsis, based upon "open source" information, gleaned from our investigation <u>and</u> excerpts from the 2015 New York State Inspector General's Report.[23]

At 5:17 AM, on Saturday morning, June 6, a correction officer discovered Matt and Sweat's empty cells, while conducting the morning count.

Matt and Sweat had begun plotting their escape in late January 2015, and had enlisted the aid of Joyce Mitchell, a Civilian Employee of the facility, assigned as the Civilian Supervisor in Tailor Shop 1; a Division of CORCRAFT prison industry. Over the years, Matt, a current inmate employee, and Sweat a former inmate employee, of Tailor Shop 1, (later assigned to Tailor Shop 8, as a result of internal discipline) had both cultivated highly inappropriate relationships with Mitchell, leading to the criminal introduction of contraband, directly facilitating, aiding, and abetting their escape. When Sweat first proposed the idea of escape to Matt, he said, according to Sweat, "She's fucking nuts, she'll bring us whatever we want, just tell me what you need, and I'll get her to bring it in," and he did.[24]

That same month, Sweat, who had previously been moved out of his adjacent cell, away from Matt, in September 2014 (for allegedly threatening an inmate, who had accused him of being an "Aryan" and allegations of an inappropriate relationship with Mitchell), claims he enlisted the aid of Correction Officer Palmer, who requested the Honor Block housing officer and Industry Supervisor, to allow Sweat an opportunity to return to Industry. Approval to return to Industry and assignment to Tailor Shop 8, paved his way for return to Six Company Honor Block. Ultimately, with the aid of a C.O., he facilitated a move back to his "old" cell, A 23, back adjacent to Matt in A 22, where they could freely communicate, share tools and act as lookouts for each other during the work that lay ahead.

Sweat, familiar with the catwalk behind his cell on the tier, from Palmer allowing him access to perform unauthorized electrical enhancements on junction boxes behind the cells (to increase amperage for hotplates), knew that the catwalk offered the best opportunity for escape. If he could just get back, behind the cells, the catwalk would afford him access to the myriad of tunnels and catacombs of the 170-year-old prison. However, he would need cutting tools to breach the cell's steel wall first.

In mid-February, Matt approached Mitchell about smuggling in tools and hacksaw blades; she readily complied, purchasing $6 dollars worth of blades at Walmart, smuggling them into the prison, past and through the front gate security in her bag, finally placing them in a box next to Matt's work station in the Tailor Shop. According to Sweat, Matt initially taped the blades to his torso and carried them back to his cell, either directly or by way of the infirmary, where he frequently requested to be taken for actual or feigned attacks of sciatica. The IG's report revealed that while it is unclear who escorted Matt that day, "Palmer testified that he escorted Matt from the shop to his cell on a number of occasions, without frisking him, on exiting the shop and bypassing the metal detector on the route."

The inmates later broke the blades in half, wrapped cloth and rubber bands around the blades as a handle and began cutting around an air vent, behind their bed, at the back corner of the cell wall. Sweat described the procedure as: using one single tooth of the saw, at the end of the blade, to scratch repeatedly in one spot, until a hole finally developed, then inserting the blade through the 3/16-inch steel and sawing away. This method proved to be effective and would be employed again. Sweat informed investigators that it took about three weeks and a single blade, to cut his 17 by 12 1/2- inch rectangular opening. Matt took an extra two weeks, and advised Mitchell when they had finished the breach, as they would routinely keep her up to date on their progress.

Both inmates took great care to conceal their work. During the cutting process, Sweat, introduced magnets, he had procured from the Tailor Shop, as a way of collecting the metal filings in the cell, then, flushing the dust down the toilet. Additionally, and most importantly, they carefully concealed the holes behind their bunks by replacing the grates, then taping and painting over the saw marks with paint, provided at will by the C.Os.

Now, Sweat had access to the facility, and began his reconnaissance behind the walls without Matt.

Sweat would face many obstacles and challenges along the way, but overcame them through stealth, ingenuity, perseverance, and opportunity. The last, while taking advantage of abandoned tools, accessing a gang box that is supposed to be locked and inaccessible, *and* good fortune, when the prison steam-heating system was shut off for the summer. This allowed the pipes to cool and an unexpected opportunity to present itself.

Repeatedly, Sweat fashioned and placed a "dummy" in his bed and took a set of "work clothes" along, that he would use exclusively in the dirty environment behind the walls. He exited the rear of the cell and climbed down multiple levels, descending the tiers to reach the subterranean level. Following a variety of tunnels and passage ways, he remained observant of utility pipes, that he correctly reasoned would lead him in the direction of the exterior south wall and the Power Plant. Earlier, from his elevated location at the Tailor Shop, he (and other inmates) could see over the walls, out onto the village streets and down several blocks to the Power Plant. Thus, it was no real mystery where all the main utility lines and pipes led. One could reasonably assume, the pipes passed under or through the wall, and it would be obvious where the pipes led if you could access that point underground.

While exploring the substructure, Sweat met his first major obstacle, a steel brace supporting a cluster of pipes running through an opening between B- and C-Block, and dispatched it in two nights, by cutting through it. On the other side, he found exactly what he was looking for: a "large diameter pipe bearing the letters 'LPS' for low-pressure steam." *"Oh, this is it. That's what I was looking for,"* he told investigators.[25] Following the pipe, Sweat, encountered another significant challenge. The pipe passed through a brick wall, separating C-Block and the Industry Building. Sweat needed to find the strength and wherewithal to penetrate it, or his journey ended right there.

Scrounging around the labyrinth, with an LED light provided to him by Mitchell, Sweat ultimately found an eight-pound sledge hammer, next to a gang box, which along with a makeshift pry bar, allowed him over many nights (two-weeks) to deconstruct a portion of the brick wall, just large enough for him and Matt to scoot through. This was tedious, but critical work. Sweat was careful to stack and replace the bricks nightly, so that in the (unlikely) event of a tunnel inspection, it would go unnoticed.

A clock watcher...each night Sweat, would consult his wrist watch, and be careful to leave himself enough time to cover evidence of his work, retrace his steps, change his clothes, reenter his cell, replace his cut-out ventilation grate, and clean up-all by 4:30 AM, before the mandatory 5:30 AM standing count.

In late April, Sweat faced his penultimate and most challenging obstacle, the seven-foot-thick base of the prison wall. With the steam pipe hot and active, Sweat focused on attempting to breach the base of the wall. Chipping away with his sledge hammer and various other scavenged implements, he was making scant progress. Up to this point Sweat had worked alone, and Matt finally persuaded him to take him behind the walls. Matt, being far less capable and fit than Sweat, proved to be a hindrance, and after a couple nights of less-than-productive work, Sweat refused, telling Matt: *"I'm not taking you down till I'm done 'cause it's too much work and I don't get nothing done."* [26]

Sweat had even managed to pick the lock on a gang box, acquiring some items of assistance, such as a two-pound sledgehammer, but what he desired most, he did not find – suitable concrete bits for the drills or power-capable cutting tools. Interestingly, while he was careful to return most items nightly, there were a few things: dust masks, a light, and a broken steel punch, that he did not return and were never reported as missing by the contractor. Sweat then went through Matt once again, requesting, two concrete drill bits, two chisels, and a steel punch. Mitchell agreed, smuggling these items into the prison by inserting them in two pounds of hamburger meat, freezing the package, bringing it through the front gate, placing it in an employee freezer, where Palmer, per Mitchell, allegedly, picked it up and transported it to Matt's cell. According to Palmer, not knowing it contained tools. Furthermore, as a C.O., there was no requirement for Palmer to proceed through metal detectors along the way.

Sweat testified he received the tools, including concrete drill bits, in late April or early May, returning to the gang box for the drill, but found the box had been removed. Nonetheless, Sweat persisted chiseling away at the wall. Then, on May 4, 2015, maintenance staff shut down the heating system and Sweat correspondingly observed that the pipe was cooling down. "Placing his hand on the steam pipe, *'I realized it's cold.'* He then, *'tapped on it and realized there was no water in it. Fuck it, if they drained that pipe and it's empty, I might be able to cut into that and go through that and cut my way back out."* [27] So, replicating the use of the hacksaw blades used to cut through the cell walls, he set about cutting his way into the 18-inch steam pipe. Meanwhile, in Tailor 1, Matt was continuing to woo and manipulate Mitchell, telling her everything she wanted to hear. Simultaneously, Sweat was sending her daily "love" notes through Matt, as he was, according to him (Sweat), just trying to "placate" her, keep her engaged. Sweat later told our investigators, "I just wanted a ride." [28]

It worked. Mitchell, increasingly becoming fixated on Matt and Sweat, with Sweat commenting that they exchanged notes, practically on a daily basis, again facilitated by Matt. Matt, for his part, was spending an increasingly inordinate amount of time daily with Mitchell in Tailor 1, right under the noses of civilian supervisors and correction officers. Inexplicably, this included several sexual encounters in the shop. According to Mitchell, *"one day while she and Matt were alone in the adjoining Tailor Shop 9, to retrieve a machine part, 'Matt grabbed me...and he kissed me...'* She admitted that a second sexual encounter occurred, where she performed oral sex on Matt, in Tailor Shop 9." [In fact, Mitchell admitted further sexual contact with Matt after the incidents in Tailor Shop 9.] Almost "daily," she testified, Matt stood by her desk and asked her to fondle his penis by reaching into his pants through a hole he had cut in his prison clothing." [29]

As the plan to escape unfolded, talk included the notion of running off together with the inmates, after they killed her husband, Lyle. Sweat testified that the idea was Mitchell's, stating she said: *"Oh, pop my hus-*

band, he's worth more to me dead than he is alive." Sweat said she once wrote in a note, *"Oh, you guys gotta get rid of the glitch."* [30] Mitchell provided a different account, admitting she made the remarks in the Tailor Shop, but she was joking, *"I was being a smart aleck. Every husband and wife have arguments and say, 'I can just kill him,' you know? Every couple does that."* She went on to say, murdering her husband was Matt's idea, and she only went along because she was afraid he would have him killed, either inside or outside the prison. However, Mitchell <u>did</u> accept two pills given to her by Matt, purportedly to knock Lyle out, so that they could return to her home and murder him. Only after the escape, did she reportedly flush them down the toilet.[31] Regardless, Sweat, was adamant, *he* did <u>not</u> plan to kill Lyle Mitchell.

As the time drew nearer, Mitchell researched cabins in Vermont, but after Matt decided they were too expensive, he decided to head to Mexico. Eventually, they settled upon her picking them up at the manhole, after which they would drive all night, spend time in West Virginia, while things cooled down, and continue down to Mexico, where Matt claimed he had connections with a drug cartel. Additionally, at the request of the inmates, Mitchell procured an [atlas], "compass, tent, sleeping bags, fishing poles, a hatchet, a rifle, shotgun and ammunition – she and her husband already owned." [32]

Near the end of May, Matt told Mitchell they were almost ready to go. "When asked for assurance she would meet them with her vehicle as planned, Mitchell, according to Sweat, told Matt: *I'll be there. I'll be there. I haven't failed you guys yet.* " [33]

As Sweat continued his work, it became clear, he would need more blades to finish the job and cut out of the pipe. Once again, he had Matt advise Mitchell; once again, she complied, utilizing the frozen hamburger technique, to introduce two more hacksaw blades on Friday, May 29. Palmer again, was the unwitting conduit for the delivery of blades in frozen hamburger to the Honor Block and Matt's cell, noting with investigators it *"was odd,"* that the meat's wrapping lacked a price bar code or store label.[34]

Over the next two weeks, Sweat, spent every night fixated on the task of cutting his way through the 3/8-inch steel, first *into* and then *out of* the steam pipe. Cutting out, some 14 feet from where he entered, presented its own challenges, as Sweat had to work from within the confined space of the 18-inch pipe itself. Then, on June 5, he completed the final cut in the 17x16-inch exit hole and shimmied out of the pipe and into the sewer tunnel, *outside* the wall of the prison. Proceeding several hundred yards underground, he passed a couple of locked manhole covers on his way to his destination, the Power Plant. Arriving there, he observed a steel gate entrance was open, but due to the intense lights on in the plant and the assumption there may be workers present, he backtracked 200 yards to one of the locked manhole covers. "With only a small piece of hacksaw blade remaining, Sweat, cut the chain, pushed up the manhole cover just enough to see *'the old school building,'* that he recognized from his observations from the Industry Building, and said *'...I knew where I was.'* This spot, in the intersection of Barker and Bouck Street, was *'perfect,'* he recalled. It will be an easier place for (Mitchell) to see to pick us up."[35]

Sweat would later tell investigators, that during the time he was working to affect his escape, he'd felt *"Free."* Now, he was about to experience it for real. Due to the "dry run," Sweat had been out of his cell longer than usual that night, and had to race back, covering his tracks along the way, in time for the morning count. Matt and Sweat had also agreed that the signal, between the two of them, of a successful breach, was to share a cigarette, when he returned to his cell. Sweat told investigators, *"...before I got him up, I lit the cigarette and knocked on his wall and stuck a mirror over so he seen me, seen the cigarette."* He goes, *'Are you serious, are you kidding me, you made it through?'* And he thought that you know, I just made it through the pipe. I said, 'No, dude, I made it out, twice, and came back.'"*[36]

That day, both Sweat by note, and Matt in person, told Mitchell *"tonight's the night"*; Sweat instructing her to *"leave the car running, but get out and act like you're talking on the phone, because everybody knows you're not allowed to drive and talk on the phone."* According to Sweat, later that night, as they were packing, Matt said he'd told Mitchell, *"Listen, you have to be there at twelve. If you're not there, we're dead, they're going to kill us."* Matt then told Sweat, for her part, Mitchell said: *"No, no, I'm going to be there. I'm going to be there."*[37]

The inmates packed items they'd procured for the journey, Sweat said, *"...like 20 packs of peanuts...40 granola bars...probably 12 sticks of pepperoni."* [38] Loading them into a soft-guitar case, in an effort to throw off anyone who may notice them on the outside. Immediately following the 11:00 PM headcount, Matt and Sweat placed "dummies" in their beds, breached their cell walls, and were on their way. Sweat said he proceeded through the steam pipe first, and extended a bedsheet back to Matt, who arms outstretched, was more or less pulled through the pipe. Reaching the sewer manhole cover, some 400 feet south of the prison wall at 11:50 PM, ten minutes early, they waited. At midnight, they climbed out onto street level.

According to Sweat, "Almost immediately after exiting the manhole, an approaching car caused Matt to panic and run into the backyard of a nearby home. Worried that Matt's actions would betray them as escapees, Sweat yelled to him, *'What the fuck are you doing, man? Where are you going?'* At that point, the car turned into the same driveway, and the driver, who resided there, got out and yelled, *'Hey, what are you fucking scumbags doing in my yard?'* Sweat replied, *'Oh, man, I'm sorry. I apologize. We were just cutting through. We were on the wrong street.'* Sweat's explanation and appearance satisfied the individual, as no further words were exchanged." [39] Later, the couple would recount this chance encounter to investigators.

Sweat's concerns were justified. Joyce Mitchell, Plan A, was a *no show*!

Meanwhile, that same Friday afternoon, while Matt and Sweat were packing, Joyce and Lyle Mitchell finished work for the day at Clinton and headed home, stopping along the way for dinner. Later that night, the very night she was supposed to drug Lyle and meet Matt and Sweat, she declared she was having a "panic attack" and was transported by her husband to the Emergency Room at Alice Hyde Medical Center, in Malone. There, she was admitted for observation. A convenient place to be, to establish an alibi, or so she thought. At approximately 11:30 AM the next morning, Saturday, after the escape, she was preparing to be discharged, when she turned on her cell phone and found that the State Police had been trying to contact her.

Officers conducting the 5:30 AM master standing count on Honor Block, which requires inmates to be sitting up in bed or standing, discovered Matt and Sweat were missing. Subsequently, the C.O.s phoned the prison's watch commander, a lieutenant, who telephonically notified the first deputy superintendent, who responded immediately from his nearby residence. Proceeding to the Honor Block, the first deputy noted the holes in the cell, ordered the area secured as a "crime scene," and proceeded to the roof, which he reasoned was also accessible from the catwalk. Seeing no evidence of escape there, he and a sergeant commenced a search of the subterranean tunnels, where he found evidence of the breach through the brick wall and the note left by Sweat. Receiving a radio transmission from a C.O. that they'd found a cut into the steam pipe at the main wall, the first deputy, obtained a firearm from the prison armory, and accompanied by a trooper, and his canine, proceeded to the Power Plant. Once at that location, the first deputy entered the sewer tunnel, containing the steam pipe, and made his way, backtracking, toward the prison. Along the way, he found the severed chain at the manhole, and, continued toward the facility, until he reached the exit hole, where Sweat and Matt had cut out of the pipe, confirming the escape.

At least six-hours earlier, with Mitchell as a no-show, the inmates had embarked on an overland route, which would subsequently (a month later) be described by investigators as: exiting the Village of Dannemora to the west, heading up SR 374, then turning left (south) onto Hugh Herron Road, then Clark Hill Road; Town of Saranac. Then, quickly ditching westbound, into the wilderness, where they spent the next several weeks, enduring miles of rugged, cross-country travel, at times hiding out in random deer blinds, lean-tos, and hunting camps. Along their way, they approached: Standish Road; Wolf Pond Road; Town of Bellmont; climbed mountains and traversed swamps; ultimately splitting up, within days after their incident at the Twisted Horn camp; because Matt's drinking was out of control, he was physically drained and was "slowing" Sweat down. After the split, the inmates remained at large in the wilderness, generally handrailing the following independent routes:

<u>Matt</u> – Northwest to Fayette Road (CR 41); Webster Street Road; and SR 30; in the vicinity of Elephant Head Mountain and Lake Titus, in the Town of Malone, Franklin County.

<u>Sweat</u> – East of Franklin CR 25, from Hamlet of Chasm Falls, then north to Badore Road; Town of Malone; Perham, Pikeville, Vincent, Finney, Fleury, Spencer, and Coveytown Roads; Town of Constable, Franklin County.

Sweat would later inform investigators, that they traveled mostly at night. The inmates procured food, guns, and other supplies from seasonal hunting camps.[40] In one of the cabins, Sweat claimed they monitored media reports of the search and were surprised that we were still searching so intently. Finally, after two weeks, they realized we weren't "giving up," forcing them to forgo Mexico and focus their real attention on Canada. Additionally, Sweat claims he was almost discovered twice. First, by three civilians who went to check their camp, when he and Matt were hiding near the cabin. Second, when he was hiding in a tree stand, after he had split off from Matt.[41] This greatly increased his sense of desperation.

On Day 23, Sweat observed law enforcement coalescing in the area, but also knew he was tantalizingly close to the border. Fearing he was about to be boxed in and apprehended, he moved out of his hide site and proceeded steadily north. He'd observed patrols with ATVs and troop cars, intently roving the surrounding roads, and attempted to time his movements to avoid detection. Ultimately, just two and a half miles from the Canadian border, near one of the last tree-lines and roads in New York State, Sergeant Jay Cook spotted him. When challenged, Sweat, initially tried to dupe the sergeant into thinking he was a fellow searcher, but Cook was too sharp for that, and the chase was on. *Both* men knew reaching the far side tree line represented Sweat's ticket to freedom. In Sweat's view, he had just spent six months crafting his escape from Dannemora and the last three-weeks on the run, eluding capture, and was trying to seal the deal. For Sergeant Cook, a tremendous 21-year career with the New York State Police had prepared him for this moment, yet everything seemed to hang in the balance...

Upon capture, Sweat later likened his effort and escape to: "The Shawshank Redemption," telling investigators that, he'd joked with Matt, "While it took Tim Robbins' character in the movie 20 years, it would only take them 10."

As elusive as Sweat had turned out to be, that day he had met his match in Sergeant Cook. Cook was indeed the right man, in the right place, at the right time.

Our strategy of **_Relentless Pursuit_** had paid off!

CHAPTER 19

WHERE ARE THEY NOW?

M uch was written, said, and investigated, both criminally by the State Police, and administratively by the Inspector General's Office, following the manhunt. Chapter 19, will bring you up to speed with some of those revelations, as a *"Where are they now?"* for the main characters, while Chapter 20, will reveal the results of the IG's investigation, what factors led to the escape, recommendations, and overall lessons learned.

Immediately following Sweat's capture and the conclusion of the manhunt, Governor Cuomo shared additional information with the national and local media. Filling in some of the most significant informational gaps at the time, he carefully avoided speculation on territory the IG was actively investigating. As evidenced by excerpts from an article in the *Press-Republican* Governor Cuomo stated, *"David Sweat has told investigators that he and Richard Matt planned to head to Mexico with Joyce Mitchell's car; they would kill Mitchell's husband, Lyle, and then get in the car and drive to Mexico, on the theory that Mitchell was in love with one, or both of them. When Mitchell doesn't show up, the Mexico plan gets foiled, and then they head north toward Canada. He continued, Sweat felt that Matt was slowing him down. Older and less fit, Matt had blisters on his feet, and the socks with blood found in Owls Head were his, adding Sweat actually disengaged from Matt about five days ago, which answers why there was no DNA of Sweat in the last cabin. Sweat was captured carrying a backpack with supplies for flight: maps, tools, bug repellent, wipes and Pop Tarts."* [42] [Note: in fact, Sweat was also in possession of a hunting knife.] The Governor also confirmed that, in addition to what was supplied by Joyce Mitchell, Matt and Sweat had used tools that belonged to outside contractors and that Sweat had been working on the escape for weeks.

These were significant revelations, in the days immediately following Sweat's apprehension.

MATT

On Friday, June 26, 2015, Matt was shot and killed in the Town of Malone, NY, nearly 30 miles west of the prison. The autopsy showed Matt died of multiple skull fractures and massive brain trauma from gunshots to the head. Additionally, the fugitive presented a strong odor of alcoholic beverage, with a .18 BAC.

SWEAT

On Sunday, June 28, 2015, Sweat was shot and captured, in the Town of Constable, NY, about 35 miles northwest of Clinton Correctional Facility and just two and a half miles south of the Canadian border. Clearly, New York State Police Sergeant Jay Cook was justified in taking the action he took to apprehend Inmate Sweat. *"State and Federal law allows the use of deadly force to prevent an escape if the officer believes the escapee poses a significant threat."* [43] Sergeant Cook's actions would be deemed fully justified by an investigation conducted by the Franklin County District Attorney, as filed in the official report dated November 12, 2015.

Sweat already serving life, without the possibility of parole, was additionally sentenced to 3 1/2 to 7 years for each of two counts of escape, and ordered to make a payment of $79,841 in restitution.

Sweat is currently in solitary confinement, in the Special Housing Unit (SHU), at Five Points Correctional Facility, in Central New York. Confined 23 hours a day, he resides in a pre-fab cell, with electronically controlled lighting and is monitored by surveillance cameras. Corrections officers remotely open a door at the rear of his cell one hour a day for exercise. Food is passed through a portal in the door. The prisoner's activities are strictly controlled and coordinated, to ensure the safety and security of the inmate, staff, and public. This setting does <u>not</u> resemble his previous residence in the Honor Block at Dannemora.

JOYCE MITCHELL

Mitchell plead guilty to Promoting Prison Contraband (Felony) and Criminal Facilitation (Misdemeanor) and was sentenced to 2 1/3 to 7 years, the max, indeterminate sentence allowed by law. Her plea agreement included not facing other charges, such as: conspiracy to murder her husband and sexual assault or rape (prisoners cannot consent), as the DA cited an inability, after consultation with NYSP, of being able to prove those charges beyond the "reasonable doubt" required for conviction. Stunningly, New York State law allows her to collect her pension.

Assemblywoman Janet Duprey, who represented the North Country until 2017, was appalled by the arrangement and voiced her significant opposition. Additionally, she took the opportunity to acknowledge the many members of her district, saying: *"The majority of the Correction Officers and Civilian Employees do their jobs incredibly well, every day, in a difficult setting. They are professionals who take pride in serving with dignity and ensuring the safety of our communities."* [44]

Mitchell is currently serving 2 1/3 to 7 years at Bedford Hills Correctional Facility for Women, a maximum-security prison in Westchester County, NY, and was eligible for merit parole by hearing in January 2017, which was DENIED.

GENE PALMER

Among other things, Gene Palmer stated that he knew Matt and Sweat at least five years, often relying on them for information. The inmates' benefit, was favorable treatment and being able to manipulate several aspects of the system. Palmer, admitted as much, saying: *"Matt provided me with elaborate paintings, and information on the illegal acts that inmates were committing within the facility,"* telling authorities. *"In turn, I provided him with benefits such as paint, paintbrushes, movement of inmates, hamburger meat, altering of electrical boxes in the catwalk areas."* Clinton County DA Wylie said, based on Palmer's statements and polygraph, investigators have *no reason* to believe he was knowingly involved in the breakout. Palmer stated, *"I did not realize at the time that the assistance I provided to Matt or Sweat made their escape easier."* [45]

That said, upon receiving notice of the escape, Palmer immediately realized he would be a person of interest, due to his relationship with the inmates, leading him to burn and bury the paintings given to him by Matt, in an apparent attempt to minimize the connection and cover the fact that the prohibited transactions had occurred.

Gene Palmer served six months in Clinton County Jail. He accepted a plea that convicted him of Promoting Prison Contraband First (Felony), which was reduced, to a Misdemeanor, because there was *no evidence* he knew the hamburger packages contained hacksaw blades; and Official Misconduct (Misdemeanor), for interactions with both inmates.

CCF Superintendent STEVEN RACETTE (Retired)

DOCCS suspended Superintendent Racette, a 37-year veteran of the agency, his first deputy superintendent, the deputy superintendent for security, and nine other employees, several having since retired. Racette, maintains he was forced out; threatened with demotion if he refused. He had been the Clinton Correctional Facility Superintendent for 14 months, was assigned there in 2014, to address morale (problems), and was never told there were security issues. To this day, he contends, had DOCCS Central Office approved his request for a "lockdown," that action may have foiled the escape the week before it occurred.

USCBP Supervisory Special Agent CHRISTOPHER VOSS

BORTAC Team Leader - recognized within his agency, among all law enforcement entities participating in the investigation, and nationally, for his courageous effort, and the exemplary performance of BORTAC, in capturing Richard Matt.

New York State Police Sergeant JAY COOK

Recognized within New York State, among <u>all</u> law enforcement entities participating in the investigation, and nationally, for his courageous effort and exemplary performance of duty, in capturing David Sweat *and* bringing the largest manhunt in NYS history to a close.

New York State Police Sergeant MIKE PENA

Recognized within the NYSP and among select law enforcement entities participating in the investigation for his outstanding effort and exemplary performance of duty, during the largest manhunt in NYS history.

New York State Forest Ranger Captain JOHN STREIFF

The *Press-Republican*, in an article titled: "In The Line Of Fire," quoted me as follows: State Police Troop "B" Commander Major Charles Guess, who led the manhunt, has said, *"Forest Rangers proved indispensable,"* and indeed they were. In addition to being local area experts, they were "force multipliers." Perhaps, most importantly, when the breaks came, the rangers, under the leadership of John Streiff, were ready to assist in exploiting them. Consider on June 20, when the sighting at the Twisted Horn Hunting camp occurred, rangers had a Quick Response Team staged near Wolf Pond Road, consisting of ATVs and approximately 90 CERT personnel, expediting our response. Then, on June 26, after Matt was shot, FROST (the ranger's tactical team), deployed on ATVs and marine assets, to clear several hard-to-reach targets. Finally, when it became apparent Sweat was still in the wind, Forest Ranger Dan Fox, led teams that pushed north on June 27, the day *before* Sweat's capture, deploying to the Canadian border, north of Constable, to cut off escape. Fox was later quoted in the article as saying: *"I was just thrilled to know we were in the right place with the right strategy. We were just a day early."*[46] No doubt, those actions, in concert with others, kept Sweat boxed-in, and ultimately influenced him to make his desperate, daytime move towards the border.

NYS DOCCS Colonel DENNIS BRADFORD, Lieutenant DARRYL MENARD, and the Corrections Emergency Response Team

Of all the difficult assignments, perhaps no one would draw the "short straw" more frequently than Colonel Dennis Bradford and his CERT members. These highly trained correction officers were everywhere you looked: manning road checks, searching tunnels, trekking endless miles, searching unforgiving terrain, providing sniper over watch, deploying canines, day and night. They came up big, time and time again, with important finds. They are a credit to their agency, and their importance cannot be overstated.

New York State Police Major CHARLES GUESS (Retired)

As a result of my role as Incident Commander, and acting as what Superintendent D'Amico had once described as the "public face of the investigation," I received numerous requests for interviews and television appearances, both during and after the manhunt, to which I only granted a few. During the manhunt, I limited myself exclusively to sanctioned press conferences. I felt it was essential that in an ongoing investigation, my attention remained focused, *without exception*, on the task at hand. Besides, there was no shortage of so-called *"experts"* ready to offer their opinion. *Some of whom would simply end up on the wrong side of history.*

After the manhunt, with the encouragement and approval of the State Police Public Information Office, I participated in several exclusives: ABC's 20/20, NBC's Dateline, and among print journalism, two professional, award-winning North Country newspapers, the *Press-Republican* and the *Adirondack Daily Enterprise*, which contributed to the historical significance of this book. Much of their work is often cited within this book with their permission, particularly, as their reporting pertained to quotes and updates derived from press conferences where I was the lead, or a ranking partner. *Those two papers are models of professional journalism.*

During the days and weeks immediately following the manhunt, I was honored to receive my third Superintendent's Commendation and the

NYSP Commissioned Officer of the Year Award from our Police Benevolent Association.

Additionally, after the manhunt I received countless congratulatory e-mails, messages, and phone calls, some from around the country. I always responded, accepting these kind words on behalf of each and every member of the investigative team. Two, in particular, I will relate below, as I am most-appreciative for the expressed sentiments:

First, Clinton County District Attorney, Andrew Wylie, upon conclusion of the manhunt was quoted as saying, *"…it was an incredible collaboration of law enforcement agencies that represented us here and participated in the search. Major Guess, of the New York State Police, he's been in Troop B for less than a year; and he did an outstanding job organizing this investigation and manhunt that took place."* [47]

Second, I began this book with a famous quote strategically placed inside the front cover, **"The Man in the Arena,"** by former President Theodore Roosevelt. Over the years, that quote has inspired me, and countless others, to strive and persevere, despite seemingly insurmountable odds. It might have been tempting to hope for someone of higher rank to come in and take command, or root for the inmates to "pop up" in another jurisdiction, thus becoming *somebody else's problem*, but that's not how I roll, or who we are in Troop "B".

When I announced my retirement, more than a year later, I received dozens of emails from colleagues who wished me well. Perhaps the most meaningful of the messages, was from a lieutenant, that I hardly know; barely an acquaintance. He wrote a year after the mission:

> "Major Guess, I was assigned to the Dannemora detail in my previous assignment in the Office of Emergency Management (OEM). I was only there for one week, filling in for the northern region OEM LT. During that time, I did learn a great deal about leadership from observing you. Despite a tremendous amount of pressure, and literally, the entire world watching our operation, you maintained a positive, professional demeanor. People from all walks of

life, from national news commentators, to the people working at the Dunkin Donuts I went to each morning, were very comfortable questioning the detail. I tried to stay solely focused on the mission, and actions to accomplish that mission, not rumor or speculation, and that tone came directly from you.

During the entire incident, I was reminded of the "Man in the Arena" speech given by Theodore Roosevelt. *You were the man in the arena* and there certainly were many critics. *This time, the man in the arena won.* We were lucky to have had you, in that position, at that time.

I hope to carry with me the leadership lessons from Dannemora during the rest of my career.

Best of luck in retirement.

Lieutenant Robert J. McConnell Jr
Internal Affairs – Northern Region

CHAPTER 20

LESSONS LEARNED

C learly, there would be many lessons to be learned from this incident. Some of them pertained to operations _outside_ the walls, when the State Police was given authority and responsibility to conduct the search. To that end, a comprehensive After Action Review (AAR-draft) was completed by Troop "B", based upon surveys and assistance compiled and analyzed from the input provided by members of the SP and participating Outside Agencies. For brevity, those lessons, which do not necessarily represent the views of the NYSP, have been distilled below, as the:

INCIDENT COMMANDER'S TOP 10 PRINCIPLE FACTORS FOR SUCCESS:

1) **LEADERSHIP BY EXAMPLE** – goal of any professional development program.
   a) Through _training_ and _experience_ (lessons learned), develop a track record of success, <u>and</u> the _credibility, integrity, and confidence_ to lead a coalition.
   b) Ideally, this should be developed and evident at _multiple_ levels, allowing the IC to _delegate_ authority to subordinate leaders to act!

2) **MANAGING EXECUTIVE EXPECTATIONS**
   a) Embrace the reality...you (IC) need the support of the upper echelon, to provide resources and facilitate outside agency and governmental interaction.
   b) Expect ongoing interactions (visits, conference calls, etc.). Use them as opportunities to shape strategy and identify key decision points.
   c) Keep partners _informed_ and remain _flexible_.

3) **INTER-AGENCY/DEPARTMENTAL COOPERATION**
   a) Building a coalition – embrace partners and solicit input. Establish consensus outcomes from the start.
   b) Establish a Unified Command, tailored for purpose; a truly collaborative effort. Organization and structure are paramount!
   c) Remember, the spirit of cooperation is tenuous…Solicit feedback, employ checks and balances, and integrate *course corrections*, when required.

4) **COMMANDER'S INTENT AND ESTABLISHING STRATEGIC FOCUS**
   a) The goal is Unity of Command! Staff must be provided with a clear view of the strategy, objectives, and guiding principles.
   b) Ultimately, the IC speaks with one voice (briefings, press, public) to present commonality of purpose.
   c) Conduct routine systems checks and promote <u>candor</u> among entities.

5) **DEVELOPING TACTICAL APPLICATIONS - OPERATIONS**
   a) Key: An integrated staff with FOCUS.
   b) Identify dedicated subordinate branch director(s) to manage high-risk units.
   c) Break out planning cells, integrate intel, and focus on future OPS.
   d) Resist/guard against over reliance on any one piece of information, tactic, type of technology, or individual.
   e) Do not arbitrarily abandon your objectives or principles, and constantly improve your position.
   f) Remain *flexible* and *welcome new concepts*.

6) **MOTIVATING SUBORDINATES**
   a) Often dependent upon the professional credibility of organizational leader(s).

b) Define the mission. Describe what success looks like.

c) Provide the resources and minimize distractions.

d) Confer authority to act and establish Rules of Engagement enabling success.

e) Focus (i.e. "Today is the Day") and battle complacency.

f) Make Safety a *Command Priority*…people will notice!

7) MANAGING CONFLICT AND OUTSIDE INFLUENCES

a) **Elected Officials**

- Prepare to receive inquiries and offers of assistance. Cut through the nonsense. Identify and leverage legitimate offers.
- Ensure your deputy (Operations Officer) is prepared to make *early* decisions, as you (IC) address initial inquiries, challenges, and concerns.
- Safeguard <u>sensitive</u> information – provide operational overviews on a need-to-know basis only.

b) **Outside Agency Leaders** - <u>must</u> be afforded a seat at the table.

- This ensures the strategy is *cohesive*, fosters *buy-in*, enables clear, concise messaging and *resolves problems* (real and perceived) in a timely manner.
- Assign a Liaison, when necessary.
- CONFIDENTIALITY - <u>must</u> be *stressed and maintained*.

c) **Media** – engage the media early and often.

- *Leverage* briefings to present information *and* instill a sense of confidence.
- Ensure *transparency* – The "Cover Up" is always worse than the crime!

8) SUPPORTING THE OPERATION

a) Communications

- Dedicate a Communications Branch Director *immediately*!
- Goal: Integration/Interoperability, with common action language.

- Secure communications when viable.

b) Logistics – *can be* the Achille's Heel…prevent it!
- Designate a LOG Branch Director early on!
- *Prioritize* this aspect of the operation; forecast the predictable, and establish emergency channels.

9) DEVELOPING A CULTURE OF SAFETY

a) You operate in a dynamic environment.

b) Designate a Safety Officer immediately!

c) Make Safety a Command priority.

10) IDENTIFYING AND APPLYING LESSONS LEARNED

a) Corrective action is an ongoing process.

b) Upon conclusion, develop an After Action Report (AAR), based upon input from partners. Timeliness of outreach matters!

c) Address the gaps!

Additionally, at the direction of Governor Cuomo, a comprehensive review was conducted by the NYS Inspector General's Office, regarding activities and conditions *inside* the prison that led to the prison break. Accordingly, I have distilled key elements of the report titled: *"Investigation of the June 5, 2015, Escape of Inmates David Sweat and Richard Matt from Clinton Correctional Facility,"* for the reader's review.

As a lead-in to the summary discussion of the report, the *Press-Republican* appropriately wrote: "The 150-page report says a combination of factors made the escape possible: '*Sweat's ingenuity and persistence, Matt's ability to manipulate Joyce Mitchell and Gene Palmer, Mitchell's willingness to commit criminal acts and Palmer's negligence in delivering escape tools.*'" But, it also said, *"The breakout would not have occurred without 'failures in fundamental security' at the prison and 'inadequate supervision' by management and DOCCS."* Furthermore, DOCCS Deputy Commissioner Joseph Bellnier told the IG that, the multiple breakdowns stemmed from a *"culture of carelessness"* at the prison.[48]

Additionally, according to an in-depth interview conducted by accomplished, veteran reporter Joe LoTemplio, of the *Press-Republican*, NYS Inspector General Catherine Leahy Scott, addressed the 150-page report issued Monday, June 6, 2016, in an article titled: *"All Has To Change,"* excerpts below:

Leahy Scott, brought in by Governor Cuomo, on June 15, 2015, said: *"It's three: the boots-on-the-ground folks, the administration at Clinton and Albany at DOCCS central. Those three entities, when you bring it all together, they are responsible for this escape. And all three will be addressed."* She also seized on Bellnier's previous comment, agreeing with the First Deputy Commissioner's characterization that a *"Culture of complacency,"* existed at Clinton.

She continued, *"...there were a lot of employees who forgot they worked at a maximum-security facility."* Troublingly, the IG added, some C.O.s were *"uncooperative,"* claiming they couldn't remember certain events, or they were improperly trained; but others were helpful and honest. She characterized Joyce Mitchell as, *"difficult to interview, not always cooperative and remorseful only that she got caught." "She lied, and she consistently lied. But when pressed and pressed hard and presented with evidence, she had to cave in and tell us the truth."*

Additionally, she added, *"Investigators were leery of Sweat's statements and worked to corroborate them, and much of it checked out."* She described Sweat as *"very smart, very cunning, very narcissistic."* Thinking of himself as, *"the smartest person in the room."*

Regarding the Clinton Correctional Facility Superintendent's denied request for lockdown, the IG *said, "...it was not her role to form an opinion on whether it was a good decision to deny the lockdown request,"* but, she was skeptical as to whether it would have prevented the escape. Pointing out, *"There was plenty of opportunity to check the cells,"* referring to the report's findings that there were 400 other cell inspections that were not properly performed. Additionally, the report cited, *"Officers failed to properly conduct at least 15 required weekly inspections of "cell integrity," including examination of bars, floors, vents, walls and rear of cell from catwalks."*

Finally, Inspector General Leahy Scott said, *"Racette has to shoulder blame for the escape from the prison he led, whether he knew about specific* practices or not. '*Leadership is always responsible,*' "she said. '*It is unacceptable to say you don't know.*'" [49]

Ms. Leahy Scott was further quoted in the IG's report and other media outlets: "*The extent of complacency and failure to adhere to the most basic security standards uncovered by my investigation was egregious and inexcusable.*" [50]

For example, according the report, it was common practice for officers to skip required rounds, and *pre-sign* inmate-count slips, turning them into the watch commander <u>before</u> the actual count had been conducted. Clearly, DOCCS policy requires the certification to be done hourly, commensurate with completion of the count, and <u>not</u> before. The report went on to say, that the watch commander, on the night of the escape, "…had already completed the 5:30 AM opening master count sheet that reported all members of the block were in their cells and had signed it in pencil, which he later erased, the report said, "testifying, he '*may have*' signed the count before 5:30 AM, but claimed he had '*signed by accident*' and then '*erased it right away*' because '*the count wasn't certified.*'" The report asserted that: "*…it is almost certain that the Watch Commander completed and signed the master count in advance and only erased his signature after learning that Sweat and Matt were missing.*" [51]

Disturbingly, Honor Block inmates who had been interviewed, testified that officers did <u>not</u> conduct counts or rounds, after the 11:00 PM count, or before the 5:30 AM count. Regardless of who you believe, one thing is certain, as the report intones, during the three months (85 nights) Sweat was out of his cell leading up to the escape, more than 400 counts should have been conducted, <u>and</u>, "*If only one count was done properly, the escape plan would have been instantly stopped.*" [52]

A summary of the <u>specific findings and recommendations</u> from the State of New York Office of the Inspector General: ***"Investigation of the June 5, 2015, Escape of Inmates David Sweat and Richard Matt from Clinton Correctional Facility,"*** is as follows:

FINDINGS:

Clinton Correctional Facility
- Failure to properly search employee bags at the front gate
  - Failure to properly screen and inventory contractors
- Failure to conduct or properly conduct inmate night counts
  - Guards not conducting, or improperly conducting required counts and rounds
  - Guards certifying and turning in counts in advance/prior to actual count
  - Failure to observe inmate's "skin and breathing"
  - Watch Commander certifying count in advance
  - Management claimed to be unaware of "longstanding" practice
- Cursory cell searches omitted cell wall/bar integrity checks
  - Failure to conduct required number of cell searches
  - C.O.s employed discretion as to what inmate cells were checked from random, computer generated list
  - Matt's cell allegedly searched, according to records, on 3-21-15 did *not* identify breach, although Matt had already cut through the back wall
  - "IG's analysis of "all reported cell searches in all housing units at Clinton during the 12 months prior to the escape revealed that no contraband was found in 6,665, or more than 96%, of the 6,894 searches." [Clearly, an implausible number.]
- Failure to conduct catwalk inspections
- Tunnel inspections did not occur as frequently as intended
- Lapses in contractor tool control
- Limited utilization of metal detectors
- Breakdown in security and Civilian Employee supervision in the tailor shop
  - Mitchell's improper interactions with inmates
  - Failure to identify and enforce standards of conduct

DOCCS Central Office

- Audits and inspections of Clinton's security, were "so superficial as to be virtually without value."
- Failure to take sufficient action to ensure security lapses that contributed to an earlier escape, at another facility, did not occur at ALL facilities.
- IG acknowledged the superintendent's request for full lockdown was "Denied;" but, DOCCS asserted it was a "judgement call." [This assertion was not challenged in the report.]
- OSI investigation into Mitchell was "deficient."
- Deficiencies in DOCCS training of Security and Civilian staff.

RECOMMENDATIONS:

- IG oversight (audit) of DOCCS to ensure integrity of operations, policies, and practices
- OSI restructured to enhance investigative ability and independence
- Front gate security enhancements, retraining and increased supervision
- Enforce night count protocols, enhance supervisory oversight, and install cellblock cameras for monitoring
- Cell searches for contraband and integrity – retraining, increase frequency, and remove discretion
- Comprehensive tunnel and catwalk inspections; add sensors
- Tailor Shops – enhance training of Security staff, Civilian Employees, and supervisors, to address and enforce policies governing proper inmate conduct and staff interaction
- Honor Block – "new" policy will "exclude inmates with histories of escape, and require greater scrutiny of inmates serving life sentences
- Internal Controls – revise and implement improved auditing practices

- Training – enhance and standardize training

In an article assembled by the *Adirondack Daily Enterprise*, titled: *"By the #s,"* [53] several interesting facts emerge, per the IG's report:

- 85 nights – Sweat worked in tunnels
- 400+ – inmate bed checks that should have occurred
- 15 – weekly inspections of "cell integrity" that failed detect holes in cells
- $573,000 – spent on CCF repairs and security upgrades
- $23 million – OT as a result of the manhunt
- 19, or more – paintings and drawing Gene Palmer accepted from Matt and Sweat
- 70+ – containers of black and cayenne pepper Joyce Mitchell smuggled into Matt and Sweat, starting in October 2014
- 29 – IG staff who worked on report
- 175 – interviews under oath
- 11 – inmates among those interviewed
- 2,653 – inmates at CCF at time of escape; 1,283 – staff

During the year that the IG was conducting its investigation and gathering the data necessary to render the report, many of these deficiencies had been addressed by DOCCS, under the leadership of newly appointed CCF Superintendent Michael Kirkpatrick. Mike, a close friend of mine, from years of interaction between NYSP and DOCCS special operations units, was the right person to take on this seemingly insurmountable challenge. A 30-year veteran of DOCCS, Kirkpatrick had come up through the ranks, serving in many of the agency's key positions, including eight years on CERT, the last four of which were as the colonel-in-charge. His last assignment, immediately prior to assignment to Clinton on July 1, 2015, was the First Deputy Superintendent of Elmira Correctional Facility.

A sampling of enhanced, or now-enforced, protocols was depicted in a newspaper article published by the *Press-Republican* on July 7, 2015; one year <u>before</u> the IG completed its investigation.[54]

- Cell integrity inspections
- Tripled number of daily, random searches
- Each cell, at least every two months
- Required bed checks
- Electrical panels inspected/set correct amperage
- Executive staff (captain or higher) present 11:00 PM to 7:00 AM and, required to make a visual inspection of staff performing count
- Manning wall posts (towers)
- Supervisors assigned to facility entrance points (i.e. front gate) during shift change to ensure compliance with screening procedures
- C.O.s at remote locations to check in every half hour
- Tunnel inspections monthly and security gates installed
- Construction job boxes (gang boxes) to be kept in gated area and inspected COB

Clearly, this suggests, and it is abundantly evident, that DOCCS *did* ***not wait*** for the report to be published, but took many of the much-needed steps immediately. This is a credit to the thousands of professionals within the agency, that grasped the seriousness of this event, and who were personally determined to *immediately* address the conditions that led up to and facilitated the escape.

Beyond the very nature of the constructive criticism and mandated changes, the spirit of this review should be embraced by future leaders and administrators, who should vow, as I did after the Phillips investigation, to ensure these problems are not repeated.

This then, can be the *positive* legacy of the Dannemora Manhunt, for:

"Those who do not learn (the lessons of) history, are doomed to repeat it." – George Santayana

ACKNOWLEDGEMENTS

B y any measure, I enjoyed a tremendous career with the New York State Police. Along the way, I encountered but a few naysayers and obstructionists. However, surrounded by exceptional colleagues who shared my vision, sometimes when it wasn't popular, I remained focused and faithful to the cause. I approached each and every assignment and opportunity with vigor, and I truly believe "I left it all on the field."

Looking back on the early days of the escape from Dannemora, when some in the media proclaimed the inmates were long gone, I was determined to maintain our team's focus and bolster morale. Subsequently, I reminded our folks that they must approach each shift and every search as though that *one moment* could be the decisive encounter in the manhunt. Thus, the phrase "Today is the day!" was born. My colleagues adopted this mindset, and together, we turned sometimes-demoralizing coverage and uncertainty into a strategy of **Relentless Pursuit**.

Many thanks to the men and women of the New York State Police, our law enforcement partners, and members of the community, who are especially deserving of recognition, including many who played a significant role, relentlessly pursuing the ever-increasing number of leads (more than 3,400) during the manhunt, ultimately leading to victory:

<u>Division Headquarters</u>
Superintendent Joseph D'Amico
Colonel Patricia Groeber
Lieutenant Colonels George Beach and Frank Koehler
Inspectors Keith Corlette and Steve James
Majors Dave Krause and Chris Fiore
Captains John Agresta and Eric Underhill
Lieutenants Bill Carraher, John Healy, and Scott Reichel
Senior Investigator John Brooks (Troop "G")
Sergeants Ron Pastino, Derek Cerza and SORT
Sergeant Jason Brewer, Trooper Kevin Beattie and K9
NYSIC, CNET, FIC, DETF, et al

NYSP Public Information Office
Director Beau Duffy
Deputy Director Kristin Lowman
Trooper Jennifer Fleishman (Troop "B")
Trooper Jack Keller (Troop "D")

Troop "B" Staff
Captains Brent Gillam, Mike Girard, Bob LaFountain, Walt Teppo, and John Tibbitts
Lieutenants Kevin Boyea, John Coryea, Brent Davison, Pat Ryan, and Shawnda Walbridge
First Sergeant Steve Lacey
Zone Sergeants Fred Atkinson, Jim Busquet, Charlie Dutko, Garett Brown, Pat Jones, Mike Snell, and Mike Trimboli
HQ's Sergeants Jay Cook, Chris Giovazzino, Mike Pena, and Chad Niles
Plus, the other *outstanding* NCOs, Senior Investigators, Investigators, Troopers, specialized units, and the *tremendous* Civilian Employees of Troop "B"

NYST PBA
President Thomas Mungeer
Troop "B" Delegate – Trooper Roger Riuta

Public Officials
Assemblywoman Janet Duprey
State Senator Betty Little
Congresswoman Elise Stefanik
Clinton County DA Andrew Wiley
Acting Franklin County DA Glenn MacNeill
Saranac School District Superintendent Johnathan Parker

Local Agencies
Franklin County Sheriff's Department
Clinton County Sheriff's Department
Essex County Sheriff's Department

Jefferson County Sheriff's Department
City of Plattsburgh Police Department
Saint Regis Mohawk Tribal Police Department
Local City, Town, and Village Police Departments throughout the North
    Country, et al

State Agencies
NYS DHSES
NYSDEC Forest Rangers and ENCON Police
Vermont State Police, et al

Federal Agencies
U.S. Customs and Border Protection and BORTAC
DHS
FBI and HRT
US Marshals Service and SOG, et al

Media
Press-Republican, especially Lois Clermont, Joe LoTemplio, Rob Fountain
    and Gabe Dickens
Adirondack Daily Enterprise, especially Catherine Moore, Chris Knight,
    Peter Crowley, and Matthew Turner
North Country Public Radio, Brian Mann

Community…last, but certainly not least!
Communities of Franklin, Clinton, Essex, and Jefferson Counties; numer-
    ous Towns, Villages, and Hamlets therein; *especially* the Villages of
    Dannemora and Malone

*Most-importantly, a "special thanks," to the multitude of private citi-
zens, volunteers, commercial businesses, schools, establishments, civic
groups, and others!*

ENDNOTES

1. State of New York Office of the Inspector General: "Investigation of the June 5, 2015 Escape of Inmates David Sweat and Richard Matt from Clinton Correctional Facility," Catherine Leahy Scott, Inspector General, June 2016.

2. "Serving the Public Since 1917." *Troopers.ny.gov.* New York State, Web. 2 January 2016.

3. "Newburgh, NY, Crime Rates and Statistics – Neighborhoodscout." *neighborhoodscout.com.* Location, Inc., Web. 4 January 2016.

4. Moore, Suzanne and Health, Dan. "Dannemora under a microscope." *Press-Republican* 9 June 2015: p. A+1.

5. LoTemplio, Joe. "Guards: Many factors led to escape." *Press-Republican* 11 June 2015: p. A1+.

6. Livingston, Ashleigh. "Dannemora residents, businesses adjust to new normal." *Press-Republican* 11 June 2015: p. A3.

7. Trombly, Justin. "Community rallies around searchers." *Press-Republican* 13 June 2015: p. A3.

8. LoTemplio, Joe. "Policies may have left prison vulnerable." *Press-Republican* 16 June 2015: A1+.

9. Raymo, Denise. LoTemplio, Joe. Heath, Dan and Trombly, Justin. "Searchers "tightening the perimeter" after DNA evidence at camp linked to fugitives." *Press-Republican* 23 June 2015: p. A1+.

10. Crowley, Peter and Knight, Chris. "Search moves to Franklin County." *Adirondack Daily Enterprise* 22 June 15: p. A1+.

11. Knight, Chris. "Camp owners, caretakers watchful for escapees." *Adirondack Daily Enterprise* 24 June 2015: p. A1+.

12. Editorial Board. "VIEWPOINT." *Press-Republican* 25 June 2015: p. A7.

13. ibid

14. Smith Dedam, Kim. Raymo, Denise and Tobias, Susan. "Day of tension ends without full relief." *Press-Republican* 25 June 2015: p. A7.

15. Lotemplio, Joe. "I Knew It Was Him." *Press-Republican* 9 March 2016: p. A1+.

16. ibid

17. ibid

18. ibid

19. Turner, Matthew. Knight, Chris and Crowley, Peter. "Party atmosphere as three-week search ends." *Adirondack Daily Enterprise* 29 June 2015: p. A1+.

20. ibid

21. Balsamo, Michael. "David Sweat shot, captured." *Adirondack Daily Enterprise (AP)* 29 June 2015: p. A1+.

22. Turner, Matthew. Knight, Chris and Crowley, Peter. "Party atmosphere as three-week search ends." *Adirondack Daily Enterprise* 29 June 2015: p. A1+.

23. State of New York Office of the Inspector General: "Investigation of the June 5, 2015 Escape of Inmates David Sweat and Richard Matt from Clinton Correctional Facility," Catherine Leahy Scott, Inspector General, 2016.

24. ibid

25. ibid

26. ibid

27. ibid

28. ibid

29. ibid

30. ibid

31. ibid

32. ibid

33. ibid

34. ibid

35. ibid

36. ibid

37. ibid

38. ibid

39. ibid

40. Belsamo, Michael. "Sweat said Matt was slowing him down." *Adirondack Daily Enterprise (AP)* 30 June 2015: p. A1+.

41. Kreig, Felicia. "Prison escapees were almost seen, Sweat says." *Press-Republican* 2 July 2015: p. A3.

42. Smith Dedam, Kim. Livingston, Ashleigh and Health, Dan. "Cuomo: Fugitives had sights set on Mexico." *Press-Republican* 30 June 2015: p. A1+.

43. Long, Colleen. "Trooper had law on his side when he shot Sweat." *Adirondack Daily Enterprise (AP)* 30 June 2015: p. A1+.

44. LoTemplio, Joe. "Duprey angered by plea deal." *Press-Republican* 30 July 2016: p. A1+.

45. Ghosh, Bonny. "Guard did not know he aided escape." *Adirondack Daily Enterprise* 26 June 2015: p. A1+.

46. Smith Dedam, Kim. "In The Line Of Fire." *Press-Republican* 30 July 2015: p. A1+.

47. Chapman, Cara. "Wylie shares impact of manhunt." *Press-Republican* 2 August 2015: p. A1+.

48. Clermont, Lois. "Scathing report on escape." *Press-Republican* 7 June 2016: p. A1+.

49. LoTemplio, Joe. "All Has to Change." *Press-Republican* 8 June 2016: p. A1+.

50. Virtanen, Michael. "Escapees wanted to go to Mexico with fake names." *Adirondack Daily Enterprise (AP)* 7 June 2016: p. A1+.

51. ibid

52. Heath, Dan. "Investigation: Escape facilitated by Honor Block protocols." *Press-Republican* 8 June 2016: p. A1+.

53. Virtanen, Michael. "By the #s." *Adirondack Daily Enterprise (AP)* 7 June 2016: p. A1.

54. LoTemplio, Joe. "Clampdown at Clinton Correctional." *Press-Republican* 7 July 2015: p. A1+.

CPSIA information can be obtained
at www.ICGtesting.com
Printed in the USA
BVOW10s0302290917
496081BV00011BB/354/P